EPIC BRITISH
WALKS

TERRY MARSH

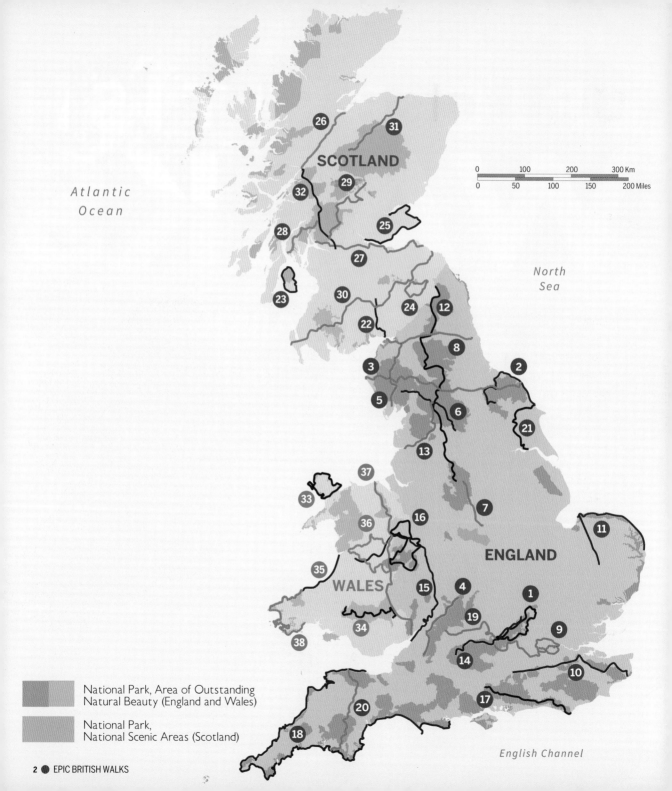

Atlantic
Ocean

SCOTLAND

26   31

32   29

28   25

27

23   30

22   24   12

3   8

5   6

13

North
Sea

2

21

37

33   16

36

35   15   4

WALES   19   1

34   9

38   14

ENGLAND

11

10

17

20

18

English Channel

0   100   200   300 Km
0   50   100   150   200 Miles

National Park, Area of Outstanding
Natural Beauty (England and Wales)

National Park,
National Scenic Areas (Scotland)

Contents

Front cover: Hadrian's Wall, Northumberland.
This page: Beside the Severn, near Bridgnorth.
Following page: Buttermere.

Long-distance walking

If there's one thing Britain excels in, it's long-distance walks. From north to south, east to west, if you're up for a walk of 50 miles or more, the choice is immense … and there are many people to thank for that.

From seeds of discontent earthed in the campaign for access to England's uplands during the late 19th-century and inter-war years of the 20th, the desire for recreational walking opportunities has always been great. Hundreds and thousands of walks, written by a reliable and knowledgeable army of authors, from professional guidebook writers to parish council clerks and even school children, are the bedrock of today's legacy of those early struggles. A desire for fitness and an appreciation of our natural heritage spurred that network of local pathways, which has been augmented by an even greater tangle of regional and national trails, middle- and long-distance treks.

Ironically, over the centuries the British have rarely looked on walking as a pleasure – it was a necessity, just that, the poor man's mode of transport, Shanks's pony … and to be avoided as much as possible. Yet the country is laced with ancient paths that collectively feed into the network

of long-distance paths: prehistoric routes such as the Ridgeway; pilgrim routes; numerous drove roads, even coffin roads that linked remote villages with places of sanctity where the dead could be buried in consecrated ground.

Hilaire Belloc in his Introduction to *The Footpath Way: an anthology for walkers*, writes: 'Of the great many things which man does which he should not do or need not do … you may count walking'. He goes on to say, '… walking will always be to [man's] benefit – that is, of course, so long as he does not warp his soul by the detestable habit of walking for no object but exercise'. Thankfully, there were opposing views. George Macaulay Trevelyan, British historian, academic and first president of the Youth Hostels Association, writing in *Clio, A Muse and Other Essays Literary and Pedestrian* (1913) said: 'I have two doctors, my left leg and my right. When body and mind are out of gear … I know that I have only to call in my doctors and I shall be well again'. And in a remarkable *volte face*, Belloc himself went on to become a legendary walker, honing his walking style in 1901 when he undertook a 700-mile (1,100-km) wander around Europe, from Moselle to St Peter's in Rome, walking 30 miles a day, taking 'advantage of no wheeled thing', though he did break that resolve a few times.

Today, something like 20 million people in Britain enjoy a regular countryside walk, mostly at weekends. On the stunning West Highland Way alone, no fewer than 120,000 people are to be encountered throughout a year. This keenness to indulge in multi-day walks is a logical extension of an evolving need for self-actualisation, for exercise, for removing oneself from the demands of life's daily tread. Small wonder then that, as one-day walking became two days, and two became three, in the end a demand grew for walks that were more tooting, offering longer periods of absence from 'home', more escapism, more rejuvenation.

These days it is a perfectly reasonable thing to walk ... for the sake of walking and for the benefits it brings: health and well-being, appreciation of our rural heritage, a break from the routine, good company and conversation. Walking for recreation – that is, re-creation – is today an end in itself, and in the wake of the 2020 pandemic, never more in demand.

But, an 'end in itself' need not necessarily be the quintessence of long-distance trails. Of course, there will always be those, rightly so, who seek to tackle the entire walk in one go, though even those contemplating the South West Coast Path must surely think twice about that. One of the 'at-odds' characteristics of all of the national and great multi-day trails is that they don't have to be a full-on commitment; they can be accomplished piecemeal by those with less available time, less inclination to plod onward day after day, and those with more willingness to take in leisurely what the routemasters have devised, what secrets they are inviting you to experience, what delights they are sharing with you.

Whatever your plans, Britain's long-distance trails await. The landscapes are there, waiting to be walked, touched, inhaled, listened to and appreciated in all their splendour; appreciate the sense of change that comes as you move on, enjoy everything on its own merits. There is a remarkable synergy about long, distance trails: the whole truly is greater than the sum of its parts: two plus two really does make five!

Long-distance paths

It all began with the Pennine Way, when a Lancashire-born young man, Tom Stephenson (1893–1987), a journalist and campaigner for the legal right of access to the countryside, was motivated by correspondence with two American girls who wrote to him asking for advice about a walking holiday in England, Stephenson went on to posit in the *Daily Herald* (22 June 1935), '… why should we not press for something akin to the Appalachian Trail – a Pennine Way from the Peak to the Cheviot?' The rest, as they say, is history … though it was not that simple. A communal and long-held desire to freely explore our countryside has led to a host of national trails and 'great' trails, a stunning network of regional and local trails, with more than enough for one lifetime.

National Trails are middle- and long-distance walking routes, ranging from 79 miles/126km (Yorkshire Wolds Way) to a staggering 631 miles/1,016km (South West Coast Path), which explore the best landscapes in Britain. Designated by the Government and managed by Natural England and Natural Resources Wales to a set of quality standards, national trails stand apart from the many other routes. For a start, each trail is well waymarked with the distinctive acorn symbol, and each is looked after by a dedicated officer often with teams of volunteers. In Scotland they are known as 'Great Trails' – see opposite.

These trails present a range of experiences, from the striking and scenic Pembrokeshire Coast Path to the splendid Norfolk Coast Path, a place of big skies and abundant and diverse wildlife. Along Hadrian's Wall Path you walk in the footsteps of Roman legionnaires, and along the North Downs Way follow in the tread of pilgrims. For a more serious challenge, the Cleveland Way offers outstanding heather moorland and craggy coastal walking, while the Pennine Way with its considerable length and constantly changing landscapes may appeal to those determined to test themselves.

In addition to these walking trails, there is the Pennine Bridleway (205 miles/330km) running roughly parallel with the Pennine Way but with its focus on access for horse riders and cyclists.

Taking things up several notches, the England Coast Path is a National Trail officially opened in 2020. Although many sections are open and well-used, others are still to be completed, but when finished, the path will stretch for almost 3,000 miles (4,800km) and be the longest continuous walking route in the world. Not to be outdone, Wales has its own coast path, launched in 2012 and, at 870 miles (1,400km), is celebrated as the first dedicated footpath in the world to cover the entire length of a country's coastline.

SCOTLAND'S GREAT TRAILS 〈〉

Analogous to the national trails of England and Wales, Scotland's 'Great Trails' are designated routes primarily intended for walkers. They developed from the former Long Distance Routes (LDRs) proposed and financially supported by Scottish Natural Heritage (SNH), in 2019 re-branded as NatureScot. These routes are clearly waymarked with a thistle symbol and are largely off-road. And, as with the English and Welsh national trails, walkers can tramp them secure in the knowledge that the way forward is generally well-trodden and certain to lead from one stunning vista to another.

At the time of writing, there are no fewer than 29 Great Trails. The first to be inaugurated was the West Highland Way in 1980, and is today one of the most popular trails, arguably, in Britain. The longest Great Trail is the delectable Southern Upland Way (214 miles/344km), while the John Muir Trail runs for (134 miles/215km), and is named after the conservationist and founder of America's National Parks, East Lothian-born John Muir (1838–914).

The trails range in length from 25 miles (40km) to 214 miles (344km), and are intended to be covered over several days, either as a combination of day trips or as an end-to-end trip. While they are indeed primarily for walkers, many have stretches that will appeal to cyclists and horse riders, and one – the Great Glen Canoe Trail – is designed for canoeists and kayakers.

REGIONAL TRAILS 🚶

Woven into the fabric of the national and great trails, Britain has a plethora of outstanding walks that collectively are very much the icing on the cake; walks that have been fashioned by local and regional enthusiasts and evolved in stature and popularity beyond local renown. Linking Ilkley in West Yorkshire with Bowness-on-Windermere in the Lake District, the Dales Way is typical of this wealth of regional trails. Likewise, the Coast-to-Coast Path links the Irish Sea and North Sea coasts in much the same way as the Two Moors Way spans Devon crossing from the English to the Bristol Channel.

Elsewhere, trails of varying length and difficulty abound; trails such as the Severn Way, which traces the river from its source, as does the Ribble Way through much of Lancashire; the Anglesey Coast Path speaks for itself, while the Shropshire Way must be the finest underrated circuit in Britain.

One thing is certain, when you also take into account shorter day walks that festoon the countryside, in Britain you're never far from somewhere to walk. The scope really is *epic*.

This page: Wildmoorway Lock, South Cerney.
Previous page: Wain Stones Shard, North Yorkshire.

At a glance

Walk	Status	Rating	Start	Finish	Distance miles	km	Height Gain feet	metres
England								
① Chiltern Way	🚶	♦♦	Hemel Hempstead, Hertfordshire	Hemel Hempstead, Hertfordshire	134	215	12,865	3,920
② Cleveland Way	⬤	♦♦♦♦	Helmsley, North Yorkshire	Filey, North Yorkshire	109	175	20,550	6,265
③ Coast to Coast Path	🚶	♦♦♦♦	St Bees, Cumbria	Robin Hood's Bay, North Yorkshire	188	302	29,125	8,880
④ Cotswold Way	⬤	♦♦♦	Chipping Campden, Gloucestershire	Bath, Somerset	101	161	15,545	4,740
⑤ Cumbria Way	🚶	♦♦♦	Ulverston, Cumbria	Carlisle, Cumbria	70	113	8,415	2,565
⑥ Dales Way	🚶	♦♦	Ilkley, West Yorkshire	Bowness-on-Windermere, Cumbria	78	125	6,805	2,075
⑦ Derwent Valley Heritage Way	🚶	♦	Heatherdene, Derbyshire	Shardlow, Derbyshire	52	82	2,985	910
⑧ Hadrian's Wall Path	⬤	♦♦♦	Wallsend, Tyne and Wear	Bowness-on-Solway, Cumbria	84	135	6,945	2,115
⑨ London's Capital Ring	🚶	♦	Woolwich Foot Tunnel, Woolwich	Woolwich Foot Tunnel, Woolwich	78	126	4,050	1,235
⑩ North Downs Way	⬤	♦♦♦	Farnham, Surrey	Dover, Kent	133	214	14,070	4,290
⑪ Peddars Way and Norfolk Coast Path	⬤	♦♦	Knettishall, Suffolk	Hopton-on-Sea, Norfolk	131	211	6,395	1,950
⑫ Pennine Way	⬤	♦♦♦♦♦	Edale, Derbyshire	Kirk Yetholm, Scottish Borders	268	429	36,065	10,995
⑬ Ribble Way	🚶	♦♦	Longton, Lancashire	Gayle Moor, North Yorkshire	70	113	6,200	1,890
⑭ Ridgeway	⬤	♦♦	Overton Hill, Wiltshire	Ivinghoe Beacon, Buckinghamshire	87	139	7,115	2,170
⑮ Severn Way	🚶	♦♦	Pumlumon (Plynlimon), Powys	Severn Beach, Gloucestershire	209	336	8,330	2,540
⑯ Shropshire Way	🚶	♦♦♦	Shrewsbury, Shropshire	Shrewsbury, Shropshire	203	327	18,565	5,660
⑰ South Downs Way	⬤	♦♦♦	Winchester, Hampshire	Eastbourne, East Sussex	101	163	13,185	4,020
⑱ South West Coast Path	⬤	♦♦♦♦♦	Minehead, Somerset	South Haven Point, Dorset	631	1,016	108,595	33,110
⑲ Thames Path	⬤	♦	Kemble, Gloucestershire	Thames Barrier, Greenwich	183	294	3,525	1,075
⑳ Two Moors Way	🚶	♦♦♦♦	Wembury, Devon	Lynmouth, Devon	117	187	15,825	4,825
㉑ Yorkshire Wolds Way	⬤	♦♦	Hessle, East Yorkshire	Filey Brigg, North Yorkshire	79	126	8,265	2,520

Walk	Status	Rating	Start	Finish	Distance miles	km	Height Gain feet	metres
Scotland								
22 **Annandale Way**	◈	◆◆	Moffat, Dumfries and Galloway	Newbiebarns, Dumfries and Galloway	56	90	4,970	1,515
23 **Arran Coastal Way**	◈	◆◆◆	Brodick, Arran	Brodick, Arran	65	104	6,295	1,920
24 **Borders Abbeys Way**	◈	◆◆	Melrose, Scottish Borders	Melrose, Scottish Borders	68	108	6,595	2,010
25 **Fife Coastal Path**	◈	◆◆	Kincardine, Fife	Newburgh, Fife	117	187	8,330	2,540
26 **Great Glen Way**	◈	◆◆	Fort William, Highland	Inverness, Highland	78	125	7,920	2,415
27 **John Muir Way**	◈	◆◆	Helensburgh, Argyll and Bute	Dunbar, East Lothian	134	215	8,855	2,700
28 **Loch Lomond and Cowal Way**	◈	◆◆◆	Portavadie, Argyll and Bute	Inveruglas, Argyll and Bute	57	92	8,595	2,620
29 **Rob Roy Way**	◈	◆◆◆◆	Drymen, Stirling	Pitlochry, Perth and Kinross	79	127	9,675	2,950
30 **Southern Upland Way**	◈	◆◆◆◆◆	Portpatrick, Dumfries and Galloway	Cockburnspath, Scottish Borders	214	344	28,290	8,625
31 **Speyside Way**	◈	◆◆◆	Buckie, Moray	Newtonmore, Highland	86	138	6,805	2,075
32 **West Highland Way**	◈	◆◆◆◆	Milngavie, East Dunbartonshire	Fort William, Highland	96	154	12,375	3,775

Walk	Status	Rating	Start	Finish	Distance miles	km	Height Gain feet	metres
Wales								
33 **Anglesey Coastal Path**	🚶	◆◆◆	Holyhead, Anglesey	Holyhead, Anglesey	132	212	13,990	4,265
34 **Beacons Way**	🚶	◆◆◆◆	Abergavenny, Monmouthshire	Llangadog, Carmarthenshire	99	159	21,295	6,490
35 **Ceredigion Coast Path**	🚶	◆◆◆	Cardigan, Ceredigion	Ynyslas, Ceredigion	59	95	12,515	3,815
36 **Glyndŵr's Way**	◉	◆◆◆◆	Knighton, Powys	Welshpool, Powys	135	217	23,355	7,120
37 **Offa's Dyke Path**	◉	◆◆◆◆	Chepstow, Monmouthshire	Prestatyn, Denbighshire	177	285	28,845	8,795
38 **Pembrokeshire Coast Path**	◉	◆◆◆◆	St Dogmaels, Pembrokeshire	Amroth, Pembrokeshire	186	299	35,140	10,715

Using this guide

ROUTE INFORMATION

Distance Given to the nearest whole mile/kilometre.
Height gain The cumulative total ascent along the whole route, given to the nearest five feet/five metres.
Difficulty rating An indication of the level of challenge presented by each route:
♦ least challenging and most suitable for novice multi-day walkers
♦♦♦♦♦ most challenging.

These ratings take into account:
Physicality Not just the overall distance and height gain, but more pertinently the length and total ascent of intermediate stages; general underfoot-conditions and ruggedness of the paths; the typical degree of exposure to the elements, whether moorland hilltop or coastal clifftop; and the relative remoteness of the route from towns and villages and requirement to carry kit and provisions.
Navigation The long-distance paths in this collection are waymarked but signage on some can be infrequent. This can be an issue on routes crossing remote or more difficult terrain where paths may be faint and/or where a sudden change in the weather can quickly reduce visibility, making wayfinding difficult, especially for walkers inexperienced in such conditions and where good navigation skills are called for.

Facilities The proximity of the route to services such as shops, pubs and cafés; the availability of a range of accommodation; and the relative connectedness of intermediate route stages to the public transport network.

Note: The factors relating to navigation and facilities may be mitigated if walking a route as part of a guided holiday or using a baggage transfer service. Unless you are a fit and experienced multi-day walker with good navigation and forward planning skills, tackling the most challenging routes as an end-to-end walk is not advised. Walking them piecemeal in convenient short-break stages, having pre-booked accommodation and travel is the best way to enjoy these wonderful trails.

DAY-WALK TASTER MAPS

See front cover flap.

ITINERARY DISTANCE TABLES

The suggested itineraries for end-to-end completion are for guidance only. On some longer routes, in addition to a typical schedule, an easier-paced regimen is listed. Fitness levels and walking experience, as well as location of accommodation and other facilities along a route, must be borne in mind when determining personal schedules.

In the **tables**, distances are rounded to the nearest ¼-mile/kilometre.

Key to Trail maps

② ——— ③ Route and suggested end-to-end itinerary day stages

④ ——— ⑤ Best weekend/short break section

⑥ ——— ⑦ Best day-walk taster section

★ Featured place of interest

National Park, Area of Outstanding Natural Beauty (England and Wales)

National Park, National Scenic Areas (Scotland)

Walking safely

Although few of the trails in this book tackle high mountains, they all deal with landscapes that need to be treated with respect, whether a modest hill, rugged sea cliff, undulating downland or upland moorland. Benign and thoroughly enjoyable in good weather conditions, all can be startlingly transformed into wet, misty, windswept and dangerous areas in poor conditions. Even on a fine day, weather can change rapidly, and anyone venturing onto these trails needs to be capable of coping with anything the countryside and its attendant weather throws at you.

Apart from the evident need to have warm and waterproof clothing, footwear, high-calorific food and drink, mapping and navigational devices (see *Navigation Skills for Walkers* by the author of this title, (ISBN 978-03190917530, available in bookshops and online at www.os.uk/shop), there is a need to be prepared both physically and mentally.

Walking on multiple days in variable weather presents its own repertoire of dirty tricks, so it is essential to be confident of your health and well-being to be fully prepared. Everyone benefits from regular exercise, but shouldering a hefty rucksack and striding out on a long and potentially arduous trek without preparation is foolhardy and likely to lead to demoralising and painful inconvenience.

On a multi-day walk, at the end of each day you have to be ready, willing and able to tackle the next day, and the next, and the next. Nor is it purely a physical thing; it's mental, too. You need to know what you can accomplish, and this can only be achieved by preparation: a couple of consecutive days walking will prepare you to do four; then four days will prepare you for a week or more, and so on. Only by acclimatising your body to these unusual demands can you become confident in your abilities and mentally prepared for any adversity that comes

your way. If all goes well, it will be a breeze and you may wonder what all the fuss is about. When it goes wrong, you'll find out. Being prepared is vital.

This book provides all the national trails alongside several of Scotland's Great Trails and an eclectic pick of regional trails. Some are comparatively short and easy, suitable for those wanting to advance to some of the more tough options, while those more difficult trails will appeal to experienced and strong walkers. For everyone, it is important to use the itineraries provided as guidelines only, and to adjust your days according to your own needs and abilities. If you look like finishing a day section earlier than you planned, so what? – the countryside has much to offer, make use of the time to earth yourself and engage with what nature is giving you and take an interest in what's around you.

Further information

ACCOMMODATION

All of the trails in this book have accommodation in some form along their length, though there are some remote stretches where it is limited. Each walk has a note indicating any problems that exist, but it is safe to say that booking accommodation well in advance will be critical during the summer months.

Information about accommodation along National Trails is available on www.nationaltrail.co.uk, and about hostels on www.yha.org.uk and www.independenthostels.co.uk. Hostel information for Scotland is at www.syha.co.uk. Details of other forms of accommodation and campsites are listed on the individual walk websites.

Wild camping is illegal in England and Wales, but not in Scotland if practised responsibly, although there are some stretches of the West Highland Way where camping has to be managed. Elsewhere, wild camping can be accommodated with the consent of the relevant landowners, but otherwise formal campsites must be used.

The Countryside Code for England and Wales

Published April 2021; for details see: www.gov.uk/government/publications/the-countryside-code

Respect everyone
- be considerate to those living in, working in and enjoying the countryside
- leave gates and property as you find them
- do not block access to gateways or driveways when parking
- be nice, say hello, share the space
- follow local signs and keep to marked paths unless wider access is available

Protect the environment
- take your litter home – leave no trace of your visit
- take care with BBQs and do not light fires
- always keep dogs under control and in sight
- dog poo – bag it and bin it – any public waste bin will do
- care for nature – do not cause damage or disturbance

Enjoy the outdoors
- check your route and local conditions
- plan your adventure – know what to expect and what you can do
- enjoy your visit, have fun, make a memory

BAGGAGE TRANSFER

Many of the trails are supported by commercial companies that offer baggage transfer facilities, enabling you to travel with just a day pack, while your main baggage is moved on to your next overnight halt.

TOURIST INFORMATION

The incidence of tourist information centres across all the walks in this book is not something to be relied on. However there are three umbrella organisations that can be relied on:
Visit England (www.visitengland.com),
Visit Scotland (www.visitscotland.com)
and **Visit Wales** (www.visitwales.com).

USEFUL WEBSITES

National Trails (England and Wales)
www.nationaltrail.co.uk

Scotland's Great Trails
www.scotlandsgreattrails.com

Natural England
www.gov.uk/government/organisations/natural-england

NatureScot www.nature.scot

Natural Resources Wales
www.naturalresources.wales

Forestry England www.forestryengland.uk

Forestry and Land Scotland
www.forestryandland.gov.scot

National Parks www.nationalparks.uk

Areas of Outstanding Natural Beauty
www.landscapesforlife.org.uk

Campaign to Protect Rural England
www.cpre.org.uk

Association for the Protection of Rural Scotland
www.aprs.scot

Countryside Council for Wales www.ccw.gov.uk

National Trust (England and Wales)
www.nationaltrust.org.uk

National Trust for Scotland www.nys.org.uk

English Heritage www.english-heritage.org.uk

Ramblers www.ramblers.org.uk

Long Distance Walkers Association
www.ldwa.org.uk

The Scottish Outdoor Access Code

1. Take responsibility for your own actions.

2. Respect people's privacy and peace of mind. When close to a house or garden, keep a sensible distance from the house, use a path or track if there is one, and take extra care at night.

3. Help land managers and others to work safely and effectively. Do not hinder land management operations and follow advice from land managers. Respect requests for reasonable limitations on when and where you can go.

4. Care for your environment. Do not disturb wildlife, leave the environment as you find it and follow a path or track if there is one.

5. Keep your dog under proper control. Do not take it through fields of calves and lambs, and dispose of dog dirt.

6. Take extra care if you are organising an event or running a business and ask the landowner's advice.

Further guidance is available at:
www.outdooraccess-scotland.scot.

ENGLAND

Warbarrow Bay, Dorset

Chiltern Way

Making the most of the stunning landscapes of the Chiltern Hills, the Chiltern Way paints a route across a canvas of appealing old villages, glorious beech woodland, bounded fields and downland with extensive views. The Way was created by the Chiltern Society as its Millennium Project, and passes through many of the most attractive parts of the Chilterns, notably the Chess, Misbourne and Hambleden valleys, Penn Country, Stonor Park, Swyncombe Down, Bledlow Ridge and Dunstable Down.

A chalk escarpment, the Chiltern Hills cover an area of 660 sq miles (1,700km²) north-west of London, from Goring-on-Thames to Hitchin, a distance of 45 miles (72km) rippled across the counties of Oxfordshire, Buckinghamshire, Hertfordshire and Bedfordshire. In 1965, almost half of the Chilterns was designated as an Area of Outstanding Natural Beauty (AONB). Its north-west boundary is clearly defined by the escarpment, while the south-west end point is the River Thames. The Thames, in fact, claims the greater part of the Chilterns, which lie within its drainage basin; although another curious feature of the Chilterns are its dry valleys, perfect for trouble-free walking.

This is a fecund scene: enclosed fields account for two-thirds of the AONB, but these are adorned with rich woodlands and copses, making this one of the most heavily wooded areas in England. During the Iron Age, the Chiltern ridge provided a comparatively safe and navigable route across southern Britain; the Icknield Way (one of England's ancient prehistoric trackways) follows the line of the hills, several of which exceed 650 feet (200m) in height.

The Chiltern Way is suitable for walkers of all abilities, and the route is well waymarked and managed by a team of volunteers. Given its nature, the Way perfectly lends itself to being tackled piecemeal, although its 134 miles (214km) are unlikely to trouble seasoned walkers intent on doing the complete round.

By way of added appeal to an already sumptuous menu, since the Way was opened in 2000, there have been three extensions that explore new areas and add a further 90 miles (144km) to the route. The 31-mile (50-km) Southern Extension runs from Bix Bottom via Mapledurham on the Thames, the Berkshire Loop is a 28-mile (45-km) ring crossing the Thames, while the North Chiltern Trail adds a further 27 miles (43km) running from Sharpenhoe Clappers via the Icknield Way and the outskirts of Hitchin to Peters Green. The route is signposted in both directions, and can be started at several locations.

> **AMAZING BUT TRUE ...**
> In the 1971 film version of *Dad's Army*, land-locked Chalfont St Giles served as the setting for the fictional Walmington-on-Sea. Its photogenic qualities and proximity to London make the Chilterns a favourite with big and small screen production companies.

Ashridge Estate

If taken in its entirety, the Chiltern Way will occupy 11 days at an average daily walk of around 12 miles. An itinerary of nine days takes the daily mileage up to around 15, but this still gives plenty of time to enjoy the scenery without it feeling like a route march. Such is the nature of the route and its transport links, however, that it is a simple task to determine the best breakdown of stages to suit your own abilities.

11 days

Start	Hemel Hempstead	Day 6	Wendover Dean *14¾mi/23.75km*
Day 1	Chalfont St Giles *13mi/21km*	Day 7	Aldbury *9½mi/15.25km*
Day 2	Marlow Bottom *14½mi/23km*	Day 8	Chalk Hill *12mi/19.25km*
Day 3	Stonor *12½mi/20.25km*	Day 9	Streatley *10¾mi/17.25km*
Day 4	Ewelme *7¾mi/12.5km*	Day 10	Peter's Green *13mi/21km*
Day 5	Stokenchurch *12mi/19.25km*	Day 11	Hemel Hempstead *15¼mi/24.5km*

Fingest

FACTS AND FIGURES

START AND FINISH Hemel Hempstead station (TL 042059)

DISTANCE 134 miles (215km)

HEIGHT GAIN 12,865 feet (3,920m)

DIFFICULTY RATING ♦♦

IS IT FOR ME? A well-waymarked route favourable for year-round walking with good access to facilities and reasonable public transport.

MAPS

OS Explorer
171, 172, 181, 182, 192, 193.
OS Landranger
164, 165, 166, 175, 176.

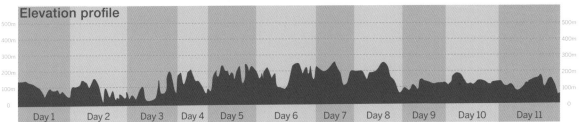

Elevation profile

GETTING THERE AND BACK
The main starting point, historic Hemel Hempstead, is served by rail on the West Coast mainline; its station is on the western edge of the town. Several other towns and villages are also served by rail on four main lines, as well as bus transport.

ACCOMMODATION
The Chilterns are a popular tourist destination, and accommodation of all standards is in plentiful supply, but very much in demand during the summer months.

WEBSITES
https://chilternsociety.org/the-chiltern-way
www.visitchilterns.co.uk

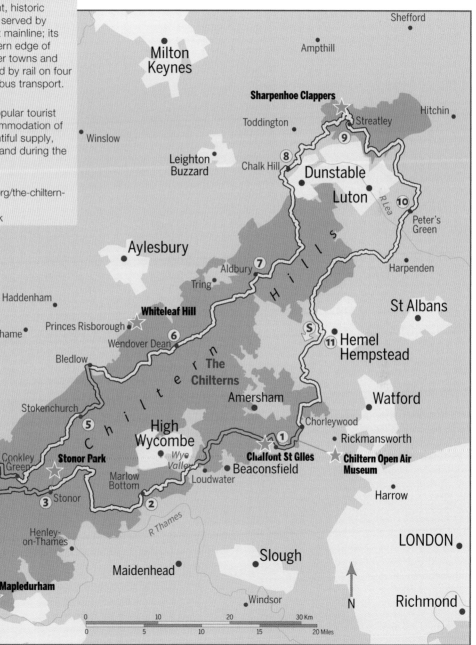

CHORLEYWOOD TO WYE VALLEY
(12½ miles/20km)

After Chorleywood and Newland Park, the way descends into the Misbourne Valley and photogenic Chalfont St Giles, a pretty village that doubled as Walmington-on-Sea in the 1971 film version of *Dad's Army*. The Way then crosses quiet upland Penn country, passing Coleshill, Winchmore Hill and Penn to reach the Wye Valley east of Loudwater.

STONOR TO COCKLEY GREEN
(12 miles/18km)

Shunning a more direct and shorter route between these two small settlements, the Chiltern Way launches itself westwards from Stonor to the ancient village of Ewelme – its church and almshouses are particularly attractive – and from there up onto the escarpment of Swyncombe Downs – one of the most stunning projections of the Chiltern escarpment, its ridge earthwork is thought to date from around 870, when the Danes reached the area – before heading for the hamlet of Cockley Green, a small group of houses set around a traditional village green.

★ Whiteleaf Hill

Not far from Princes Risborough, and well worth the brief diversion, Whiteleaf Hill Local Nature Reserve has five scheduled ancient monuments, some dating to the Neolithic and Bronze Ages, along with Whiteleaf Cross – a cross-shaped chalk hill carving, the date and origin of which are unknown. The southern part of the nature reserve is ancient semi-natural beech woodland dating from at least 1600.

★ Mapledurham

On the north bank of the Thames is a small village and country estate that has been used in several film sets, notably the 1976 thriller *The Eagle has Landed*, and for several television series, including *Midsomer Murders*. The village watermill dates from the 16th century and is the last operational watermill on the Thames. Mapledurham House is one of the largest Elizabethan houses in Oxfordshire.

Stonor Park is an historic country house and private deer park; it has been the ancestral home of the Stonor family for more than 800 years. Even older than this historic house was a stone circle formed of giant boulders, known as erratics, left behind at the end of the last Ice Age, and fashioned into a circle by prehistoric people. In 601, the Pope called on priests in England to adopt Pagan sites of worship for the Catholic faith, and so the chapel at Stonor was built on the site of the circle. One of the original stones has been symbolically incorporated into the foundations of the chapel.

The escarpment of Swyncombe Downs – one of the most stunning projections of the Chiltern escarpment

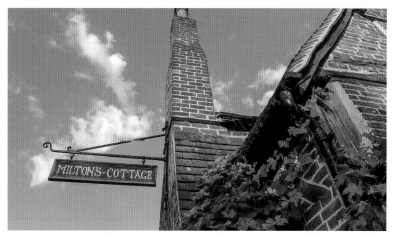

★ Chalfont St Giles

This charming village lies on the edge of the Chiltern Hills and has been home to some interesting personalities, including Ozzy Osbourne, Noel Gallagher and Nick Clegg, the sometime deputy prime minister of England. During the Great Plague of London in 1665, poet and intellectual John Milton retired to Chalfont St Giles to complete his epic poem *Paradise Lost* in safety. The 16th-century Milton's Cottage still stands in the village, and is open to the public.

STOKENCHURCH TO BLEDLOW
(5½ miles/9km)

If truth be known, then, probably, the best bit of the Chiltern Way is all of it; there are just so many delightful stretches that finding one that stands out from the rest is impossible. But this undulating route out of the ancient village of Stokenchurch, across Bledlow Ridge and by way of Rout's Green to the village of Bledlow, is as good as any. A large chalk cross carved into the side of Wain Hill above Bledlow is worth a visit.

Another curious feature of the Chilterns are its dry valleys, perfect for trouble-free walking

★ Sharpenhoe Clappers

Host to an Iron Age fort, Sharpenhoe Clappers, a classic chalk escarpment to the south of the hamlet of Sharpenhoe, is one of a series of defended sites established along the Chiltern ridge during the Late Bronze Age and Iron Age. Today, it is the only regional example of a promontory fort that relied for its defence on the strength of its topographical location – its commanding position dominating the local landscape, providing not only defence but also displaying the status of its former inhabitants.

SPARKING REBELLION

The Chiltern Way passes through the former estate villages of Great and Little Hampden. The most famous member of the Hampden family – the lords of the manor – was John (1595–1643), a Parliamentary opponent of King Charles I, whose refusal to pay ship money in 1641 helped to trigger the Civil War. He was killed in 1643 while fighting for the Parliamentary army at the Battle of Chalgrove Field.

★ Chiltern Open Air Museum

Just outside Chalfont is the Chiltern Open Air Museum, a place that takes visitors back in time. Here a plethora of reconstructed historic buildings include an Iron Age roundhouse, a Victorian toll house, wartime Nissen huts and a working historic farm with goats, sheep, cows and cats, all of which is embraced in 45 acres of the beautiful Chiltern countryside. Given such a range of buildings, it is not surprising that several films and television dramas have been set here, including *Downton Abbey*, *Call the Midwife* and *Grantchester*.

Nature on the trail (clockwise): The rare Chiltern gentian; red kite; nuthatch; marbled white butterfly.

Cleveland Way 🔔

Along the Cleveland Way, officially opened in 1969, lush heather moorland contrasts strikingly with exceptional coastal scenery, making this a trail of two halves. Much of the Way falls within the North York Moors National Park, and it is a testament to the quality of the landscapes that two other challenging walks – the Lyke Wake Walk and the Coast to Coast Walk – run concurrently with the Cleveland Way.

The moorland, rich in heathered expanses, is a managed red grouse habitat; at its most vibrant in summer, it is a delight to traverse. In contrast, the coastal settings bring dramatic cliffs, coastal scars and skerries and a union with the England Coast Path.

The varied nature of the landscapes through which the Way passes is such that many days have their own unique characteristics, starting with the charming market town of Helmsley (home base of the North York Moors National Park), which still has its compact medieval layout. Close by the centre stand the remains of Helmsley Castle, destroyed during the Civil War, and once owned by Richard III who was granted it in 1478.

On leaving Helmsley, the Cleveland Way soon reaches the Hambleton Down racecourse, once one of the top racecourses in the country. Beyond, the Way traverses a fine escarpment to Sutton Bank and on across the limestone Hambleton Hills to the village of Osmotherley, following an 18th- and 19th-century drove road.

The undulations of the Cleveland Hills now await, rising abruptly from the flat Tees valley, including the distinctive cone-shaped peak of Roseberry Topping near Great Ayton, the childhood home of Captain James Cook. This invigorating section crosses five moors: Scarth Wood Moor, Live Moor, Cringle Moor, Cold Moor and Hasty Bank, all of which have needed major path restoration in recent times. Along this stretch, keep an eye open for evidence of alum, jet and ironstone mining.

Having passed through Guisborough Woods, the longest stretch of forestry on the Way, the route finally reaches the coast at Saltburn-by-the-Sea, a place much favoured by Victorian excursionists. Now it's all coastline, and Heritage Coast at that, through Staithes, Whitby, Robin Hood's Bay (the end of the Coast-to-Coast Walk), Ravenscar and the busy resort of Scarborough, before finally coming to rest on the long, narrow peninsula of Filey Brigg.

AMAZING BUT TRUE ...
At Sutton Bank, the Cleveland Way crosses the A170 at the top of one of the most notorious sections of A-class road in Britain. The ascent has a 25% gradient (1 in 4) and an acute hairpin bend midway up. Vehicles towing caravans are prohibited.

Whitby

END TO END

The Cleveland Way falls into nine convenient stages, the longest of these is just 17½ miles (28km), making the route ideal for tackling on a day-by-day basis, although not all days end at convenient places to find accommodation.

9 days

Start	Helmsley	Day 5	Saltburn-by-the-Sea 15mi/24km
Day 1	Sutton Bank 10mi/16km	Day 6	Sandsend 17½mi/28km
Day 2	Osmotherley 11½mi/18.5km	Day 7	Robin Hood's Bay 10½mi/16.5km
Day 3	Clay Bank 11¼mi/18km	Day 8	Scarborough 12¼mi/19.5km
Day 4	Kildale 9½mi/15km	Day 9	Filey Brigg 10½mi/17km

Lush heather moorland contrasts strikingly with exceptional coastal scenery, making this a trail of two halves

FACTS AND FIGURES

START Helmsley, North Yorkshire (SE 612838)

FINISH Filey Brigg, North Yorkshire (TA 130815)

DISTANCE 109 miles (175km)

HEIGHT GAIN 20,550 feet (6,265m)

DIFFICULTY RATING ◆◆◆◆

IS IT FOR ME? Some strenuous sections with no access to facilities or public transport; good fitness levels and forward planning essential.

PRACTICALITIES

GETTING THERE AND BACK
Helmsley is served by a regular bus service from Scarborough, while Filey has both rail and bus connections.

ACCOMMODATION
The Cleveland Way has plentiful accommodation in several sections, but hardly anything along the Cleveland Hills themselves, though there are camping pods (and a café) on Carlton Bank at the Lord Stones.

WEBSITES
www.nationaltrail.co.uk/cleveland-way
www.clevelandway.co.uk

MAPS

OS Explorer
OL26, OL27, 301, 306.
OS Landranger
93, 94, 99, 100, 101.

Top: Captain Cook monument, Whitby.
Left: Robin Hood's Bay.

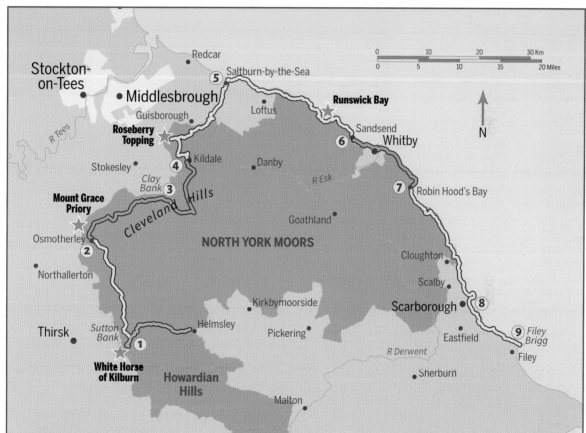

Map labels:

Stockton-on-Tees

Redcar

Saltburn-by-the-Sea ⑤

Middlesbrough

Runswick Bay

Guisborough

Loftus

Sandsend

Roseberry Topping ⭐

Whitby

Stokesley

Kildale

Danby ⑥

R Esk

④

Clay Bank

Cleveland Hills

③

⑦ Robin Hood's Bay

Mount Grace Priory ⭐

Goathland

Osmotherley ②

NORTH YORK MOORS

Northallerton

Cloughton

Scalby

Kirkbymoorside

Scarborough ⑧

Thirsk

Helmsley

Pickering

Eastfield

⑨ Filey Brigg

Sutton Bank ①

R Derwent

Filey

White Horse of Kilburn ⭐

Sherburn

Howardian Hills

Malton

R Tees

0   10   20   30 Km
0   5   10   15   20 Miles

N

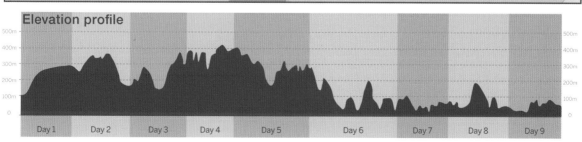

Elevation profile

500m · 400m · 300m · 200m · 100m · 0

Day 1 · Day 2 · Day 3 · Day 4 · Day 5 · Day 6 · Day 7 · Day 8 · Day 9

OSMOTHERLEY TO KILDALE
(20¾ miles/33km)

A long day, or two shorter ones, that will be filled with joy. Anyone staying in Osmotherley may be tempted to visit the nearby Mount Grace Priory, one of only nine Carthusian priories founded in Britain, and the best preserved (see page 30).

From Osmotherley, perched on elevated ground at the western edge of the North York Moors, the route crosses the Cleveland Hills, taking in five moors. En route, there is plentiful evidence of the mining activity that occurred here, including for alum, ironstone and jet; jet became de rigueur mourning jewellery in Victorian times following the death of Prince Albert.

On Urra Moor, beyond the convenient halt at Lord Stones on Carlton Bank (camping and camping pods), the Way crosses the highest point of the North York Moors, where there are several stone markers and crosses. Further on are the fascinating gathering of rocks known as the Wain Stones. At Bloworth Crossing, the Way strikes north along the continuing escarpment before leaving the hills to drop into the village of Kildale.

★ Runswick Bay

In 2020, Runswick Bay was chosen by the *Sunday Times* as 'Beach of the Year'. Runswick Bay, which also gives its name to the nearby cliff-side village, is a popular tourist attraction famed for its white sand beach. The original village suffered devastation during a landslide in the 17th century, but was rebuilt further to the south. The village is divided into two parts: the 'lower' densely packed, red-roofed, cliff-side, former-fishing village with narrow winding streets and steep steps; and Runswick Bank Top, a hamlet located adjacent to farmland overlooking the bay. The Cleveland Way follows the steep lane that links the two parts.

SANDSEND TO ROBIN HOOD'S BAY
(10½ miles/16.5km)

Making the most of outstanding coastal scenery, this stretch of the Way grew in popularity during the Victorian era. On leaving Sandsend, the route soon reaches Whitby, a settlement that prospered from whaling, shipbuilding and the trade in jet. However, it seems a high percentage of today's visitors are bent on that great British classic, fish and chips. The abbey above the town gave inspiration to author Bram Stoker, who used tales he had gleaned there to fashion his infamous character, Dracula.

Robin Hood's Bay, an old fishing village, has a notorious history of smuggling and piracy; notably between 1700 and 1850, it was reportedly the busiest smuggling community on the Yorkshire coast, protected by marshy moorland on three sides. Man is believed to have first inhabited this area 3,000 years ago, during the Bronze Age, and continuously since. In spite of its name, there is no evidence that the famed outlaw ever visited the area, and it may have derived from a folkloric name for a woodland sprite or spirit.

For many who roll down its narrow, twisted, cobbled streets and alleyways today, however, it represents the eastern end of the Coast-to-Coast Walk (page 33). Here, red-roofed cottages huddle together in a companionship that has lasted for centuries, many said to be inter-connected by secret passageways through which contraband could be passed unobserved.

★ White Horse of Kilburn

Just before reaching Sutton Bank, near Roulston Scar, on the edge of the Hambleton tableland, the Way passes the White Horse of Kilburn. This is a hill figure cut into the hillside, and is the largest and most northerly hill figure in England. It was created, allegedly, by a local school master and his pupils in 1857; although other accounts link it to a native of Kilburn, Thomas Taylor, who is known to have visited the prehistoric Uffington White Horse in Oxfordshire in 1857 and came home inspired to provide his home village with its own version.

The route crosses the Cleveland Hills, taking in five moors

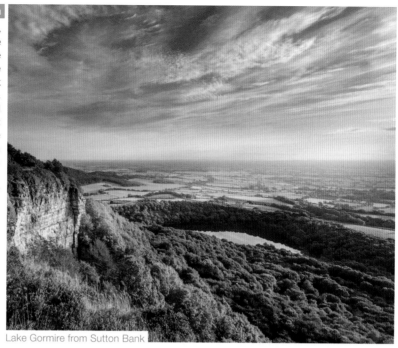

Lake Gormire from Sutton Bank

★ Roseberry Topping

Once thought to be the highest hill in the North York Moors (1,049 feet/320m), Roseberry Topping – 'Yorkshire's Matterhorn' – is today managed by the National Trust. It has a distinctive half-cone shape flanked by a rugged cliff, and may well have been held in special regard by the Vikings who inhabited this area during the medieval period and, as elsewhere in Britain, gave the region many of its place names. A spur from the Cleveland Way runs up to its summit, and it has been a popular ascent for centuries, having unrivalled views of the valley below.

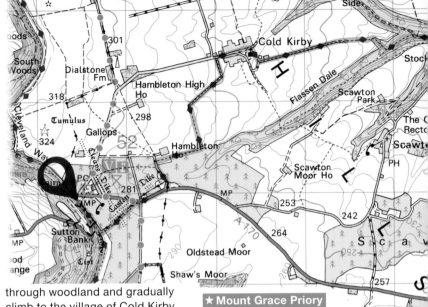

HELMSLEY TO SUTTON BANK
(10 miles/16km)

There is much of interest in the delightful market town of Helmsley, not least the ruins of Helmsley Castle surrounded by banks and a huge double ditch, and Duncombe Park, home to the Duncombe family, and one of Yorkshire's finest historic houses (www.duncombepark.com).

This initial stretch of the Cleveland Way is a great introduction, and the walking not too demanding. Shortly after leaving Helmsley, the route passes Rievaulx Abbey, ensconced in the wooded Rye valley, where it has dominated the region for over 800 years. Onward, you walk through woodland and gradually climb to the village of Cold Kirby and on past Hambleton Down Racecourse onto the dramatic escarpment of Sutton Bank. The Vale of York author James Herriot (*All Creatures Great and Small*) claimed the view from Sutton Bank to be 'the finest in England'.

★ Mount Grace Priory

Close by the village of Osmotherley, Mount Grace Priory is the best preserved and most accessible of the nine medieval Carthusian charterhouses in England. The individual cells emphasise the isolation of the monks who lived as hermits, each in his own cell, coming together only during nocturnal hours, Sundays and feast-days. They were a silent order, and lived on a diet that was strictly vegetarian (www.nationaltrust.org.uk/mount-grace-priory).

This page (top): The Wain Stones; (bottom): Robin Hood's Bay. **Opposite page**: Whitby Abbey.

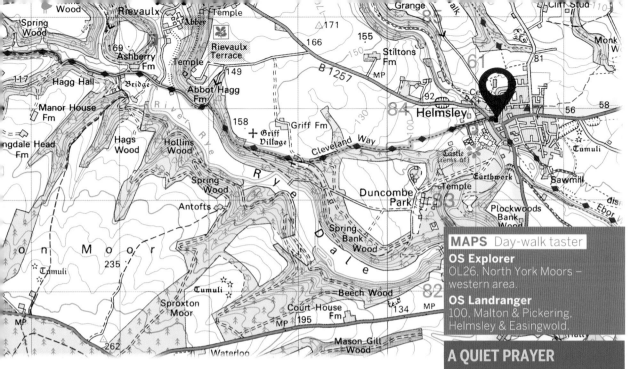

MAPS Day-walk taster

OS Explorer
OL26, North York Moors –
western area.

OS Landranger
100, Malton & Pickering,
Helmsley & Easingwold.

A QUIET PRAYER

Daily monastic life had a
regular structure of prayer
at eight appointed times:

Matins or *Vigils*: at nighttime,
a period from 2am up
to, but before dawn.

Lauds: at dawn, the time varying
according to seasonal first light.

Prime: during the first hour of
daylight, typically at 6am.

Terce: at the third hour of
daylight, typically at 9am.

Sext: at the sixth hour of
daylight, typically at noon.

None: at the ninth hour of
daylight, mid-afternoon,
typically at 3pm.

Vespers: at sunset, with
seasonal variation but
typically at 6pm.

Compline: at the end of the day
before retiring to bed, after 7pm.

The times of these canonical
hours would be sounded
by the tolling of a bell.

Nature on the trail (clockwise):
Emperor moth; merlin; kittiwake;
red grouse.

Coast to Coast Path ▶

WALK 3

Usually tackled west to east, the northern England Coast-to-Coast walk is hugely popular, and rightly so, connecting as it does the coastline of Cumbria with that of North Yorkshire, running from St Bees to Robin Hood's Bay. En route, the walk ventures into three national parks: the Lake District, Yorkshire Dales and the North York Moors, and takes its pick of the finest countryside in between.

The original idea is credited to the late Alfred Wainwright, who put his route forward simply as one of many possible ways from which he encouraged walkers to devise their own. Over the years the route has largely remained static, although a way across the Vale of Mowbray has evolved that avoids much of the original road walking into Danby Wiske, largely making use of field-edge paths on rights-of-way; elsewhere variants have been devised that avoid the most sensitive landscape areas.

Combining both high- and low-level sections, the C2C (as it has become branded), is neither an easy ramble nor a major mountain challenge. If extravagant beauty taken at a leisurely pace is your bag, then the C2C fits perfectly. With only a little bit of difficulty does it lend itself to completion on a piecemeal basis – some start points are awkward to get to.

Fundamentally, there are five distinct sections, and anyone unable to devote the time for a complete undertaking may well consider a fragmented approach. First, across the Lake District is certainly the most arduous section for finding routes between several Lakeland dales and fells, before ambling easily across outstanding countryside to Shap. The section through the Dales largely follows the course of rivers; while that through the North York Moors blends bucolic landscapes with heathered upland and far-reaching views.

In between, there are two relatively lowland sections: from Shap on the edge of Lakeland into the Dales, and further east across the delectable Vale of Mowbray. These are agreeable interludes of unadulterated pleasantness, but should not be underestimated; enjoy but certainly don't be beguiled into thinking it's as easy as it sometimes appears. Use these sections to recharge body and soul.

Taken as a whole, the Coast to Coast may appear daunting, but if you think of it as five consecutive linear walks, each with their own challenges, history, landscapes and uniqueness it becomes less so. To misappropriate Keats, the Coast to Coast is 'A thing of beauty … a jot for ever.'

> ## AMAZING BUT TRUE …
> The total ascent along the entire 188-mile length of the C2C between St Bees and Robin Hood's Bay is the equivalent of climbing to the summit of Mount Everest from sea level, at 29,125 feet (8,880m). The highest point on the route is the Lakeland fell top of Kidsty Pike, 2,560 feet (780m).

Haweswater

END TO END

The Coast to Coast Walk falls into five distinct 'main' stages and several shorter stages that lend themselves to a comfortable trek of 13, 15 or 19 days, averaging 14½, 12½ and 10 miles a day respectively. The following itineraries are merely suggestions.

	13 days	**15 days**	**19 days**
Start	St Bees	St Bees	St Bees
Day 1	Ennerdale Bridge *14¼mi/23km*	Ennerdale Bridge *14¼mi/23km*	Cleator *7½mi/12km*
Day 2	Rosthwaite *14½mi/23.25km*	Rosthwaite *14½mi/23.25km*	Ennerdale Bridge *6mi/11km*
Day 3	Patterdale *17¾mi/28.5km*	Grasmere *8½mi/13.75km*	Black Sail Hut *10mi/16km*
Day 4	Shap *16mi/25.75km*	Patterdale *9¼mi/15km*	Rosthwaite *4½mi/7.25km*
Day 5	Kirkby Stephen *20mi/32km*	Shap *16mi/25.75km*	Grasmere *8½mi/13.75km*
Day 6	Keld *12¾mi/20.5km*	Kirkby Stephen *20mi/32km*	Patterdale *9¼mi/15km*
Day 7	Reeth *11¼mi/18km*	Keld *12¾mi/20.5km*	Shap *16mi/25.75km*
Day 8	Richmond *10½mi/16.75km*	Reeth *11¼mi/18km*	Orton *7¾mi/12.5km*
Day 9	Danby Wiske *13mi/21km*	Richmond *10½mi/16.75km*	Kirkby Stephen *12¼mi/19.5km*
Day 10	Ingleby Cross *8½mi/13.75km*	Danby Wiske *13mi/21km*	Keld *12¾mi/20.5km*
Day 11	Blakey Ridge *18½mi/29.5km*	Ingleby Cross *8½mi/13.75km*	Reeth *11¼mi/18km*
Day 12	Grosmont *13¼mi/21.25km*	Clay Bank Top *10mi/16km*	Richmond *10½mi/16.75km*
Day 13	Robin Hood's Bay *14¼mi/22.75km*	Blakey Ridge *8½mi/13.75km*	Bolton-on-Swale *6½mi/10.5km*
Day 14		Grosmont *13¼mi/21.25km*	Danby Wiske *6½mi/10.5km*
Day 15		Robin Hood's Bay *14¼mi/22.75km*	Ingleby Cross *8½mi/13.75km*
Day 16			Clay Bank Top *10mi/16km*
Day 17			Glaisdale *17½mi/28km*
Day 18			Grosmont *4½mi/7.25km*
Day 19			Robin Hood's Bay *14¼mi/22.75km*

FACTS AND FIGURES

START St Bees, Cumbria (NX 962117)

FINISH Robin Hood's Bay, North Yorkshire (NZ 951053)

DISTANCE 188 miles (302km)

HEIGHT GAIN 29,125 feet (8,880m)

DIFFICULTY RATING ◆◆◆◆

IS IT FOR ME? A mix of challenging sections and comparatively easy-going ones; not for the novice long-distance walker.

PRACTICALITIES

GETTING THERE AND BACK
St Bees is accessible by both rail and bus; Robin Hood's Bay just by bus, the nearest railhead being at Whitby.

ACCOMMODATION The Coast to Coast Walk route is generally well served with accommodation for walkers, but at busy times of the year some forward planning will be needed if you are to avoid long deviations to find somewhere to sleep.

CAMPING There are several formal and informal campsites dotted across the Coast to Coast, in addition to which many landowners will allow one-night camping on their land in return for a polite request to do so.

WEBSITES
www.coasttocoast.uk
www.coastto.co.uk
There is a Facebook group that provides information on current activities and recommendations for the Coast to Coast Path; see www.facebook.com and search for 'Coast to Coast Walk'.

MAPS
OS Explorer
OL4, OL5, OL19, OL26, OL27, OL30, 303, 304.
OS Landranger
89, 90, 91, 92, 93, 94, 98, 99, 100.

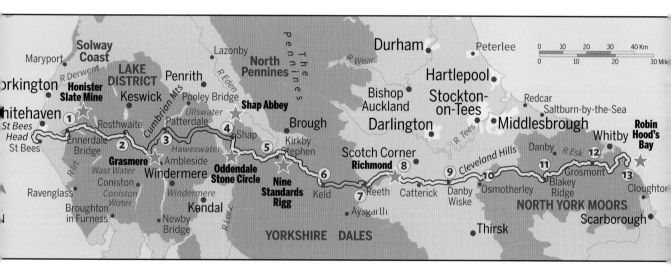

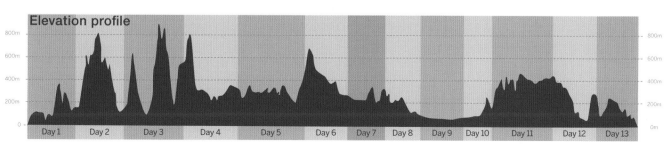

GRASMERE TO PATTERDALE
(9¼ miles/15km)

Taking the line of least resistance between these two villages, the C2C squeezes between the fells of Seat Sandal and the higher Fairfield and through Hause Gap to Grisedale Tarn, before taking a choice of ways down the valley of Grisedale to Patterdale at the southern end of Ullswater.

PATTERDALE TO SHAP
(16 miles/25.75km)

On leaving Patterdale, the route tackles the knobbly terrain to the east, passing Angletarn Pikes and Angle Tarn itself before rising to a high point on Rampsgill Head, from where a steep descent leads to an excellent shoreline walk along Haweswater Reservoir to the hamlet of Burnbanks. Beyond, farmland awaits, the route twisting and turning first to the ruins of Shap Abbey before finally exiting the Lakeland fells and heading for Shap.

★ Grasmere

This appealing village lies a short way off the line of the Coast to Coast, but is invariably visited by most walkers. It is of great attraction and sometime home base of Lakeland poet, William Wordsworth, who lies buried in the churchyard. Grasmere is also the home of Grasmere Gingerbread, a unique, spicy-sweet cross between a biscuit and cake.

★ Nine Standards Rigg

Arrival on Nine Standards Rigg deserves a moment of appreciation, sitting as it does on the great watershed, that imaginary line dividing the waters of Britain east and west. The large cairns that comprise the Nine Standards sit on the border between the former counties of Westmorland and the North Riding of Yorkshire, but no one has yet come up with any historical fact to account for them.

★ Honister Slate Mine

C2C walkers cannot avoid this mine, which was the last working slate mine in England, and in operation since the late 17th century, quarrying the attractive Westmorland green slate. Today it is also the focal point of several adventure activities, including via ferrata and cliff camping.

St Bees Head

★ Robin Hood's Bay

A picture-postcard village on the North York Moors Heritage Coast, this was a noted place of smuggling and piracy between 1700 and 1850. It's narrow and twisting cobbled streets and alleyways, so evocative of these illicit times, are today lined with a wide range of interesting places to eat and drink. There's a sandy beach, popular with families, with opportunities for rock pooling and fossil hunting.

KELD TO REETH
(11¼ miles/18km)

or

KELD TO RICHMOND
(21¾ miles/34.75km)

The remote hamlet of Keld has a limited (Monday–Saturday) Little White Bus service (Route 30) from Catterick and Richmond (www.dalesbus.org).

Shortly after leaving Keld, crossing the River Swale very briefly in company with the Pennine Way (page 102), the walker bound for Reeth has a choice between a high-level route branching into Swinner Gill for a taste of the region's industrial archaeology, or the less demanding low-level option staying with the River Swale throughout, and continuing on to Richmond. This is delightful walking all the way, especially in spring and early summer.

★ Richmond

Totally dominated by its castle, Richmond boasts the largest horseshoe market place in England, once the outer bailey of the town's castle. Below the castle, lies a labyrinthine network of narrow alleyways and back streets, called 'wynds', formed by groups of haphazardly built houses and shops.

If extravagant beauty taken at a leisurely pace is your bag, then the C2C fits perfectly

This page (top): Richmond; (middle): Burnbanks; (bottom): Shap Abbey.
Opposite page: Overlooking Haweswater.

★ Shap Abbey

The Abbey at Shap was one of the monastic houses established during the 12th century by the order founded by the German saint, Norbert. The end of the abbey came in 1540, when the last abbot surrendered the abbey's possessions to the Crown under Henry VIII's Dissolution of the Monasteries. Today it is an evocative ruin, full of interest for those with a penchant for religious architecture.

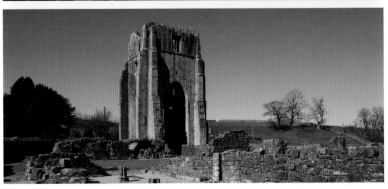

★ Oddendale stone circle

(NY 592 129) Difficult to locate because it is made up of small stones, the Oddendale circle is part of a much larger complex of cairns, stone circles and standing stones. Believed to have been constructed almost 5,000 years ago, it is just a small part of the legacy of Neolithic and Early Bronze Age field monuments around Crosby Ravensworth.

Nature on the trail (clockwise):
Red deer above Haweswater; Herdwick sheep; cottongrass; marsh trefoil.

GINGERBREAD, WHAT BETTER WAY TO FUEL YOUR COAST-TO-COAST WALK?

Grasmere Gingerbread was first made in 1854. While the recipe is a closely guarded secret, why not make you own gingerbread to provide sustenance on any long-distance walk?

Ingredients	Method
8oz/225g self-raising flour	1 Sieve together flour, salt and ground ginger
4oz/125g oatmeal	
Pinch of salt	2 Warm the butter until it melts with the black treacle
5oz/150g soft brown sugar	
2 heaped tsp ground ginger	3 Add the dry ingredients with the sugar and eggs
1 tbsp soft preserved ginger, chopped	
6oz/175g unsalted butter	4 Beat well adding the milk gradually
8oz/225g black treacle	5 Pour the mixture into a greased/lined cake tin and bake for 1½ hours at 180°C/gas 4
2 eggs	
¼ pint/130ml milk	

Cotswold Way 🔔

That a walking route through the Cotswolds was mooted as long ago as the 1950s may come as a surprise, given that it was only officially opened as a national trail in 2007. The route grew in popularity during the 1970s and 1980s, and the appeal is obvious the moment you enter the wider Cotswolds. Here, there are honey-coloured, medieval villages, pastoral landscapes with far-reaching views and prehistoric sites, through which the Cotswold Way fashions a route before concluding in the World Heritage City of Bath.

The Way meanders across the western scarp slopes of Cotswold Edge, crossed by long-established paths and trails, and characterised by undulating land forms where the escarpment is fragmented. Following a roughly south-westerly direction from the archetypal English market town of Chipping Campden to the Roman city of Bath, almost the entire Way lies within the Cotswold Area of Outstanding Natural Beauty. Along the way, the route tackles extensive rolling pasturelands, flower-filled meadows, beech woodland and, most renowned, those visually captivating villages built from the warm-hued Cotswold stone. What makes the Cotswold landscape so distinctive is its geology, of course – the underlying oolitic limestone,

a sedimentary rock formed in England during the Jurassic period 200-145 million years ago.

Elsewhere, there are Neolithic burial barrows, historic battle sites, stately homes and the stunning views from the escarpment, which, be warned, contains several unsuspected steep ups and downs. On a good day, it is possible to pick out the Clee Hills, near Ludlow in Shropshire, 60 miles (97km) to the north-west. A little closer, there are inspiring views to the Malvern Hills and the hazy blue hills of the Mendips and the Welsh borderlands.

For the most part, once away from Chipping Campden, the route involves comparatively little hard-surface walking, the greater part being on grass or compacted tracks through woodland and across fields, largely avoiding busy roads, which is a credit to the original route designers. Being a national trail, the Cotswold Way is well waymarked throughout and is one of the easier national trails. Guidebooks tend to favour a north–south direction, as designed, but there is something to be said for going the other way, too. Towns and villages pop up, often enough to provide welcome breaks, especially so if you have a hankering for the old, traditional pubs of Britain.

> **AMAZING BUT TRUE ...**
>
> Dover's Hill, encountered soon after leaving the start of the Cotswold Way at Chipping Campden, is named after a local lawyer, Robert Dover, who in 1612 founded some famous games here, known as the Cotswold 'Olympicks'. They were very popular, but eventually drunken unruliness led to their abolition in 1853. In 1951, the games were revived, albeit somewhat more sedately.

Painswick Beacon

The entire route of the Way has been completed in under 20 hours! For those with less urgency, the Way can be walked comfortably in seven days without any day being greater than 21¾ miles (35km). Extending this to eight or more days builds in time to explore the many sights and sites encountered, and to immerse oneself in the history and fabric of the Cotswolds. By keeping the days very short – perfect for exploring – it is possible to take up to 15 days for the walk. The following itineraries are suggestions only.

	7 days	8 days
Start	Chipping Campden	Chipping Campden
Day 1	Winchcombe *18mi / 29km*	Wood Stanway *12½mi / 20km*
Day 2	Birdlip *21¾mi / 35km*	Whittington *15¼mi / 24.5km*
Day 3	Painswick *7¼mi / 11.7km*	Birdlip *11¾mi / 19km*
Day 4	Dursley *16½mi / 26.5km*	Stroud *15½mi / 24.75km*
Day 5	Hawkesbury Upton *12¾mi / 20.25km*	North Nibley *10½mi / 16.75km*
Day 6	Cold Ashton *14mi / 22.25km*	Hawkesbury Upton *10¼mi / 16.5km*
Day 7	Bath *10¼mi / 16.5km*	Pennsylvania *13¼mi / 21.25km*
Day 8		Bath *11mi / 17.75km*

FACTS AND FIGURES

START Chipping Campden, Gloucestershire (SP 150391)

FINISH Bath, Somerset (ST 751649)

DISTANCE 101 miles (161km)

HEIGHT GAIN 15,545 feet (4,740m)

DIFFICULTY RATING ♦♦♦

IS IT FOR ME? More energetic than one might imagine, but the route is well waymarked and well served with facilities and public transport links.

Cleeve Hill

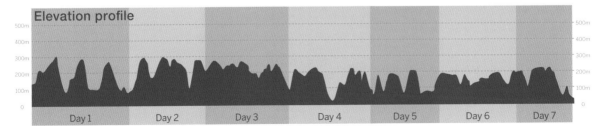
Elevation profile

PRACTICALITIES

GETTING THERE AND BACK
Chipping Campden is not the easiest of places to get to using public transport. Buses do run from Cheltenham, and there are railway stations at Moreton-in-Marsh and Stratford-upon-Avon. Bath, in contrast, is well served by buses, coaches and trains, with direct services from London and elsewhere.

ACCOMMODATION
There is ample accommodation in the larger towns, but elsewhere options are limited. Budget accommodation is virtually non-existent, likewise bunkhouses and inexpensive guesthouses, so the likelihood is that you'll need to use hotels, pubs and B&Bs. Planning ahead is essential, especially if walking the Way during the summer months; over 200,000 visitors walk the Cotswold Way each year, competing for accommodation. At a practical level, since the Cotswolds AONB area is very popular with tourists, the prices for food and drink and somewhere to stay reflect this. Campsites, too, are limited, and wild camping isn't permitted anywhere along the Cotswold Way. At a push, you could try asking farmers along the way for permission to camp overnight in a field, but don't just pitch a tent without doing so.

WEBSITES
www.nationaltrail.co.uk
www.cotswolds.com
http://cotswoldwayassociation.org.uk
www.cotswoldsaonb.org.uk

MAPS
OS Explorer
OL45, 155, 167, 168, 179.
OS Landranger
150, 151, 162, 163, 172.

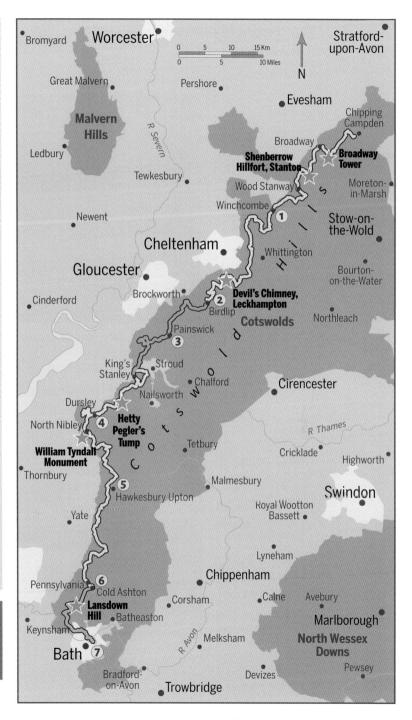

BIRDLIP TO KING'S STANLEY
(16¼ miles/26km)

On leaving Birdlip, the Way passes through splendid semi-natural beech woodlands and on to Coopers Hill, which hosts an annual cheese rolling festival. Around Painswick Beacon, the ramparts of an Iron Age hill fort can still be seen.

Descending from Painswick, the Way climbs again onto Edge Common before plunging back into woodland, heading for Haresfield Beacon with views along the escarpment and of the River Severn. Standish Woods are especially delightful in springtime, when they are lush with bluebells and wood anemone and lead down into the Stroud valley.

Coopers Hill

★ William Tyndall Monument

Constructed in 1866 and standing at 111 feet (34m) tall, the monument was built in honour of William Tyndall, a leading figure in the Protestant Reformation and translator of the New Testament. From its location on a hill at North Nibley, there is a pleasing view down the River Severn.

★ Broadway Tower

Rising from the Cotswold escarpment, Broadway Tower is an iconic landmark. It was the brainchild of that great 18th-century landscape designer, 'Capability' Brown, who built it for George William, the 6th Earl of Coventry, with the help of James Wyatt, the renowned architect, and completed in 1798. Today, the tower houses exhibitions about the history of its chequered past.

★Devil's Chimney, Leckhampton

A curious limestone rock formation standing above a disused quarry in Leckhampton, the Devil's chimney is named for its peculiar shape, which makes it look like a crooked chimney. According to legend, this is the chimney of the Devil's underground dwelling deep beneath the ground. Supposedly the Devil, provoked by the many Christian churches of the area, would sit on Leckhampton Hill and hurl stones at Sunday churchgoers.

★ Shenberrow Hillfort, Stanton

Dating from the Iron Age, Shenberrow is one of the smaller camps that once lined the western edge of the Cotswolds escarpment. Today, there is not much to see of the camp's outer ramparts, although the inner ditch and rampart on the north-east side have been well preserved by large trees.

★Hetty Pegler's Tump

More correctly known as Uley Long Barrow, but named after Hester Pegler who owned the land in the 17th century, this is a Neolithic burial mound at least 5,000 years old, and commandingly situated overlooking the Severn valley. Up to twenty skeletons have been recovered from the site over the years, though little is known about their subsequent history. Coins and broken pots found inside the barrow suggest that it had already been opened in Roman times.

COLD ASHTON TO BATH
(10¼ miles/16.5km)

From Cold Ashton, the Way drops into the secluded valley at Lower Hamswell, then climbs to the site of the Civil War battle at Lansdown (see below). Onward, the Way levels for a while, passing the promontory hill fort at Little Down and Bath Racecourse. The first views of Bath come at Prospect Stile (actually now a gate), and from there the trail traverses farmland to emerge in Weston, where it becomes more urban as it heads for the city. But there are, en route, fine interludes of parks and Regency architecture as the route heads for Bath abbey. Look for a stone disc set in the pavement outside the west door; it marks the official end of the Cotswold Way.

★ Lansdown Hill

A monument on the edge of Lansdown Hill commemorates the Civil War battle fought there in 1643 when the Royalists sought to secure the south-west of England and its rich resources for the king. The battle was an indecisive Royalist victory and did nothing to settle the issue of control; the Royalists may have won but they paid a heavy price for storming the high ground held by their opponents.

A LITERARY CRICKETING ELEVEN

After the First World War, J M Barrie, the creator of Peter Pan, became a regular visitor to Stanway House, on the Cotswold Way between Broadway and Winchcombe. His love of the game of cricket was such that he formed a team of players with notable literary connections, including at one time or another G K Chesterton, Arthur Conan Doyle, Jerome K Jerome, A A Milne, H G Wells and P G Wodehouse. The thatched pavilion raised on staddle stones, a legacy from that time, was paid for by Barrie.

Look for a stone disc set in the pavement outside the west door; it marks the official end of the Cotswold Way

Nature on the trail (clockwise):
Buzzard; European rabbit; spotted orchid; wild poppies at Snowshill.

BATH

Cumbria Way 🚶▶

Like so many middle- and long-distance trails, the Cumbria Way was the brainchild of local ramblers, in this instance devised in the 1970s and with waymarking completed in 2007. By then it had become a popular way of threading a passage through the heart of the Lake District World Heritage Site.

From the ancient market town of Ulverston on the Furness peninsula, the Way penetrates Lakeland's scenic heart, bound for the border city of Carlisle, along the way taking in Coniston, Langdale, Borrowdale, Derwent Water, Skiddaw Forest and John Peel country. For the most part, the Way is low-lying, but does involve some high-level exposed sections; the last of these is in the area known locally as Back o' Skidda', over High Pike in the grassy Caldbeck Fells. Elsewhere, it finds a way across the less well-known Blawith Fells, west of Coniston Water, and later clambers out of Langdale over the high Stake Pass into Langstrath.

Essentially, the Cumbria Way falls into five day stages with differing characteristics. In the south and the north the route is through active dairy farmland. The central stage is classic Lakeland fell country, starting to become evident as Coniston Water is approached, which the Way later courts as it heads for the village of Coniston.

Until copper mining, originally begun in Jacobean times, was revived in the mid-19th century, Coniston was a scattered settlement focused on the 16th-century farmhouse of Coniston Hall. Coniston Water is forever associated with Donald Campbell, who broke the water speed record here in 1955, and was killed attempting to regain it in 1967. He is buried in the village cemetery. There are strong literary associations here, too: Arthur Ransome based his children's book *Swallows and Amazons* on Coniston locations, while Beatrix Potter owned the vast Monk Coniston Estate, giving it on her death to the National Trust. Bound for the valley of Langdale, the Cumbria Way passes beside one of the estates most attractive locations, Tarn Hows.

The Way feeds into Langdale at Skelwith Bridge, and leaves it via Mickleden at the head of the valley, over the Stake Pass heading for Borrowdale, Derwent Water and the northern market town of Keswick. The ongoing route leaves Keswick on the customary start of the ascent of mighty Skiddaw, but soon diverts along Glenderaterra Beck as far as the lonely outpost, Skiddaw House, where it takes to the infant River Caldew, leaving it for a high jaunt over High Pike and a long easy descent to Caldbeck. Now the Way takes again to riparian wandering, re-joining the Caldew for the last stage of its journey into Carlisle.

AMAZING BUT TRUE ...

It was the raw vision of Castle Crag, stark against the brooding mountains beyond, that prompted early visitors to the Lakes to describe what is actually a geological constriction as the 'Jaws of Borrowdale'; emotive language symptomatic of a time when the mountains were fearful places inhabited by dragons.

Langdale Valley

The Cumbria Way falls into five distinct stages, with daily walking distances from 10½ to 15¾ miles (16.75 to 25.25km).

5 days

Start	Ulverston
Day 1	Coniston *15mi / 24.25km*
Day 2	Dungeon Ghyll *10½mi / 16.75km*
Day 3	Keswick *15¾mi / 25.25km*
Day 4	Caldbeck *14¼mi / 12.5km*
Day 5	Carlisle *15mi / 24km*

MAPS
OS Explorer
OL4, OL5, OL6, OL7, 315.
OS Landranger
85, 89, 90, 96.

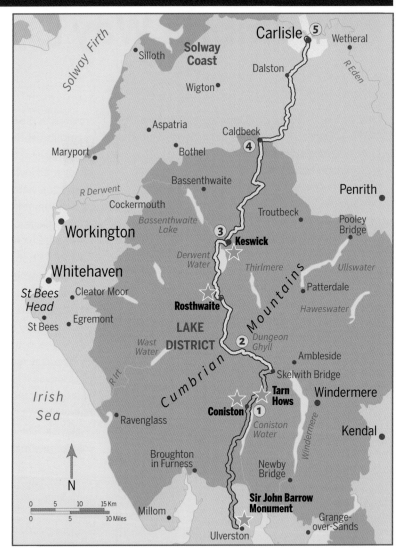

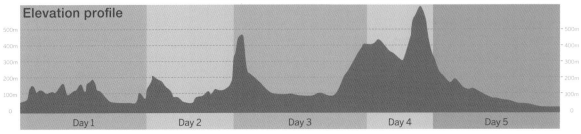

Elevation profile

FACTS AND FIGURES

START Ulverston, Cumbria (SD 288782)

FINISH Carlisle, Cumbria (NY 403560)

DISTANCE 70 miles (113km)

HEIGHT GAIN 8,415 feet (2,565m)

DIFFICULTY RATING ♦♦♦

IS IT FOR ME? Mostly a low-level route but using several high-level passes and crossing some exposed fell summits; a good mixture of Lakeland walking, facilities and reasonable public transport.

PRACTICALITIES

GETTING THERE AND BACK
Both Ulverston and Carlisle are on bus routes; Carlisle is on the West Coast Main Line rail service between London and Glasgow, while Ulverston is on a branch line from Preston that eventually runs along the north edge of Morecambe Bay.

ACCOMMODATION
The Lake District is well supplied with accommodation. Along the Cumbria Way there is plenty of choice in Ulverston, Coniston, Keswick and Carlisle, and comparatively less, but still ample, in Langdale and Caldbeck. There is the opportunity, too, to use hostels and bunkhouses (see https://independenthostels.co.uk).

WEBSITES
www.english-lakes.com/cumbria_way
www.keswick.org
www.walklakes.co.uk/cw
www.exploresouthlakeland.co.uk
www.lake-district.gov.uk

★ Tarn Hows

For more than a hundred years, Tarn Hows has been one of the most popular tourist destinations in the Lake District, and is today managed by the National Trust. Tarn Hows was once three smaller tarns and, until 1862, was part of the common grazing associated with Hawkshead parish; it is now a Site of Special Scientific Interest. Surprisingly, in his 1835 guide, Lake poet William Wordsworth encouraged visitors to come to this area, but appears not to mention Tarn Hows. When the tarns came up for sale in 1929, they were bought by Beatrix Potter, who later sold the half containing Tarn Hows to the National Trust, and bequeathed the rest of the estate to the Trust anonymously in her will.

Nature on the trail (clockwise): Water avens; Herdwick tup; mute swan; pair of goldeneye ducks.

ULVERSTON TO CONISTON
(15 miles/24.25km)

Probably, for many generations, best known as the birthplace of Stan Laurel, one half of the comedic Laurel and Hardy duo of yesteryear, the ancient market town of Ulverston has long been a thriving maritime community. Today, its labyrinthine cobbled streets are overlooked by the towering Hoad Monument, a copy of the Eddystone Lighthouse.

On the way to Coniston, the Way traverses the delectable but little known Blawith Fells, a wild and hummocky landscape of knolls, tarns and streams After leaving the fells behind, the route lies along the lake shores of Coniston Water all the way to the village. Visible on the other side of the lake, Brantwood was the home of John Ruskin, whose memorial grave stands in the churchyard in Coniston.

The Way traverses the delectable but little known Blawith Fells, a wild and hummocky landscape of knolls, tarns and streams

★ Sir John Barrow Monument

Described above as the Hoad Monument, because it stands at the top of Hoad Hill (436 feet/133m), the monument was erected in 1850 at a cost of £1,250, and commemorates Sir John Barrow, a founder member of the Royal Geographical Society, who was born in Ulverston in 1764. The monument is not a lighthouse, but a copy of the third Eddystone lighthouse, and is one of the most prominent landmarks in Cumbria, although this area was until 1974 part of the County Palatine of Lancashire.

★ Keswick

With concealed alleyways and a tight-knit centre, the market town of Keswick was granted its charter by Edward I. The town was central to an important mining area, including gold, but tourism has been popular since Victorian times, when it became widely associated with poets Samuel Taylor Coleridge and Robert Southey. Clear evidence of prehistoric occupation lies, off-route (but worth a diversion), at Castlerigg Stone circle to the east of the town, thought to be over 5,000 years old. The town has several attractions worth visiting: the Theatre by the Lake, opened in 1999; the Derwent Pencil Museum; and Greta Hall known for its links with the Lake poets.

CONISTON TO SKELWITH BRIDGE
(6¼ miles/10km)

This is just a part of the stage linking Coniston and Dungeon Ghyll (and could be extended to Dungeon Ghyll), and it winds its way through some of the most appealing scenery approaching and around Tarn Hows, a Site of Special Scientific Interest, and on to visit a couple of splendid waterfalls – Colwith Force and Skelwith Force – before entering greater Langdale. The Stagecoach bus service runs into Langdale from Kendal.

★ Rosthwaite

Not instantly evident, but passed directly by the Cumbria Way, the farmed area around Rosthwaite shows evidence of glacial lakes having formed here. The village is built on a particularly resistant upthrust of rock, a *roche moutonnée*, known as The How. Just to the north of the lane leading out of Rosthwaite, the field pattern shows a discernible 'break of slope' at its edges, a clear indicator that a large body of water once stood here, penned in by the Jaws of Borrowdale to the north.

BODIES OF WATER IN THE LAKE DISTRICT

Pedantically, there is only one 'lake' in the Lake District – Bassenthwaite Lake; all the others are meres, tarns and waters. The top ten ranked by surface area are:

Windermere
5.7 sq miles (14.8sqkm)

Ullswater
3.4 sq miles (8.9sqkm)

Derwent Water
2.1 sq miles (5.4sqkm)

Bassenthwaite Lake
2 sq miles (5.3sqkm)

Coniston Water
1.9 sq miles (4.9sqkm)

Haweswater
1.5 sq miles (3.9sqkm)

Thirlmere
1.3 sq miles (3.3sqkm)

Ennerdale Water
1.2 sq miles (3sqkm)

Wast Water
1.1 sq miles (2.9sqkm)

Crummock Water
1 sq mile (2.5sqkm)

★ Coniston

Historically part of Lancashire, the village of Coniston, hitherto a farming village raised to serve the local copper and slate mines, grew exponentially in popularity when the Coniston branch of the Furness railway opened in 1859. Poet John Ruskin popularised the village following his move to the mansion, Brantwood (above), on the eastern shore of the lake. His love of the area became even more apparent when, before his death, he rejected the option to be buried in Westminster Abbey, but instead chose a corner of St Andrew's churchyard in the village.

WALK 6 Dales Way 🚶➤

The Dales Way is a testament to cooperation, in this instance between the Countryside Commission (as it then was) and the West Riding Group of the Ramblers' Association (RA) in 1969. With inspirational vision, it was this arm of the RA that saw the incontestable appeal of a route through the Dales and across the British watershed into Cumbria; it links the historically eminent spa town of Ilkley in West Yorkshire with the equally important town of Bowness-on-Windermere, on the shores of the country's largest lake. By continuing the route into what was then the county of Westmorland, it also attractively linked two of Britain's major national parks – the Yorkshire Dales National Park and the Lake District National Park. In fact, little of the Dales Way is not within one national park or the other.

The characteristics of the countryside through which the Way passes are such that it is not an overly demanding middle-distance walk, and rarely far from civilisation. That alone makes it ideal for those who might want to complete the walk piecemeal, returning time after time until the whole is completed. But it also brings it within the orbit of those contemplating a multi-day walk for the first time, and is much like the West Highland Way in that regard. That is not to say that the Dales Way is some kind of soft option. Certainly, it is gentle, follows the course of (usually) sedate rivers and is largely benign; but adverse weather conditions can make it testing, especially on the watershed crossing from Upper Wharfedale into Dentdale. Many sections can be potentially treacherous underfoot and some even occasionally impassable; but help is never far distant.

For the curious, within close proximity to the route are numerous features of architectural, ecological or historic interest – churches, bridges, manor houses, Roman roads, ancient stone circles, viaducts and nature trails. There is also an abundance of natural history. So there is reason enough to dally; be sure to set daily walk targets with time in-built for exploring.

The Way is, too, a walk for all seasons; with careful planning, even a winter crossing is manageable and likely to throw up its own repertoire of challenges and delights. Spring and autumn tend to be the most colourful times, bursting with a vibrancy that can be flat in the long days of summer. But whenever you go, there can be no doubt that the Dales Way will be an inspiration that can lead you to greater rambling achievements.

AMAZING BUT TRUE ...

Appletreewick had its very own real-life Dick Whittington character, William Craven, born in the village in 1548. He was sent to London to be apprentice to a merchant tailor, and grew in stature and standing to become Sheriff and, later, Lord Mayor of London.

Stainforth

The Dales Way falls into six distinct stages, and these lend themselves to a relaxed trek. A six-, seven- or eight-day experience will accommodate those who want to be quicker or those who want to be more laid back. A race in 2019 to commemorate the Dales Way's 50th anniversary saw the winner home in 14 hours 35 minutes and 53 seconds. For everyone else, the Dales Way is a journey to be enjoyed at your own pace, taking your cue from the easy-going rivers that accompany you for much of the way.

FACTS AND FIGURES

START Wharfe Bridge, Ilkley, West Yorkshire (SE 112480)

FINISH Bowness-on-Windermere, Cumbria (SD 403969)

DISTANCE 78 miles (125km)

HEIGHT GAIN 6,805 feet (2,075m)

DIFFICULTY RATING ♦♦

IS IT FOR ME? A relatively benign route, but not to be underestimated; advance planning is essential for access/accommodation for piecemeal completion.

MAPS

OS Explorer OL2, OL7, OL19, OL30, 297.

OS Landranger 97, 98, 104.

PRACTICALITIES

GETTING THERE AND BACK Both Ilkley and Bowness-on-Windermere are served by bus. Ilkley has a railway station, but the nearest railhead to the end of the Way is at Windermere, a short distance away.

ACCOMMODATION
The Dales Way is tolerably well-off with accommodation, but there are stretches – from Buckden to Dentdale – where it is sparse. For this reason, and the fact that accommodation can be fully booked anything up to a year in advance, makes it prudent to plan well ahead. There are few campsites along the Dales Way, but many farmers will allow small parties to pitch tents; in the interests of fostering and maintaining good relations with farmers, please do not camp without permission.

WEBSITE
www.dalesway.org

	6 days	7 days	8 days
Start	Ilkley	Ilkley	Ilkley
Day 1	Burnsall 13¼mi/21.25km	Burnsall 13¼mi/21.25km	Burnsall 13¼mi/21.25km
Day 2	Buckden 13½mi/22km	Buckden 13½mi/22km	Kettlewell 9½mi/15.25km
Day 3	Cowgill 17mi/27.5km	Cowgill 17mi/27.5km	Hubberholme 5½mi/8.75km
Day 4	Sedbergh 8¾mi/14km	Dent 4mi/6.55km	Cowgill 15¾mi/25.5km
Day 5	Burneside 15¼mi/24.5km	Sedbergh 4¾mi/7.5km	Dent 4mi/6.5km
Day 6	Bowness-on-Windermere 9½mi/15.25km	Staveley 15¼mi/24.5km	Sedbergh 4¾mi/7.5km
Day 7		Bowness-on-Windermere 9½mi/15.25km	Staveley 15¼mi/21.5km
Day 8			Bowness-on-Windermere 9½mi/15.25km

Spring and autumn tend to be the most colourful times, bursting with vibrancy

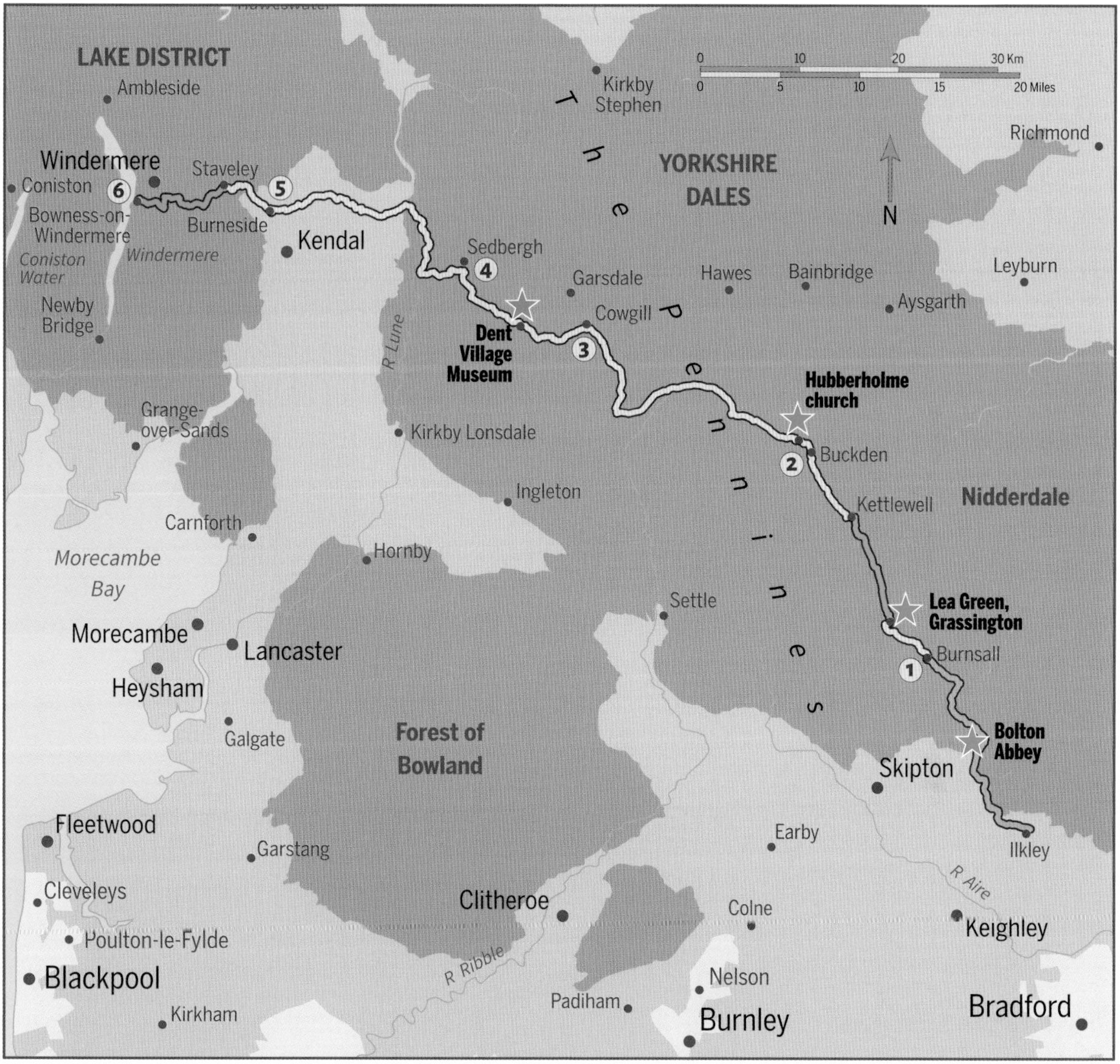
LAKE DISTRICT
Ambleside
Windermere
Coniston
Staveley
Bowness-on-Windermere
Burneside
Kendal
Coniston Water
Windermere
Newby Bridge
Kirkby Stephen
The Pennines
YORKSHIRE DALES
Richmond
N
Sedbergh
Garsdale
Hawes
Bainbridge
Leyburn
Aysgarth
Cowgill
Dent Village Museum
R Lune
Hubberholme church
Grange-over-Sands
Kirkby Lonsdale
Buckden
Ingleton
Kettlewell
Nidderdale
Carnforth
Morecambe Bay
Hornby
Settle
Lea Green, Grassington
Morecambe
Lancaster
Burnsall
Heysham
Galgate
Forest of Bowland
Bolton Abbey
Skipton
Fleetwood
Earby
Ilkley
Garstang
R Aire
Cleveleys
Clitheroe
Colne
Keighley
Poulton-le-Fylde
Blackpool
R Ribble
Nelson
Padiham
Kirkham
Burnley
Bradford
0 10 20 30 Km
0 5 10 15 20 Miles
1
2
3
4
5
6

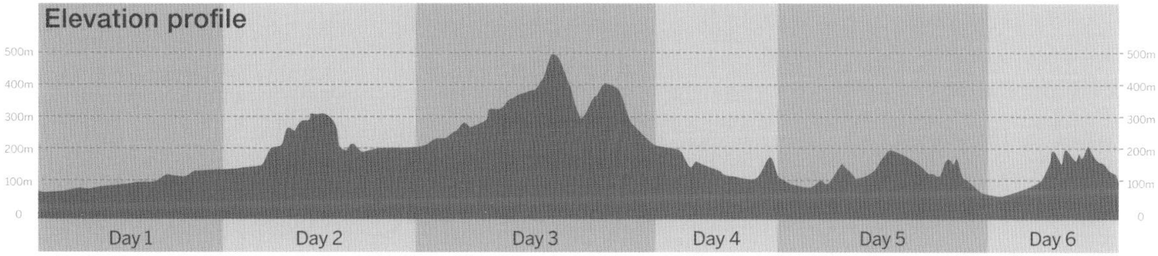
Elevation profile
500m
400m
300m
200m
100m
0
Day 1
Day 2
Day 3
Day 4
Day 5
Day 6

GRASSINGTON TO KETTLEWELL
(6½ miles/10.5km)

The village of Grassington is a delight, a market town of some antiquity having been granted a market charter in 1282. A cobbled market square is fringed by shops, cafés and pubs, and these alone make it difficult to move on. But from the top end of the main street, the Dales Way heads out onto the upland limestone expanses of Lea Green where, in earlier times, most people lived and worked. Today, this is one of the richest archaeological sites in the north of England; a place of Bronze Age burial mounds, Celtic villages, Romano-British settlements and medieval farmsteads, all in close proximity. Kettlewell, in comparison, is as far from the brouhaha of modern life as can be imagined, a laid-back place of peace and beauty, beneath limestone terraces fringed with hazel and rowan coppices.

STAVELEY TO BOWNESS-ON-WINDERMERE
(6½ miles/10.5km)

This final leg of the Dales Way tackles a landscape like no other part of the route. Ingenuity in abundance was employed to tease a route through this rocky, hummocky, twisted limestone arena; but it paid dividends, because once the initial climb from Staveley is accomplished, nothing but delight ensues as the Way wriggles ever closer to its final steep descent to the shores of Windermere with its host of shops, pubs, ice cream parlours, cafés, restaurants, hotels and B&Bs.

★ **Lea Green, Grassington**

High above the village of Grassington, Lea Green is a vast field system of an ancient British settlement, thought to be Iron Age. However, it is described by some as Romano-Celtic, which suggests that the Romans found it in working order and commandeered it before leaving Britain in the early 5th century.

Grassington's cobbled market square is fringed by shops, cafés and pubs, and these alone make it difficult to move on

★ Hubberholme church

The Church of St Michael and All Angels at Hubberholme, an outstanding Norman structure, sits in a peaceful setting above the Wharfe. The church – and the local pub (The George) – were favourite places of novelist and playwright J B Priestley whose ashes are buried in the churchyard. Within the church, other points of interest include the rood loft and the oak pews hand carved by, and bearing the famous mouse trademark of, Robert Thompson – otherwise known as the 'Mouseman of Kilburn'.

★ Dent Village Museum and Heritage Centre

Dent Village Museum hosts a wealth of information about the working lives and social customs of the Dales folk. The centre itself has been designed and built entirely with local labour, on the site of an existing building that formerly served as the filling-station for Dent town. Almost all the exhibits enjoy genuine Dales provenance.

ILKLEY TO BURNSALL
(13¼ miles/21.25km)

The start of the Dales Way is somewhat elusive, tucked away in a side street that leads down to the River Wharfe. From this first encounter with the river, an agreeable saunter leads to the village of Addingham. Originally a small agricultural community, Addingham expanded rapidly at the end of the 18th century and into the 19th to become a busy textile manufacturing centre, with five mills, five churches and five pubs.

Once beyond Addingham, the Way scarcely leaves the company of the river as it heads north to the grounds of Bolton Abbey, where the remains of the Augustinian Priory still house a place of worship spared during the Dissolution of the Monasteries. At the abbey, the Way changes banks of the river, with stepping stones offering an intrepid way across; thankfully there is a substantial bridge nearby.

Before long, however, the river returns to the true right bank, pressing on further into the Bolton Abbey estate, where woodland – and one of the largest remnants of sessile oak trees in the Yorkshire Dales – flanks the river. This area is especially renowned for its flora and fauna. Here, the Way passes above a narrow gap in the river known as The Strid, both dramatic and dangerous.

By the time Burnsall is reached, the Way has changed river banks again. Burnsall was an Anglo-Saxon settlement, to which rare Viking and Anglo-Saxon stones in the church testify. It is undoubtedly one of the most beautiful villages in Wharfedale.

Burnsall

ANCIENT NAMES

Many of the settlements across the Dales were originally founded in Anglo-Saxon times, but later Viking colonists, both Danish and Norse, settled in the area. The Danes penetrated from the east coast, moving up the Humber and Ouse and across the Vale of York, while the Norsemen came from the west. A glance at a map reveals the intermingling of typical Anglo-Saxon placename endings, such as -ton, -ham and -den with the Scandinavian endings of -by, -thorpe, -thwaite, and the predominance of Norse words such as gill, beck, fell, crag and scar, describing physical features. The word 'dale' is derived from a Danish word meaning 'valley'.

The Strid

Nature on the trail (clockwise):
Hazel trees; dipper; cranesbill; jay; sessile oak leaves; yarrow.

★ Bolton Abbey

The Bolton Abbey estate, owned by the Dukes of Devonshire since 1755, comprises 30,000 acres of outstanding countryside and boasts no fewer than 80 miles (130km) of all-weather walking routes. Bolton Abbey, founded in 1154 by the Augustinian order, was technically a priory, despite its name. The land at Bolton was given to the order by Lady Alice de Romille of Skipton Castle in 1154. The nave of the abbey church has been in use as a parish church from 1170, surviving the Dissolution of the Monasteries.

Derwent Valley Heritage Way

This delightful trail is typical of the inventiveness of local walkers in creating middle- and long-distance routes. The Way, as its name suggests, is a fascinating walk through ancient, medieval and industrial history, and yields intriguing insights into the social and work life of the 18th and 19th centuries. Starting on the banks of Ladybower Reservoir, the Way follows the River Derwent through the Peak District, visiting Chatsworth and Derwent Valley Mills World Heritage Site, until the river, meets the Trent near Shardlow. The Derwent Valley Mills World Heritage Site embraces a series of historic mill complexes, including some of the world's first 'modern' factories, where water power was harnessed for textile production.

The Derwent Valley Trust set up the walk in 1996, and not surprisingly makes the most of the riparian loveliness of the River Derwent from the outset, where the river escapes the reservoir, diving into its company as it heads for the Hope Valley. Reluctant to leave the river, the Way soon passes below the beetling gritstone 'edges' of Froggatt, Curbar and Baslow, where rock climbers play.

South of Baslow, the Way traverses the 1,000-acre Chatsworth Park, designed by Lancelot 'Capability' Brown in the 1760s. The park contains historic and modern architecture and art, including James Paine's bridges and mill, and Queen Mary's Bower

(see below). Chatsworth House is home to the Duke and Duchess of Devonshire, and has been passed down through sixteen generations of the Cavendish family.

Down river, the village of Rowsley is at the point where the River Wye flows into the Derwent, and the village benefited from the many mills built along both rivers. Five miles (8km) downstream, the Way reaches Matlock, a former spa town popular with Victorian excursionists, which prospered both from the hydrotherapy industry and its cloth mills.

Belper developed in medieval times on the strength of its nail-making industry, and expanded during the early years of the Industrial Revolution to become one of the first mill towns in England. Just north of Belper lies the Wyver Nature Reserve, a modest 19-acre site prone to flooding, which makes it good for spotting wading birds.

Before finally plunging into the centre of Derby, the Way passes through Darley Abbey, a former historic mill village that developed on the site of an Augustinian monastery. In Derby itself, the river guides the Way through the city centre to pass Elvaston Castle Country Park and its stately home, a Gothic Revival castle, and on to its conclusion near the village of Shardlow, where it meets the River Trent.

AMAZING BUT TRUE ...

During the 18th century, Betty and Luke Kenyon lived in a huge ancient yew tree, the remnants of which are still visible in Shining Cliff Woods, just south of Whatstandwell. The pair raised eight children, and legend has it they used a hollowed out bough as a cradle and that this was the origin of the *Rock-a-bye-baby* nursery rhyme.

River Derwent

The Derwent Valley Heritage Way falls into ten distinct stages, suitable for completion in one go or in sections. Only two of these sections, however, are greater than 6 miles (10km), and experienced multi-day walkers will find this too brief. Here are three suggested itineraries:

Froggatt Edge, above the River Derwent

	4 days	5 days	10 days
Start	Ladybower	Ladybower	Ladybower
Day 1	Rowsley 16½mi/26.75km	Baslow 12mi/19.25km	Hathersage 5¼mi/8.25km
Day 2	Belper 17¼mi/27.75km	Matlock 10mi/16km	Baslow 6¾mi/11km
Day 3	Derby 9¼mi/15km	Belper 12mi/19.25km	Rowsley 4½mi/7.25km
Day 4	Derwent Mouth 9½mi/15.25km	Derby 9¼mi/15km	Matlock 5½mi/8.75km
Day 5		Derwent Mouth 9½mi/15.25km	Whatstandwell 6½mi/10.5km
Day 6			Belper 5½mi/8.75km
Day 7			Little Eaton 4¾mi/7.5km
Day 8			Derby 4½mi/7.25km
Day 9			Borrowash 5mi/8km
Day 10			Derwent Mouth 4½mi/7.25km

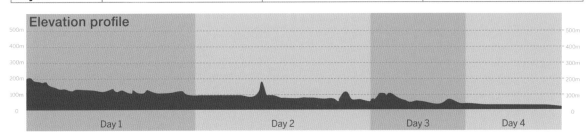

Elevation profile

500m
400m
300m
200m
100m
0

Day 1   Day 2   Day 3   Day 4

FACTS AND FIGURES

START Ladybower Reservoir, Heatherdene, Derbyshire (SK 202860)

FINISH Derwent Mouth, Shardlow, Derbyshire (SK 458307)

DISTANCE 52 miles (82km)

HEIGHT GAIN 2,985 feet (910m)

DIFFICULTY RATING ♦

IS IT FOR ME? An easy-going, well-waymarked, largely riparian trail with good access to accommodation and public transport.

PRACTICALITIES

GETTING THERE AND BACK
Buses from Sheffield and Bakewell via Bamford pass the entrance to Heatherdene car park. There are bus routes from Hathersage to Sheffield, Castleton, Bakewell and Chesterfield. Train stations at Bamford and Hathersage are on the Sheffield to Manchester Hope Valley line.

ACCOMMODATION
The Derwent Valley Heritage Way enjoys a wealth of accommodation, from grand hotels to guest houses and B&Bs.

WEBSITES
www.derwentvalleytrust.org.uk
www.visitpeakditrict.com

MAPS
OS Explorer
OL1, OL24, 259, 260, 269.
OS Landranger
110, 119, 128, 129.

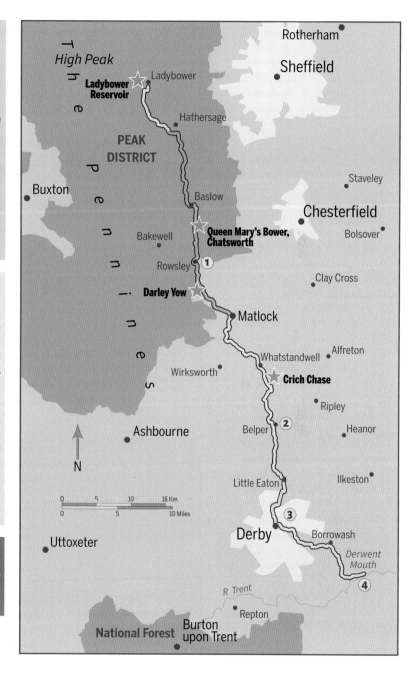

HATHERSAGE TO BASLOW
(6¾ miles/11km)

This is one of the longer sections of the Way and, being largely rural, one of the more pleasant, passing, as it does, the villages of Grindleford and Froggatt. Hathersage is delightful, and became a popular place with those in search of legendary heroes and literary heroines. By the south door of the Church of St Michael is the grave of Robin Hood's lieutenant, Little John, reputedly born in Hathersage. Charlotte Brontë, too, is associated with the village, which is said to be featured in her novels: North Lees Hall, on the route up to Stanage Edge, is believed to have been the model for Thornfield Hall in *Jane Eyre*.

Like Stanage and many other gritstone edges in the Peak, Froggatt was the source of millstones used in the many mills that occupied the valley bottoms, and many that never made it can still be found dotted around the landscape.

This page (top): Chatsworth House.
The Mills (clockwise): Cromford Mill, Matlock; Darley Abbey Mill, Derby; Caudwell Mill, Rowsley; Strutt's North Mill, Belper.
Opposite page: Ladybower Reservoir.

★ Queen Mary's Bower, Chatsworth

The fame of Chatsworth House and its grounds is legendary, but within the park stands a fascinating feature, Queen Mary's Bower. Tradition maintains that the structure was constructed in the 1570s to provide a raised exercise ground for Mary, Queen of Scots when she was detained at Chatsworth. The captive queen remained at Chatsworth for a large part of the eighteen-and-a-half years she was held in custody at the behest of Elizabeth I. While it is perfectly feasible that the bower was used by Queen Mary, the probability is that it was originally built as a garden feature.

★ Ladybower Reservoir

A large Y-shaped reservoir, Ladybower is the most southerly of three reservoirs in the Upper Derwent Valley. The River Ashop flows into Ladybower from the west, while the Derwent flows south, initially through Howden Reservoir, then Derwent Reservoir, and finally through Ladybower Reservoir. Ladybower was built between 1935 and 1943, a development that resulted in the drowning of the villages of Ashopton and Derwent. During the Second World War, Derwent Reservoir was used by pilots of the 617 Squadron to practise the low-level flights needed for the so-called Dam Busters Raids (Operation Chastise), due to its similarity to the German dams they intended to attack.

★ Darley Yew

All too easy to pass by, the Church of St Helen in Churchtown is said to be the oldest in Darley Dale, its battlemented west tower dating from the 14th century. The church was founded in the late 9th century, in or around the year 900, and substantially rebuilt following the Norman Conquest. Examples of excellent Norman, Saxon and Celtic masonry still remain. Opposite the main entrance, with an enormous girth of 33 feet (10m) round its trunk, stands the Darley Yew, reputed to be 2,000 years old. A plaque on the tree tells of the Saxon settlers who built their huts to the west of the church.

BASLOW TO MATLOCK
(10 miles/16km)

Almost entirely on the Chatsworth Estate, the first stretch of this section passes Chatsworth House (www.chatsworth.org), renowned for the quality of its art, which spans 4,000 years from ancient Egyptian and Roman, through the great masters, to more modern artists like Lucian Freud and David Nash.

South of Chatsworth, the Way stays with the river below the steep, wooded slopes of Lees Moor Wood to Rowsley. No longer operational, the village railway station is said to have been in frequent use by Edward VII when he visited Chatsworth. North-west of Matlock, the Derwent Valley is wide and flat, before it finally closes in as it heads for the centre of the former spa town.

This page (top): Chatsworth House; **(middle left)**: Wooden sculpture, Chatsworth; **(middle right)**: James Paine's three arch bridge, Chatsworth; **(bottom)**: Matlock.

In December 2001, the Derwent Valley between Matlock Bath and Derby was designated as a cultural World Heritage Site by UNESCO. The citation states:

'The cultural landscape of the Derwent Valley is of outstanding significance because it was here that the modern factory system was established to accommodate the new technology for spinning cotton developed by Richard Arkwright. The insertion of industrial establishments into a rural landscape necessitated the construction of housing for the workers in the mills, and the resulting settlements created exceptional industrial landscape that has retained its qualities over two centuries.'

Nature on the trail (clockwise):
Chatsworth's red deer herd; little grebe; kingfisher; goat willow – tree and flowerbuds; comfrey; barbel.

★Crich Chase

Between Whatstandwell and Ambergate, the eastern flanks of the valley are occupied by Crich Chase Meadows, one of Derbyshire's most important wildlife habitats, its fields never having been fertilised. Over 100 species of fungi grow here, along with just as many plant species which attract a wide range of insects, with 25 species of butterfly having been recorded.

Hadrian's Wall Path 🔔

Begun in the year 122, during the reign of the Roman emperor Hadrian, the eponymous wall ran from Wallsend on the banks of the River Tyne in the east to Bowness-on-Solway on the Irish Sea. The generally accepted reason for the wall was, according to Hadrian's biographer, 'to separate the Romans from the barbarians', although no record exists of the exact explanation for the wall, or who, precisely, they regarded as barbarians. So, explanations vary, and historians have long postulated that, in addition to keeping hostile forces out of Roman Britain, the wall served as a kind of border control, managing the passage to and fro of trade, and dissuading smuggling.

Today, while little of the wall remains, its course holds endless fascination for any enquiring mind; the interpretation facilities along the route are excellent. In 1987, Hadrian's Wall was declared a World Heritage Site, and in 2005 became part of the transnational 'Frontiers of the Roman Empire' World Heritage Site.

The path that now accompanies the wall sticks as close as feasible to its course, avoiding roads as much as possible. Unlike most 'heritage' sites, Hadrian's Wall is unprotected, and visitors are encouraged to resist the urge to stand on the wall or, for that matter, to walk the path other than during the summer months, to protect the fragile landscape.

Traditionally, the Path is walked from east to west, starting at Wallsend, where a viewing tower gives an elevated view of the Roman fort of Segedunum. The first stage of the path from the outskirts of Newcastle is urban, the wall lying under a military road built in the aftermath of the Jacobite uprising of 1745. Eventually, the path heads for Heddon-on-the-Wall, where fragmented sections of the wall are encountered.

At the Roman fort of Vercovicium, today known as Housesteads, the complexities of the original wall, its arrangement of milecastles and turrets, are splendidly explained. A tour of this English Heritage site, will consume a chunk of time but will do much to give tangible *raison d'être* to your endeavours. West of Housesteads, the Wall Path encounters the Pennine Way, and the two march in harmony over a stunning switchback that reaches the highest point of the wall on Winshield Crags (1,132 feet/345m).

Further west, although the line of the wall can be faithfully followed on field paths, little of the wall remains as the Path heads for the city of Carlisle, although its insistence on sticking close to the River Eden means that the urban aspects of the city can largely be ignored. The Eden escorts the Wall Path out beyond the city, before it is abandoned in favour of a more direct route to the Path's end at Bowness-on-Solway.

AMAZING BUT TRUE ...

There was no such thing as a standard Roman mile, 'mille passum', translating as 1,000 paces, was their equivalent of one mile. When finished, Hadrian's Wall was 80 Roman miles long – about 73½ statute miles or 118.25km. Our 'mile' comes from the Latin 'milia'. The regular gateways guarded by a fortlet were sited one mile apart, hence the name milecastles.

Sunset at Walltown Crags

The Hadrian's Wall Path arguably doesn't have clearly defined stages, but may nonetheless be divided into six convenient day-walks, ranging from 12 to 16½ miles (19 to 26.75km), although you may want to build in extra time to visit the several Roman sites you will pass.

Sycamore Gap

6 days

Start	Wallsend
Day 1	Heddon-on-the-Wall
	15mi / 24km
Day 2	Chollerford
	16mi / 25.5km
Day 3	Once Brewed
	12mi / 19.25km
Day 4	Walton
	16½mi / 26.75km
Day 5	Carlisle
	11¼mi / 18km
Day 6	Bowness-on-Solway
	14½mi / 23.5km

FACTS AND FIGURES

START Wallsend, Tyne and Wear (NZ 301660)

FINISH Bowness-on-Solway, Cumbria (NY 223626)

DISTANCE 84 miles (135km)

HEIGHT GAIN 6,945 feet (2,115m)

DIFFICULTY RATING ◆◆◆

IS IT FOR ME? Straightforward eastern and western ends bookend some energetic and dramatic parts mid-route; best tackled in summer when the Hadrian's Wall bus service operates.

PRACTICALITIES

GETTING THERE AND BACK
Newcastle-upon-Tyne is served by the national rail network, and bus services link the city with Wallsend. Occasional bus services operate between Bowness-on-Solway and Carlisle, which sits on the West Coast Mainline rail service between London and Glasgow. The Hadrian's Wall Bus (Service AD122) runs daily in the summer between Carlisle and Hexham, stopping along the route; each bus connects with rail and bus services in Carlisle, Haltwhistle and Hexham (Tel: 01434 344777/322002).

ACCOMMODATION
There is a good choice of accommodation close to the route of Hadrian's Wall Path. In addition, there are several opportunities to use youth hostels and bunkhouses – see https://independenthostels.co.uk. There are plenty of campsites along the trail, but please note that it is illegal to wild camp in England – you need to stay at official campsites.

WEBSITES
www.nationaltrail.co.uk
www.visitcumbria.com
www.visitnorthumberland.com

ROMAN NUMERALS

1	I	11	XI	21	XXI	40	XL	200	CC
2	II	12	XII	22	XXII	49	XLIX	249	CCXLIX
3	III	13	XIII	23	XXIII	50	L	250	CCL
4	IV	14	XIV	24	XXIV	51	LI	251	CCLI
5	V	15	XV	25	XXV	60	LX	399	CCCXCIX
6	VI	16	XVI	26	XXVI	70	LXX	400	CD
7	VII	17	XVII	27	XXVII	80	LXXX	499	CDXCIX
8	VIII	18	XVIII	28	XXVIII	90	XC	500	D
9	IX	19	XIX	29	XXIX	99	XCIX	900	CM
10	X	20	XX	30	XXX	100	C	1000	M

MAPS

OS Explorer
OL43, 314, 315, 316.

OS Landranger
85, 86, 87, 88.

★ Heddon-on-the-Wall

The area around the village contains the longest unbroken section of wall at its original and planned width, today known as Broad Wall. Later sections were not built to the full width to save time and expense.

Nature on the trail
Hadrian's Wall has superb habitat for butterflies.
(clockwise): Orange-tip; red admiral; painted lady; large heath.

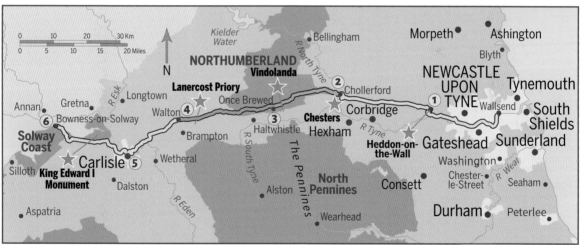

Elevation profile

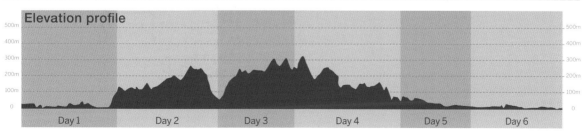

ONCE BREWED TO WALTON
(16½ miles/26.75km)

From Once Brewed, the Wall Path crosses Winshield Crags, the highest point on its journey, and still here in company with the Pennine Way. Quarrying operations have destroyed part of the wall after Caw Gap, though Milecastle 42, on a steep south-facing slope is on one of the best-preserved sections of the wall.

With the route gradually gaining height, its passes Great Chesters Fort (Aesica) and presses on to Greenhead, Gilsland and Birdoswald along which course there are several fragmented remains of the wall as well as milecastles and turrets. Gradually, the wall remains peter out, though the line of the wall can still be traced on the climb to the village of Walton.

★Chesters

The original plan for Hadrian's Wall contained no forts, but within two years the decision was taken to add 15 forts to the line, to be manned by units of auxiliary troops. These forts straddled the wall, half to its north and half to its south as was the case at Chesters, where the ditch that fronted the wall was filled in and a turret demolished to make way for the fort (www.english-heritage.org.uk).

★ Vindolanda

A Roman auxiliary fort, Vindolanda pre-dates the building of Hadrian's Wall and was in occupation between the years 85 and 370. The fort guarded the Stanegate, the Roman road from the River Tyne to the Solway Firth. The site's museum is set in gardens, and includes a full-size reconstruction of a Roman temple and other buildings. The site is managed by the Vindolanda Charitable Trust (www.vindolanda.com).

This page (top): Chesters; **(middle left)**: Wallsend – ceremonial mask; **(middle right)**: legionnaire helmet; **(bottom)**: Vindolanda.
Opposite page (top): Lanercost Priory; **(bottom)**: Edward 1 monument.

★ Lanercost Priory

To the south of the Wall, near Banks, the tranquillity of the Augustinian Lanercost Priory is at odds with the long, troubled history of the region. Close by Hadrian's Wall, the priory suffered repeated attacks during the Anglo-Scottish Wars, including by William Wallace and Robert the Bruce. Prior to his death in 1307, King Edward I of England was compelled by ill health to spend the winter of 1306–07 at the priory. Lanercost was one of the poorest of the English monasteries, and one of the first to be closed down under Henry VIII's Dissolution of the Monasteries edict.

★ Edward I monument

Lying to the north of Hadrian's Wall Path, at Burgh-by-Sands, a stone monument (NY 325 609), surrounded by an iron fence, marks the place where King Edward I of England, the so-called 'Hammer of the Scots' died, on the edge of the Solway Firth in 1307, on his way north for another assault on the Scots.

CHOLLERFORD TO ONCE BREWED
(12 miles/19.25km)

Beginning by exploring Chesters Fort, overlooking the point where a Roman bridge used to span the river, the Path soon creeps into the Northumberland National Park, encountering several sections where parts of the wall can be viewed. Once the company of the B6318 is left behind, the drama of the wall unfolds as it crosses Sewingshields Crag and heads for the fort at Housesteads – allow plenty of time to visit here – before pressing on above Crag Lough beyond Milecastle 39 to a minor road leading south to Once Brewed.

Whin Sill

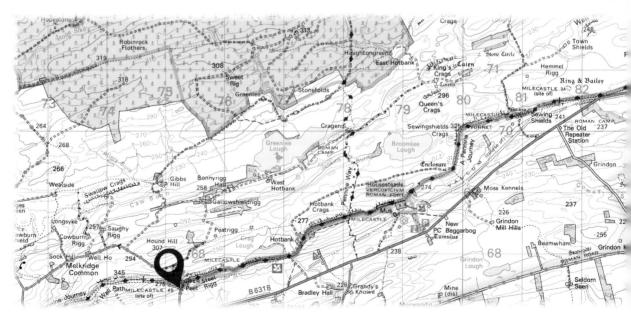

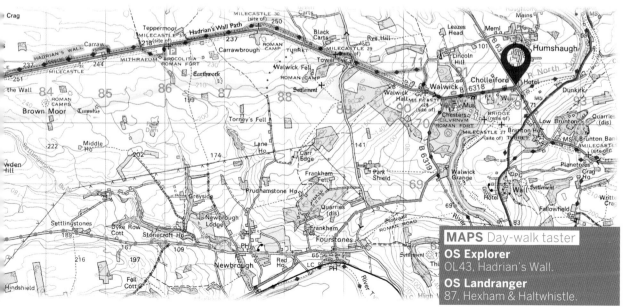

MAPS Day-walk taster

OS Explorer
OL43, Hadrian's Wall.

OS Landranger
87, Hexham & Haltwhistle.

London's Capital Ring ▶

The Capital Ring is a 78-mile (126-km) orbital walking route promoted by London's local councils and coordinated by the City of London Corporation in partnership with the Greater London Authority and its functional body for regional transport, Transport for London. The route completely encircles inner and central London, and passes through no fewer than 18 of its boroughs. The circuit may be completed as a continuous undertaking, but a piecemeal approach will allow time to gain a better understanding of the wealth of London's green spaces.

This was an idea anchored in 1990 when it was mooted as a flagship project at one of the early meetings of the London Walking Forum. Passing through green areas of urban and suburban London, the route was completed in September 2005. This is a remarkable and ingenious way of getting to see some of London's finest scenery, much of it largely unsuspected: open spaces, commons, nature reserves, ancient oak woodland, remnants of the Great North Wood, and Sites of Special Scientific Interest. Much of the trail is shared with other major routes, notably the Thames Path South-east Extension, Green Chain Walk, the Thames Path National Trail (page 160), Grand Union Canal Walk, Brent River Park Walk, Dollis Valley Greenwalk, Parkland Walk, Lea Valley Walk and The Greenway.

The route is waymarked by two distinguishable signs: in open spaces, these are a white disc on a wooden post featuring a Big Ben logo and directional arrow; on streets look for large aluminium signs featuring the walking man symbol strapped to lamp posts and other street furniture.

The circuit offers a splendid and compelling journey through London's streets, parks, riverside walks and woodland, and visits many of the city's most fascinating places, including Crystal Palace Park, Wimbledon Common, Richmond Park, Harrow on the Hill, Highgate Woods, Finsbury Park, Hackney Marshes and the Royal Victoria Docks. Intrinsically, it doesn't affect to be anything other than an urban walk that imaginatively joins up several of London's green oases and sights. Distanced from the bright lights and wealth of the city, much of the route is off-road and surprisingly green and vibrant.

AMAZING BUT TRUE ...

Almost half of the land area of Greater London is green space of one form or another with in excess of 350 parks, playing fields, gardens, allotments, cemeteries, meadows, commons, woods, wetlands and wildlife corridors along its canals, rivers and railways, making it one of the greenest capital cities in the world.

Abney Park Cemetery

The Capital Ring consists of 15 distinct stages that lend themselves, to completion entirely on a bit-by-bit, selective basis using London's abundance of public transport.

15 sections

Start	Woolwich Foot Tunnel
Section 1	Falconwood 7mi / 11.25km
Section 2	Grove Park 4mi / 6.5km
Section 3	Crystal Palace 8½mi / 13.5km
Section 4	Streatham 4mi / 6.5km
Section 5	Wimbledon Park 5½mi / 9km
Section 6	Richmond Bridge 7mi / 11.25km
Section 7	Osterley Lock 5mi / 8km
Section 8	Greenford 5½mi / 8.75km
Section 9	South Kenton 5½mi / 8.75km
Section 10	Hendon 6¼mi / 10km
Section 11	Highgate 6mi / 9.5km
Section 12	Stoke Newington 5mi / 8km
Section 12	Hackney Wick 4mi / 6.5km
Section 14	Beckton District Park 5¼mi / 8.5km
Section 15	Woolwich 4mi / 6.5km

FACTS AND FIGURES

START/FINISH Conventionally, the walk starts on the south side of Woolwich Foot Tunnel, although the nature of the walk allows it to be started almost anywhere along its route. The distance to be walked is not clear, with differing distances being given by different boroughs. But, Transport for London gives a distance of 78 miles (126km), which is near enough.

DISTANCE 78 miles (126km)

HEIGHT GAIN 4,050 feet (1,235m)

DIFFICULTY RATING ◆

IS IT FOR ME? An easy-going, green-corridor route with excellent public transport connections for piecemeal completion.

PRACTICALITIES

GETTING THERE AND BACK Ring walkers will rarely be more than a short walk from a bus stop with frequent services or a London Underground, London Overground, National Rail or Docklands Light Railway (DLR) station or London Trams stop.

ACCOMMODATION Wherever you are on the Capital Ring Walk, you will never be far from some form of accommodation or the ready means to access it by public transport or taxi.

WEBSITE https://tfl.gov.uk/modes/walking/capital-ring

MAPS
OS Explorer
161, 162, 173, 174.
OS Landranger
176, 177.

This page: Bell from opening ceremony London Olympics 2012.

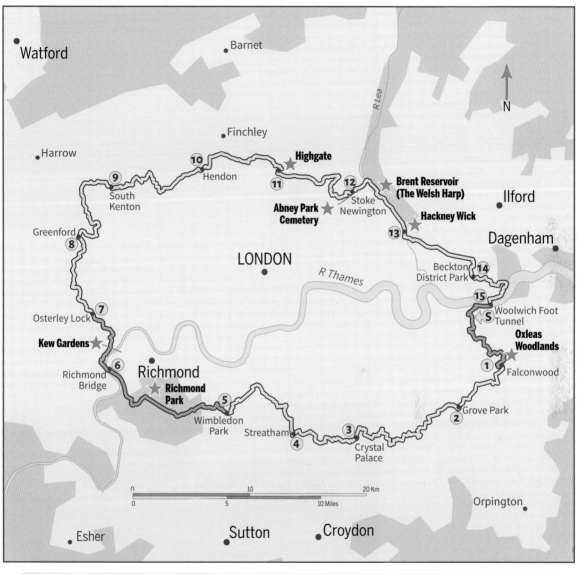

Watford

Barnet

Finchley

Harrow

Highgate

⑩

Hendon

⑪

⑫

Brent Reservoir
(The Welsh Harp)

⑨

South
Kenton

Abney Park
Cemetery

Stoke
Newington

Ilford

Hackney Wick

Greenford

⑬

Dagenham

⑧

LONDON

R Thames

Beckton
District Park

⑭

⑮

Osterley Lock

⑦

Woolwich Foot
Tunnel

S

Kew Gardens

Oxleas
Woodlands

⑥

Richmond

①

Falconwood

Richmond
Bridge

Richmond
Park

⑤

Grove Park

②

Wimbledon
Park

Streatham

④

③

Crystal
Palace

0   10   20 Km

0   5   10 Miles

Esher

Sutton

Croydon

Orpington

N

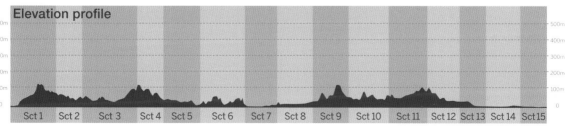

Elevation profile

500m   500m

400m   400m

300m   300m

200m   200m

100m   100m

0   0

Sct 1 Sct 2 Sct 3 Sct 4 Sct 5 Sct 6 Sct 7 Sct 8 Sct 9 Sct 10 Sct 11 Sct 12 Sct 13 Sct 14 Sct 15

WOOLWICH FOOT TUNNEL TO FALCONWOOD

(7 miles/11.25km)

Visiting the Thames Barrier, Charlton House, Shooters Hill and Sevendroog Castle (see Oxleas Woodlands below), this initial section of the Capital Ring is a good place to begin the exploration, embracing much of historic and natural history interest.

WIMBLEDON PARK TO RICHMOND BRIDGE

(7 miles/11.25km)

Once beyond Wimbledon Park close by the renowned All England Lawn Tennis and Croquet Club, this section of the route strikes across Wimbledon Common and into Richmond Park. The common is maintained for the benefit of the public for informal recreation, and for the preservation of natural flora and fauna and is the largest expanse of heathland in the London area. Richmond Bridge, at the end of this stretch, is an 18th-century stone arch bridge spanning the Thames and linking the two halves of the Borough of Richmond-upon-Thames.

★ Oxleas Woodlands

The Oxleas Woodlands consist of a series of woods and meadows of approximately 330 acres – Eltham Common, Castle Wood, Jack Wood, Oxleas Meadow, Oxleas Wood, Deansfield, Shepherdleas Wood and Falconwood Field – located on the south and eastern side of Shooters Hill in south-east London. The Woodlands are home to a varied range of wildlife, including a raucous population of ring-necked parakeets. Near the summit of Castle Wood stands Severndroog Castle – a restored 18th-century folly built in the form of a three-storey, 63-foot (19-m) high tower. www.oxleaswoodlands.uk.

★ Richmond Park

Located in Richmond upon Thames, the park was created by Charles I in the 17th century as a deer park. Today, it is the largest of the Royal Parks and of national and international importance for wildlife conservation. Remarkably, it is a National Nature Reserve, a Site of Special Scientific Interest and a Special Area of Conservation, and is included on Historic England's Register of Parks and Gardens of Special Historic Interest in England. www.royalparks.org.uk/parks/richmond-park.

★ Kew Gardens

This fabulous botanic garden in south-west London houses the largest and most diverse botanical and mycological collections in the world. Founded in 1840 from the exotic garden at Kew Park in Middlesex, its living collections includes some 27,000 species; while the herbarium, one of the largest in the world, has over 8.5 million preserved plant and fungal specimens. www.kew.org/kew-gardens.

★ Highgate

Perhaps best known for Highgate Cemetery in which the Communist philosopher Karl Marx is buried, Highgate village proves to be a delightful collection of largely Georgian shops, pubs, restaurants and residential streets. Highgate is also one of the most expensive London suburbs in which to live and has a keen conservation body – the Highgate Society – committed to protecting its character. www.highgatesociety.com.

★ Abney Park Cemetery

Located in Stoke Newington, Abney Park is one of the so-called 'Magnificent Seven' garden cemeteries of London, a woodland memorial park and nature reserve managed by the London Borough of Hackney. There is free public access to the park all year. https://abneypark.org.

★ Hackney Wick

Located in the east of London, an area undergoing tremendous change, Hackney Wick boasts a rich industrial history on which the area has founded one of the most creative and dynamic communities in London. Today, it is home to an exciting and innovative arts scene, and has become a trendsetting area with a vibrant community of galleries, exhibition spaces, cafés, restaurants, bars and boutiques. www.hackney-wick.co.uk.

RICHMOND TO OSTERLEY LOCK
(5 miles/8km)

This section of the Capital Ring is one of the easiest, never far from water and with level walking on towpaths and tracks. The route embraces Richmond waterfront, Old Deer Park, Richmond Lock, the River Thames, Syon Park – the 200-acre London estate belonging to the Duke of Northumberland – and the Grand Union Canal. The whole stretch is well served with pubs, cafés and public transport; and, in spite of its brevity, is a fair representation of the Capital Ring at its best.

★Brent Reservoir (The Welsh Harp)

Brent Reservoir, popularly called the Welsh Harp, will surprise many; a Site of Special Scientific Interest, its open water and habitats support a diverse range of bird- and plant-life, such as grebes, summer warblers and ducks, of course. The wetland areas will appeal to botanists, offering water forget-me-not, water-plantain and flowering rush. The reservoir sits on the boundary between the boroughs of Brent and Barnet, and is owned by the Canal and River Trust. https://canalrivertrust.org.uk/places-to-visit/brent-reservoir-welsh-harp.

River Thames at Richmond

The whole stretch is well served with pubs, cafés and public transport; and, in spite of its brevity, is a fair representation of the Capital Ring at its best

Architecture on the Ring (clockwise): Aquatic Centre, Queen Elizabeth Olympic Park; graffiti in Hackney; Thames Barrier with Canary Wharf; tree house at Kew Gardens.

ALONG THE CAPITAL RING

HIGH POINTS
Shooters Hill
Westow Hill
King Henry's Mound
Horsenden Hill
Harrow Hill
Highgate Hill

LONDON BOROUGHS PASSED THROUGH
Bexley
Brent
Bromley
Camden
Croydon
Ealing
Greenwich
Haringey
Harrow
Hounslow
Islington
Lewisham
Merton
Newham
Richmond
  upon Thames
Southwark
Streatham
Wandsworth

Nature on the trail (clockwise):
Ring-necked parakeet; starling; fox;
Richmond deer park; plane tree.

North Downs Way

The North Downs Way introduces walkers to a diverse and unique landscape. It follows a chalk ridge extending from Farnham in Surrey through to the Kent coast at Dover, and though the route passes through one of the most built-up areas of Britain, it contrives to winkle out plenty of open spaces, peaceful countryside and Sites of Special Scientific Interest. This is an intricate trail wending a way through woodland and open downland, through fields and orchards, and for the most part avoiding towns and villages. Passing through two Areas of Outstanding Natural Beauty – the Surrey Hills and the Kent Downs – the Way also takes in castles, cathedrals, archbishops' palaces, stately homes and gardens, several Neolithic sites, Roman and Napoleonic forts and Second World War fortifications.

This national trail can be enjoyed at any time of year, and is usually followed from west to east. For the most part, it keeps to level ground – the first 14 miles (22.5km) over sandy countryside to the south of the Downs – but a few ups and downs are introduced on reaching the scarp slope of the North Downs, the effort involved being rewarded with fine views across the High Weald. The stretch from Guildford to Reigate is the most challenging section, taking in, as it does, Albury Down, White Down, Box Hill and Colley Hill; there are several steepish ascents here, where the chalk upland ridge is cut by valleys.

The North Downs Way's signposts from Canterbury to Dover include the logo of the Via Francigena European Pilgrimage route to Rome, which serves as a reminder that the modern route is founded on, and a celebration of, an older 'Pilgrims' Way' that linked Winchester with the shrine of Thomas à Becket in Canterbury. After Boughton Lees, the path divides, with the northern section running via Canterbury and the southern via Wye; the two sections reunite at Dover. The Way underfoot is mixed, varying from footpath to bridleway, byway and some (mostly minor) road walking.

Becoming fully open in 1978, the Way is not far from the urban sprawl of London and suburban Surrey, yet it offers some of south-east England's most accessible and beautiful countryside. The Kent Downs that stretch from the London/Surrey border to the White Cliffs of Dover embrace biodiversity-rich habitats, farmed landscapes, water, woodland and wetlands topped off with a surprising dose of tranquillity and remoteness.

AMAZING BUT TRUE ...

The often heard expression "leafy Surrey" is not without foundation for with woodland comprising just over 22 per cent of its surface area, Surrey has the highest proportion of tree coverage of any county in England.

River Mole, Box Hill

END TO END

The North Downs Way can be completed comfortably in as few as nine days, while a more leisurely 13-day itinerary builds in more time to explore. The following itineraries, following the northern fork via Canterbury, are merely suggestions.

	9 days	11 days	13 days
Start	Farnham	Farnham	Farnham
Day 1	Guildford 10½mi/17km	Guildford 10½mi/17km	Guildford 10½mi/17km
Day 2	Westhumble 10½mi/17km	Westhumble 10½mi/17km	Westhumble 10½mi/17km
Day 3	Godstone 17½mi/28.25km	Reigate 10½mi/17km	Reigate 10½mi/17km
Day 4	Otford 15¾mi/25.25km	Westerham 14½mi/23.25km	Oxted 10¼mi/16.5km
Day 5	Cuxton 15mi/24km	Wrotham 14mi/22.75km	Otford 12½mi/20km
Day 6	Lenham 21½mi/34.5km	Rochester 10¾mi/17.25km	Cuxton 15mi/24km
Day 7	Wye 9mi/14.75km	Thurnham 11¾mi/18.75km	Detling 12mi/19.5km
Day 8	Canterbury 12½mi/20.25km	Lenham 8mi/13km	Lenham 9¼mi/15km
Day 9	Dover 20½mi/33km	Wye 9mi/14.75km	Wye 9mi/14.75km
Day 10		Canterbury 12½mi/20.25km	Chilham 5½mi/8.75km
Day 11		Dover 20½mi/33km	Canterbury 7mi/11.5km
Day 12			Shepherdswell 10½mi/17km
Day 13			Dover 10mi/16km

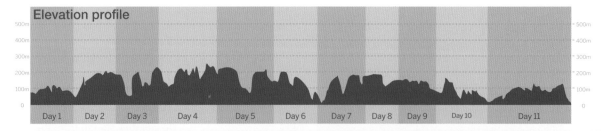

Elevation profile

Reigate Hill

FACTS AND FIGURES

START Farnham, Surrey (SU 839468)

FINISH Dover, Kent (TR 315417)

DISTANCE (via Canterbury route) 133 miles (214km)

HEIGHT GAIN (via Canterbury route) 14,070 feet (4,290m)

DIFFICULTY RATING ◆◆◆

IS IT FOR ME? A well-waymarked route suitable for year-round walking, with some energetic parts; good access to facilities and public transport.

PRACTICALITIES

GETTING THERE AND BACK
Virtually the entire walk has good transport links to London.

ACCOMMODATION
In this densely populated and touristy part of the country, there is no shortage of accommodation, but some forward planning will be needed during the summer season.

WEBSITE
www.northdownsway.co.uk

MAPS

OS Explorer
137, 138, 145, 146, 147, 148, 149, 150, 163.

OS Landranger
177, 178, 179, 186, 187, 188, 189.

Nature on the trail (clockwise):
Adder; common rock rose; nightjar; hops.

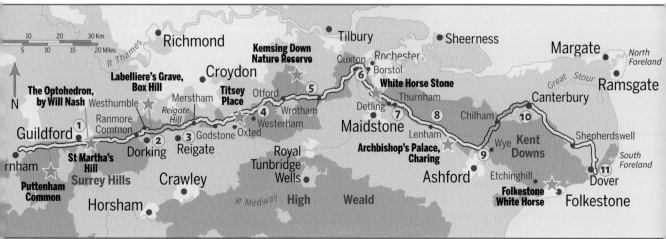

WYE TO CANTERBURY
(12½ miles/20.25km)

Leaving the village of Wye and crossing the Great Stour, the Way to Canterbury provides an opportunity to visit Boughton Aluph church to see the Pilgrims Porch, where medieval pilgrims gathered. Godmersham Park is where Jane Austen's brother lived, and is thought to be the inspiration for *Mansfield Park*, her third published novel. Keep an eye open here for deer in the woodlands, which in springtime are lush with bluebells, an ancient woodland indicator species. A choice of inns and a tea room will encourage you to take lunch in the medieval village of Chilham, before the final stage through hop gardens and apple orchards to Canterbury.

A choice of inns and a tea room will encourage you to take lunch in the medieval village of Chilham

★ Puttenham Common

Privately owned by the Hampton Estate, Puttenham Common has considerable archaeological interest, not least the hill fort at Hillbury. There is evidence, too, in the form of slit trenches and rifle range butts, of the area's use during the Second World War. The common in summer is swathed in bell heather and ling, with several areas of oak and Scots pine. Adders may be seen basking here, while among the birdlife, the elusive nightjar is particularly fond of this heathland habitat.

★ Folkestone White Horse

Not so old as many other chalk figures in England, this Millennium landmark, stands on Cheriton Hill, near Folkestone, directly above the Channel Tunnel Terminal. Its design was drawn by local artist, Charlie Newington, who was inspired by a nearby Iron Age fort in an area known as Horse Hill dating from three millennia ago and the prehistoric White Horse of Uffington in Oxfordshire.

★ St Martha's Hill

The wooded rise of St Martha's Hill features several Megalithic and Neolithic artefacts, dating back 5,500 years. Below the summit church, five circular earthworks can be found, believed to date to the Bronze Age. Some suggest that the name of the hill is a reference to a martyr, in this case St Thomas of Canterbury.

MAJOR
PETER LABELLIERE
AGED 75
AN ECCENTRIC RESIDENT
OF DORKING WAS BURIED
HERE HEAD DOWNWARDS
11TH JULY 1800

★ Labelliere's Grave, Box Hill

Peter Labelliere, a British army major, was born in Dublin in 1725 to a family of French Huguenot descent. He joined the army at the age of 14, but on leaving military service became a political agitator and was accused of bribing British troops not to fight in the American War of Independence. After moving to Dorking in the late 18th century, Lablliere often visited Box Hill to meditate. In old age he became increasingly eccentric, neglecting his own personal hygiene to such an extent that he acquired the nickname 'The walking dung-hill'. He died in 1800, and, in accordance with his wishes, he was buried head downwards on the western side of Box Hill above The Whites.

★ White Horse Stone

The White Horse Stone (TQ 753603) is a name given to two separate sarsen megaliths on the slopes of Blue Bell Hill, near the village of Aylesford, although only one survives. The White Horse Stone is seen as a sacred site by members of a modern Pagan religious persuasion that seek to copy pre-Christian belief systems, while others take the view that the stone is connected to 'earth energies' that pre-modern people were 'in tune with'.

★ Archbishop's Palace, Charing

The Archbishop's Palace at Charing is an important 8th-century heritage site, one of the earliest of 17 medieval palaces owned by the see of Canterbury. The current palace dates back to the late 13th century, with later additions and rebuilding.

WESTHUMBLE TO REIGATE HILL
(10½ miles/17km)

This stretch of the North Downs contains an outstanding range of wildlife habitats, including large areas of woodland and chalk grassland. Box Hill gets its name from the ancient box woodland found on its west-facing chalk slopes, overlooking the River Mole; it lies within the Surrey Hills AONB. The western part is managed by the National Trust.

This leg of the North Downs Way forms part of the Mole Gap to Reigate Escarpment Site of Special Scientific Interest, noted for its orchids and other chalk downland-favouring plant species. At the eastern end, Reigate Hill and nearby Gatton Park, landscaped by 'Capability' Brown, are also in the custody of the National Trust; while sitting prominently at the top of the hill is the 19th-century Reigate Fort, a historic defensive position overviewing the Weald towards the South Downs.

MAPS Day-walk taster
OS Explorer
146, Dorking, Box Hill & Reigate.
OS Landranger
187, Dorking & Reigate.

Box Hill

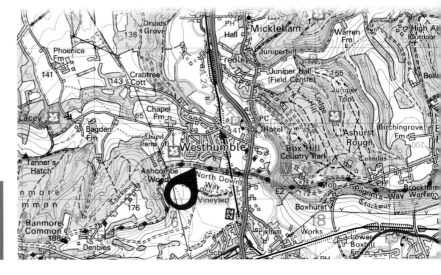

THE *OPTOHEDRON*, BY WILL NASH

Located near Newlands Corner on the Albury Downs, just east of Guildford and one of the finest viewpoints on the North Downs way, the *Optohedron* is an inspiring outdoor artwork by artist Will Nash, embodying his fascination with geometry and patterns in nature – in this case, the multifaceted structure of an insect's eye.

★Titsey Place

Near Oxted, Titsey Place is an English country house with a pedigree extending back to Tudor times, though little of the original mansion survives. The house, which is open to the public, is noted for its fine collection of family portraits and other paintings, including works by Joshua Reynolds and Canaletto. see www.titsey.org.

Box Hill gets its name from the ancient box woodland found on its west-facing chalk slopes overlooking the River Mole

★Kemsing Down Nature Reserve

Just the slightest of deviations facilitates a visit to this nature reserve, which is splendid not only for its panoramic views but for its ancient woodland and the orchids that grow here, including pyramidal orchid and common spotted-orchid. Other grassland flora species include common rock-rose and burnet-saxifrage. Butterflies, too, find this an ideal habitat, notably the brown argus, common blue, dingy and grizzled skipper.

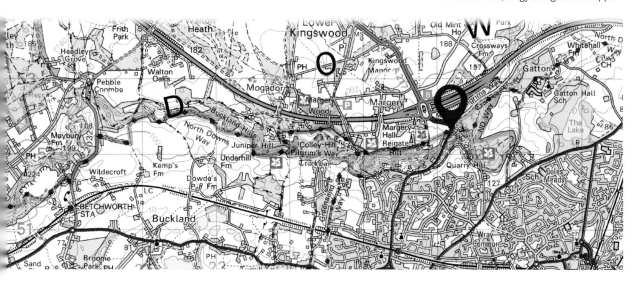

Peddars Way and Norfolk Coast Path 🐚

Trails upon trails is what the Peddars Way and Norfolk Coast Path National Trail is about, as it combines two separate trails which run in a great arc from inland villages to and along the coast. It was opened in 1986 by Prince Charles. The Peddars Way is one of a number of components of a prehistoric route, the Greater Ridgeway, that ran from The Wash to the South Devon Coast. The Norfolk Coast Path is a key part of the as yet incomplete England Coast Path, and runs from Hunstanton to Hopton-on-Sea, linking with the Peddars Way at Holme-next-the-Sea. The greater part of the trail runs through the Norfolk Coast Area of Outstanding Natural Beauty, and the whole is a golden opportunity to become immersed among sand dunes, reedbeds, tidal salt marshes rich with wildlife, huge beaches, militaria, ancient churches and pine woodland. Birdwatchers, like the birds they seek, flock to the Norfolk Coast, particularly Titchwell Marsh and Cley Marshes.

The first stretch of the trail starts in the Brecks, a unique expanse of forest, heath and river valleys, and roughly follows tracks, footpaths and minor roads along the course of the Peddars Way (a part of the Icknield Way, one of only a few long-distance tracks that pre-date the Roman occupation of Britain; the extant sections are a Scheduled Ancient Monument). The terrain overall is varied but generally flat, making this one of the easier national trails and suitable for walking at any time of year. Winter brings changeable but often pleasant weather, while the proverbial Indian summer is certain to bring colour to cheeks; spring and autumn are great for migrating birdlife; while in summer the hedgerows bloom and the skies are blue – usually, this is Britain, after all.

The Norfolk Coast section, unlike the Peddars Way, is a contemporary development that has grown from a network of footpaths old and new. The richness of the hedgerows and ancient field patterns that flank the Peddars Way, however, are a clear indicator of its ancient pedigree. The section southwards along the Norfolk Coast from Cromer to Hopton-on-Sea only opened in 2016, and here there are beaches and cliff tops, sites of special scientific interest, sand dunes, marram grass and river valleys. Also unlike the Peddars Way, none of the Norfolk Coast is far from civilisation and ideal for a disconnected, pick 'n' mix approach to multi-day walking.

> **AMAZING BUT TRUE …**
> There's plenty of history along this walk. Not only does the Peddar's Way go back to Roman times (look on the map to see how straight it is), but it also formed part of a pilgrimage route to Walsingham and the priory there.

Wreck of the Steam Trawler *Sheraton*, Hunstanton cliffs.

The Peddars Way and Norfolk Coast Path perfectly lends itself to completion as two distinct walks: Peddars Way (46 miles/75km) and the Norfolk Coast Path (85 miles/136km). As a combined national trail, however, it can be accomplished in 10 days, with no single day more than 17½ miles (28.25km). The following itinerary is merely a suggestion.

FACTS AND FIGURES

START Knettishall Heath Country Park, Suffolk (TL 943807)

FINISH Hopton-on-Sea, Norfolk (TM 524999)

DISTANCE 131 miles (211km)

HEIGHT GAIN 6,395 feet (1,950m)

DIFFICULTY RATING ♦♦

IS IT FOR ME? Comparatively level and easy-going throughout; on Peddars Way, accommodation en route is scarce and access by public transport difficult at start.

PRACTICALITIES

GETTING THERE AND BACK
The Peddars Way may be accessed by public transport, although the start at Knettishall Heath is not the easiest place to get to, so a taxi may be the best approach; be sure to book overnight accommodation, which is in short supply. Holme-next-the-Sea, at the northern end, has a regular bus service to King's Lynn and Hunstanton. For the Norfolk Coast Path, regular bus services run to Great Yarmouth, from where trains and buses connect to London. A 'Coastline' bus service runs from Hunstanton to Cromer.

ACCOMMODATION
Accommodation may not always be found at day's end, but there will be some close by; it just need's some advance planning to get to and from the route without too much additional walking.

WEBSITES
www.nationaltrail.co.ukwww.visitwestnorfolk.com

10 days

Day 1	Merton 12¾mi/20.5km	Day 6	Cley-next-the-Sea 10mi/16km
Day 2	Castle Acre 12¾mi/20.5km	Day 7	Cromer 12¼mi/19.75km
Day 3	Ringstead 17½mi/28.25km	Day 8	Happisburgh 13¼mi/21.25km
Day 4	Brancaster 15mi/24km	Day 9	Caistor-on-Sea 15½mi/24.75km
Day 5	Wells-next-the-Sea 12½mi/20km	Day 10	Hopton-on-Sea 9mi/14.5km

MAPS

OS Explorer
229, 230, 236, 237, 238, 250, 251, 252.

OS Landranger
132, 133, 144.

This page (left): Groynes on Hunstanton Beach; **(right):** Salt marsh at Wells-next-the-Sea.

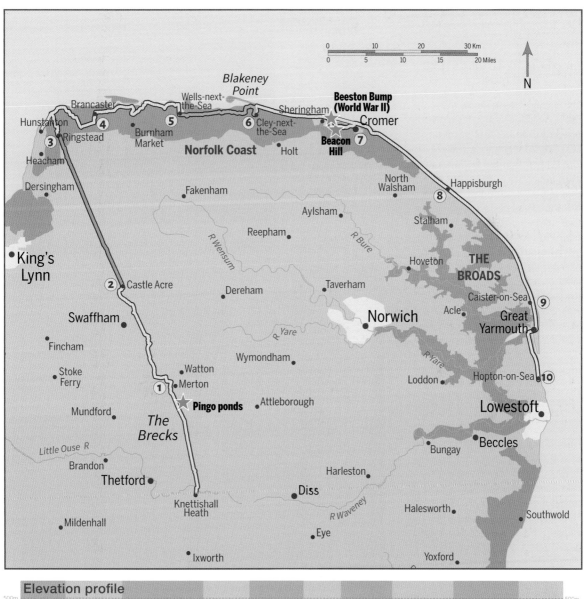

Blakeney Point

Beeston Bump (World War II)

Wells-next-the-Sea

Brancaster

Sheringham

Cromer

Beacon Hill

Hunstanton

Ringstead

Burnham Market

Cley-next-the-Sea

Holt

Norfolk Coast

Heacham

Dersingham

Fakenham

North Walsham

Happisburgh

Aylsham

Stalham

King's Lynn

Reepham

R Wensum

R Bure

Hoveton

THE BROADS

Castle Acre

Dereham

Taverham

Caister-on-Sea

Swaffham

R Yare

Norwich

Acle

Great Yarmouth

Fincham

Watton

Wymondham

Hopton-on-Sea

Stoke Ferry

Merton

Loddon

R Yare

Mundford

Pingo ponds

Attleborough

Lowestoft

The Brecks

Little Ouse R

Bungay

Beccles

Brandon

Harleston

Thetford

Diss

Knettishall Heath

R Waveney

Halesworth

Southwold

Mildenhall

Eye

Ixworth

Yoxford

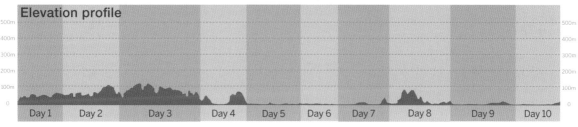

Elevation profile

Day 1 | Day 2 | Day 3 | Day 4 | Day 5 | Day 6 | Day 7 | Day 8 | Day 9 | Day 10

Best section for
Weekends/Short breaks

CASTLE ACRE TO RINGSTEAD
(17½ miles/28.25km)

On leaving Castle Acre, the route, which reaches its highest points (both 302 feet/92m) on Massingham Heath and west of Great Massingham village, closely parallels a minor road, but one that sits atop both the original Peddars Way and the Roman road that came along later. The village of Great Massingham is worth a deviation, if time allows. This is one of Norfolk's most endearing villages and is thought to date from the 5th century, when the region was occupied by Angles and Saxons following the departure of the Romans. Several ponds dominate the village, and these are thought to be associated with an 11th-century Augustinian abbey. England's first prime minister, Robert Walpole, was educated in the village school room.

As it passes on, almost arrow-straight, the route travels across gentle countryside, only undulating as it passes Fring, the traditional source of the River Heacham, and Sedgeford, a small village with a history spanning 4,000 years. Ringstead, when it comes, is renowned for no fewer than 16 listed buildings, including two churches and its 17th-century pub. The nearby Ringstead Downs is a partly wooded chalk ridge and important unimproved chalk grassland. A permissive footpath runs across the downs to Hunstanton.

★Freshwater marshes

The flooded grasslands of Norfolk are the product of ancient deforestation followed by centuries of grazing by cattle. The exception is the wet grazing marsh of the north Norfolk coast, which is the product of saltmarsh being reclaimed by the building of embankments to prevent incursion by seawater.

This page (top): Burnham Overy Staithe; **(middle):** Norfolk Coast Path; **(bottom):** Thompson Water. **Opposite page** Second World War pill box near Happisburgh.

★Pingo ponds

Also known as 'kettle lakes', pingo ponds are a rare and specific type of waterhole found by the dozen in the Brecks in Norfolk, by far the largest density in the UK. They were created at the end of the last ice age – as the glaciers retreated, 10,000 or so years ago, they left hard discs of ice compressed into the ground, over which soil later accumulated. The warmer climate caused the discs to melt, forming a depression filled with water – a pingo pond, a peculiarity of the Brecks landscape.

Many of the churchyards encountered along the trail have considerable biodiversity value as they occupy ancient meadows that were used for hay or pasture, long before the church was built. Because so many wildflower meadows have been cultivated, churchyards in Norfolk may be the only remaining areas of 'unimproved' species-rich grassland.

Norfolk as a county has the highest number of churches in the UK

★ Second World War

Along the Norfolk coast there are many pill boxes and gun turrets surviving from the Second World War. Beeston Bump (TG 168432) used to be a wireless intercept station, where radio signals from German E-boats were intercepted and relayed to Bletchley Park. Of particular interest is the Muckleburgh Collection, a military museum on the site of a former military camp at Weybourne; it was opened to the public in 1988 and is the largest privately owned military museum in the UK (see www.muckleburgh.co.uk).

WELLS-NEXT-THE-SEA TO CLEY-NEXT-THE-SEA
(10 miles/16km)

Seemingly under constant threat of flooding, the salt marshes at Wells-next-the-Sea are a rich habitat for birdlife; the village is a popular tourist destination, and its beach is one of the finest and most extensive in the country. Here you find the Holkham National Nature Reserve, one of England's largest and part of the North Norfolk Coast Site of Special Scientific Interest.

It may not seem it now, but Cley used to be one of the busiest ports in England, trading in everything from grain and spices to coal and fish. The marshes around Cley are important today for their populations of rare breeding and visiting birds, including bittern, bearded tit, avocet, black-winged stilt and spoonbill.

This page **(top)**: The lighthouse on Beacon Hill; **(middle)**: Cley-next-the-Sea; **(bottom)**: West Runton cliffs.

Cley used to be one of the busiest ports in England, trading in everything from grain and spices to coal and fish

Nature on the trail

There is plenty of wildlife on the Peddars Way, but the coastal marshes and sand banks are where the action is. **(clockwise):** Red knot (a type of sand piper) on the shoreline; dunlin (the UK's most common wader; grey seals; avocet display over the marshes.

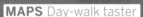

MAPS Day-walk taster

OS Explorer
251, North Norfolk Coast, Wells-next-the-Sea & Fakenham.

OS Landranger
132, North West Norfolk, King's Lynn & Fakenham; 133, North East Norfolk, Cromer & Wroxham.

Pennine Way

Conceived as a south to north route, the Pennine Way begins in Edale, Derbyshire. Immediately, wayfarers are faced with a Herculean task, the crossing of the Kinder and Bleaklow massifs, treading a peaty, gritstone course to the northern edge of the Peak District National Park at Standedge. There, the route passes into the noticeably different landscapes of the South Pennines, crossing the Calder Valley and heading for the famed land of the Brontë sisters.

Beyond, lie the unrivalled limestone delights of the Yorkshire Dales, reached near Gargrave on the River Aire and left behind at the highest pub in England, the Tan Hill. Between these bookends, the extravagant scenery for which the Dales are renowned arouses a host of feelings and emotions, contrasting markedly with the austere miles to the south.

A return to the tang of wild places lies beyond Tan Hill as the route launches into the North Pennines, a region that, in spite of having borne its share of mining activity, is nonetheless an Area of Outstanding Natural Beauty. Many consider that here the Pennine Way is at its best, as it courts the turbulent, boisterous Tees; tackles the long crossing to High Cup Nick and the remote village of Dufton, before setting off to the roof of the Pennines on Cross Fell.

From the heights of Cross Fell (2,929 feet/893m), the Way eases down to the village of Garrigill and on beside the North Tyne to the cobbled streets of Alston, a long-established market town that shares the title of the 'Highest market town in England', at about 1,000 feet (300m) above sea level, with Buxton, Derbyshire. From Alston, the Way heads along the ancient Maiden Way, a Roman supply route running between the Brough/Penrith road at Kirkby Thore, near Appleby, and Carvoran Roman Fort on Hadrian's Wall.

Another distinct change of scenery is found north of Hadrian's Wall as the Way heads into the Border forests and the Cheviot Hills, a region that in times past has witnessed inordinate savagery, bloodshed and brutality during the period known as the Border Troubles. Finally, clinging to every last vestige of high ground, the Way enters the rolling hills of Southern Scotland, a delightful prospect, but by no stretch of geological imagination part of the Pennines. But who would argue that the last stretch, as the route slips gracefully down to its end in Kirk Yetholm, is not a fitting end to an outstanding and invigorating achievement?

In short, the Pennine Way is a long and arduous undertaking, often crossing remote moorland, and suitable only for strong and experienced walkers; this is not the route on which to cut your long-distance walking teeth.

AMAZING BUT TRUE ...

Across the Kinder plateau, the Pennine Way follows in the footsteps of the famous Kinder Trespass of Sunday 24 April 1932, when 400 people marched to protest against landowner prohibition on moorland access, land over which earlier generations had once had the freedom to roam. Benny Rothman, the leader, was arrested and given a custodial sentence.

Nicol's Chair, High Cup Nick

END TO END

The Pennine Way can loosely be sub-divided into five groups: Dark Peak, South Pennines, Yorkshire Dales, North Pennines and Cheviot Hills. Anyone intending to do the whole thing must first and foremost be very good at forward planning, and able to devote a minimum of 15 days to the walk; ideally more, because 15 days makes no allowance for rest days and any days needed to cope with extreme weather conditions, and also involves several days at or above 20 miles (32km). Three weeks would be a better allocation of time, but here is a minimum outline.

15 days

Start	Edale
Section 1 Dark Peak	
Day 1	Crowden 16½mi/26.25km
Day 2	Standedge 11½mi/18.25km
Section 2 South Pennines	
Day 3	Hebden Bridge 12¼mi/19.75km
Day 4	Cowling 19mi/30.5km
Section 3 Yorkshire Dales	
Day 5	Malham 17½mi/28km
Day 6	Horton-in-Ribblesdale 14¾mi/23.75km
Day 7	Hawes 14¼mi/23km
Day 8	Keld 12½mi/20.25km

Section 4 North Pennines	
Day 9	Middleton-in-Teesdale 24mi/39.25km
Day 10	Dufton 21¼mi/34.25km
Day 11	Alston 20¼mi/32.75km
Day 12	Greenhead 16¾mi/27km
Section 5 Cheviot Hills	
Day 13	Bellingham 22¼mi/36km
Day 14	Byrness 15¼mi/24.5km
Day 15	Kirk Yetholm 27¼mi/44km

FACTS AND FIGURES

START Edale, Derbyshire (SK 122859)

FINISH Kirk Yetholm, Scottish Borders (NT 827282)

DISTANCE 268 miles (429km)

HEIGHT GAIN 36,065 feet (10,995m)

DIFFICULTY RATING ♦♦♦♦♦

IS IT FOR ME? The oldest and still the most challenging national trail with some long remote stages; best for experienced multi-day walkers.

MAPS

OS Explorer
OL1, OL2, OL16, OL19, OL21, OL30, OL31, OL42, OL43, 288.

OS Landranger
74, 75, 80, 86, 87, 91, 92, 98, 103, 109, 110.

Elevation profile

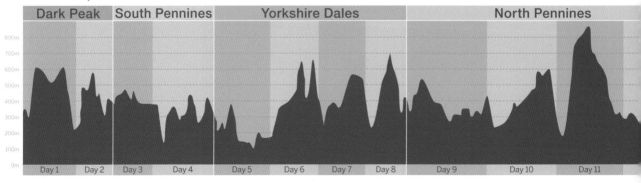

PRACTICALITIES

GETTING THERE AND BACK
Edale is served by rail connections between Sheffield and Manchester, while infrequent buses run from Kirk Yetholm and Town Yetholm to Kelso, which has good bus services to towns with railway stations. In between, the Pennine Way is networked by bus and rail services of varying frequency.

ACCOMMODATION
The Pennine Way is suitable for backpackers and youth hostellers, although there is an ample supply of other, mainly B&B, accommodation. But note, while the Pennine Way itself may not have herds of walkers tramping along it all at the same time, many of the valley stopovers are popular with day trippers; booking well in advance is essential.

CAMPING
Most of the Pennine Way is within a few miles of civilisation, apart from in the Cheviot Hills. Wild camping requires permission of the landowner, and there are countless places where wild campers would want to set down for the night.

WEBSITES
www.nationaltrail.co.uk/pennine-way
www.thepennineway.co.uk
www.penninewayassociation.co.uk
There is a Facebook group that provides information on current activities and recommendations for the Pennine Way. See www.facebook.com and search for 'Pennine Way walkers'

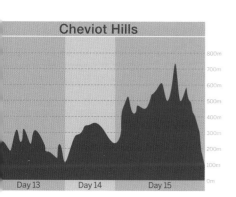

Cheviot Hills

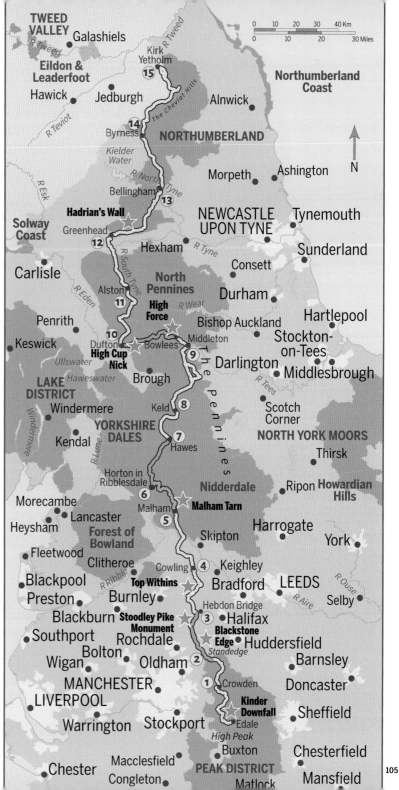

★Kinder Downfall

This is the tallest waterfall in the Peak, a 98-foot (30-m) drop formerly known as Kinder Scut (*sic* of Kinder Scout), from which the plateau above takes its name. In benign conditions, this is rarely more than a trickle, but at its best it is dramatic, often with plumes of spray being blown back upwards, drenching unsuspecting passers-by.

★Blackstone Edge

Blackstone Edge is a stark gritstone escarpment at 1,549 feet (472m) above sea level in the Pennine hills, and surrounded by moorland on the boundary between Lancashire (Greater Manchester) and Yorkshire. At the northern end of the Edge stands the Aiggin Stone, a gritstone pillar, possibly a waymarker along a 1735 packhorse route, once thought to be a Roman road, and marking the county boundary.

★Stoodley Pike Monument

This towering monument replaced an earlier structure, started in 1814 and commemorating the defeat of Napoleon and the surrender of Paris, was completed in 1815, after the Battle of Waterloo (Napoleonic Wars), but collapsed in 1854. The present tower is a replacement and long in the view of Wayfarers tramping across Langfield Common.

★Top Withins

This ruined farmhouse near Haworth is said to have been the inspiration for the location of the Earnshaw family house in Wuthering Heights, the 1847 novel by Emily Brontë. The Brontë Society remark that 'The buildings, even when complete, bore no resemblance to the house she described, but the situation may have been in her mind when she wrote of the moorland setting of the Heights'.

★Malham Tarn

This lovely expanse of water is a glacial lake seated on a bed of impermeable slate, one of only eight upland alkaline lakes in Europe and the highest marl lake in the UK. The area has been occupied since Mesolithic times, when the shores of the lake would have been a perfect camping site for hunter-gatherers. The scenery here has inspired the likes of John Ruskin, the Lakes poet, and Charles Kingsley, who wrote part of *The Water Babies* while staying as a guest at Malham Tarn House.

★High Force

This stunning waterfall lies within the North Pennines Area of Outstanding Natural Beauty, and was formed where the River Tees crosses a geological feature known as the Whin Sill, a hard layer of igneous rock. With care, it is possible to walk to the very lip of the top of the falls.

★High Cup Nick

This is the most dramatic glaciated valley in Northern England, a classic U-shaped valley at the top of which a particularly stunning piece of rock artwork, Nicol's Chair, is part of the well-known Whin Sill. From here you get a fine view of the grey-blue dolerite crags that also feature at High Force and Cauldron Snout.

In many ways, the Pennine Way is best done piecemeal rather than as one continuous trek. Many walkers will tackle it this way, choosing fair weather days, and enjoying it without the effort of multi-day walking.

STANDEDGE TO HEBDEN BRIDGE
(12¼ miles/19.75km)

Low moorlands characterise much of this stretch, which reaches north to cross the M62 motorway on a delightful footbridge to gain the gritstone crest of Blackstone Edge. At the Aiggin Stone, the Way meets an ancient paved track said to be a Roman road, while onward the route passes several reservoirs before striking across Langfield Common to the monument on Stoodley Pike (1,300 feet/400m), which commemorates the defeat of Napoleon and the surrender of Paris. The Way doesn't descend directly to Hebden Bridge, but

runs down through Callis Wood to cross the Rochdale Canal before tackling the steep valley slopes beyond. Hebden Bridge is easily reached by bus, or on foot along the canal towpath.

HORTON-IN-RIBBLESDALE TO HAWES
(12¼ miles/19.75km)

On leaving Horton, the Pennine Way finds a delightful route across the gathering grounds of the River Wharfe, bound for the distant market town of Hawes. A long stretch makes use of the high, wide and handsome, Roman Cam Road, while a brief connection ties in with a more modern trail, the Dales Way (page 54). The landscape is one of high moorland dotted with isolated farms, and provides a fine view of Yorkshire's Three Peaks. This is exhilarating walking, which contrives to avoid an otherwise hard surface tramp down into Hawes by finding a way around the lump of Dodd Fell Hill.

BOWLEES TO DUFTON
(16½ miles/26.5km)

AND DUFTON TO ALSTON
(20¼ miles/32.75km) – 2 days

This two-day trek from Bowlees in Teesdale to Alston is not for the faint-hearted, but it is one that takes in the dramatic splendour of High Force, where a step in the River Tees creates England's biggest waterfall, spectacularly dropping 70 feet (21m) into a plunge pool below. Cauldron Snout, where the river outflows from Cow Green Reservoir, is not much less dramatic; beyond which the Way tackles Maize Beck before encountering the splendour of High Cup Nick, a classic U-shaped valley that will take your breath away.

Having descended to Dufton and lost so much height, and ended the day farther from the Pennine Way's end than when it began, a steady pull leads up over Knock Fell, onto the two Dun

Fells and onward to the highest of the Pennine summits, Cross Fell. Here you feel on top of the world before taking to the long gradual descent to the River South Tyne and the market town of Alston.

THE FIRST NATIONAL TRAIL

Motivated by correspondence with two American girls who wrote to him asking for advice about a walking holiday in England, Lancashire-born Tom Stephenson (1893–1987), journalist and campaigner for the legal right of access to the countryside went on to ask in the *Daily Herald* (22 June 1935), '... why should we not press for something akin to the Appalachian Trail – a Pennine Way from the Peak to the Cheviot?' He went on, '... a meandering way deviating as needs be to include the best of that long range of moor and fell ... just a faint line on the Ordnance Maps which the feet of grateful pilgrims would, with the passing years, engrave on the face of the land.'

Given the fast-growing state of the outdoor movement at that time, the proposal was greeted with enthusiasm and support; but with numerous new rights of way needing to be created, it was 30 years before the route opened in 1965. As Britain's first long-distance trail, it was instantly popular.

The original plan was to stick as much as possible to the crest of the Pennines by linking old footpaths, drove roads, packhorse trails, bridleways, shepherds' and miners' tracks, and even Roman roads. Modifications were needed here and there, and the odd idiosyncratic lurch, as from Teesdale to Dufton, were introduced to include places of scenic interest or to reach a valley where food and lodging might be found. The end product, as several thousands of walkers have since discovered, was a superb undertaking, and one that inspired a network of trails across the whole British Isles.

Here you feel on top of the world before taking to the long gradual descent to the River South Tyne and the market town of Alston

This page (top): Cauldron Snout; **(bottom):** High Force.
Opposite page (top): Rochdale Canal, Hebden Bridge; **(bottom):** Aiggin Stone.

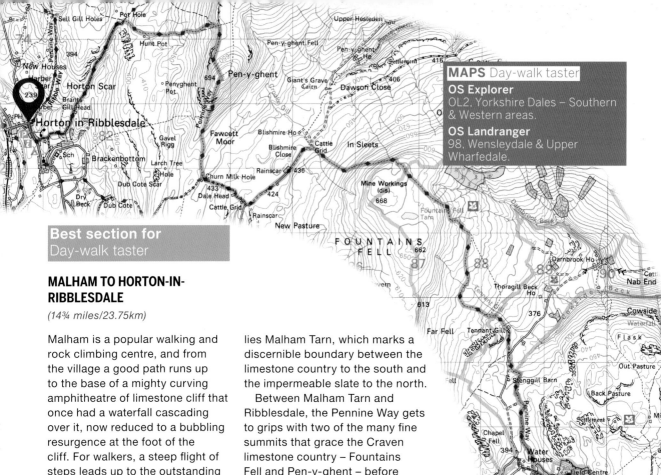

MAPS Day-walk taster

OS Explorer
OL2, Yorkshire Dales – Southern & Western areas.

OS Landranger
98, Wensleydale & Upper Wharfedale.

Best section for
Day-walk taster

MALHAM TO HORTON-IN-RIBBLESDALE

(14¾ miles/23.75km)

Malham is a popular walking and rock climbing centre, and from the village a good path runs up to the base of a mighty curving amphitheatre of limestone cliff that once had a waterfall cascading over it, now reduced to a bubbling resurgence at the foot of the cliff. For walkers, a steep flight of steps leads up to the outstanding expanse of limestone pavement above, which featured in the film *Harry Potter and the Deathly Hallows – Part 1*. Once above the cliff, the Way passes through a shallow valley, Watlowes. Ahead lies Malham Tarn, which marks a discernible boundary between the limestone country to the south and the impermeable slate to the north.

Between Malham Tarn and Ribblesdale, the Pennine Way gets to grips with two of the many fine summits that grace the Craven limestone country – Fountains Fell and Pen-y-ghent – before easing down to the small village of Horton-in-Ribblesdale, the traditional starting point for that rugged day jaunt over Yorkshire's Three Peaks, and home to two pubs, a café and tea rooms.

THE MASS TRESPASS ONTO KINDER SCOUT STARTED FROM THIS QUARRY 24TH APRIL 1932

The Pennine Way is at its best as it courts the turbulent, boisterous Tees, tackles the long crossing to High Cup Nick and the remote village of Dufton, before setting off to the roof of the Pennines on Cross Fell

Nature on the trail (clockwise): Black grouse; feral goats in the Cheviots; curlew; lady's slipper orchid; common bistort, scarlet elf cup.

This page: Malham Cove.
Opposite page: Bowden Bridge Mass Trepass plaque.

Ribble Way

There are several fine walking trails that follow a river from its source to the sea; the Ribble Way is contrary, and goes upstream, running from the Lancashire coast up into the hills above Dentdale and Wharfedale in North Yorkshire. Along the way, the trail encounters tidal marshes, riverside meadows, farmland, limestone gorges, quiet lanes and moorland terrain; it fashions an elegant route from Preston to Roman Ribchester, historic Clitheroe, Settle and Horton-in-Ribblesdale. Aiming to get the best from delightful countryside, the Way is adept at switching from one bank of the river to the other, always seeking the most attractive passage, looking for beauty … and finding it at every turn.

The coastal end of the Way is the village of Longton on the wildlife-favoured salt marshes of the Ribble Estuary, overlooking its confluence with the River Douglas. Staying close by the river, the Way passes through Preston, emerging on the other side to pass beneath the M6 motorway – the first stretch of motorway in Britain – and into the Brockholes Nature Reserve (see page 116). For a while, the river is abandoned as the trail loops across farmland, roughly following the line of a Roman road that fed into the town of Ribchester, an important Roman site as the location of a cavalry fort known as Bremetennacum, although the area has been inhabited since the Bronze Age.

Close by Clitheroe, the River Ribble is joined by the River Hodder, which flows from the rounded hills of the Forest of Bowland. Maintaining faith with the river, the Way passes round Clitheroe and on by several charming Lancashire villages: Waddington, West Bradford, Chatburn and Sawley, bound for Gisburn where the trail heads in a more northerly direction for Ribblesdale, occasionally in the company of the Pennine Bridleway.

Having entered North Yorkshire, the Way reaches Settle, historically part of the West Riding of Yorkshire, and an old market town on the fringes of the Yorkshire Dales National Park with a pedigree that is both Anglo-Saxon and Irish-Norse.

Beyond Stainforth and its rippling cataracts, the Ribble Way briefly diverts into a karst wonderland, west of Malham, before returning to the valley, heading for Horton-in-Ribblesdale. The final stage takes you through limestone country, briefly in company with the Pennine Way (page 102) and later encountering the Dales Way (page 54). Finally, touching on the head of Dentdale, the Way takes a meandering route up onto Gayle Moor to the river's source, where a stream issues from the limestone fells – a wild and lonely place so classically evocative of these upland quarters of the Yorkshire Dales.

AMAZING BUT TRUE …

J R R Tolkien stayed in the area of Hurst Green while he was working on *The Lord of the Rings* trilogy when his son studied at nearby Stonyhurst College. Could this be the place that inspired Tolkien? Could the gentle countryside of woods and meadows bisected by looping meanders of the River Ribble be the Shire? How fanciful might it be to suggest that Hurst Green is really Hobbiton?

Stainforth Force

PRACTICALITIES

GETTING THERE AND BACK
Longton is accessible by local bus services from Preston, which is on the West Coast mainline railway and national bus routes. Gavel Gap, the source of the Ribble is accessible only on foot, so time needs to be allowed to retreat to Dent or Ribblehead railway stations, to Hawes in Wensleydale, or back to Horton-in-Ribblesdale – if returning to Horton, the course of the Pennine Way along Cam High Road and then southwards is both shorter and quicker.

GETTING AROUND
The several intermediate route points are accessible by or close to local bus service routes. Clitheroe, Settle and Horton-in-Ribblesdale have a railway service, although Horton's station is a short distance away from the village centre.

ACCOMMODATION
There is plentiful accommodation, generally small hotels, B&Bs and guest houses, along the route until the final section up to the source; it may have to be shared with walkers tackling the Pennine Way or the Dales Way.

MAPS
OS Explorer
OL2, OL21, OL41, 286, 287.
OS Landranger
98, 102, 103.

FACTS AND FIGURES

START Longton, Lancashire (SD 459254)

FINISH Gavel Gap, Gayle Moor, North Yorkshire (SD 813832)

DISTANCE 70 miles (113km)

HEIGHT GAIN 6,200 feet (1,890m)

DIFFICULTY RATING ♦♦

IS IT FOR ME? A straightforward riparian route along the Ribble from sea to source; the final leg is in remote countryside, with allowance needed to return to Horton-in-Ribblesdale.

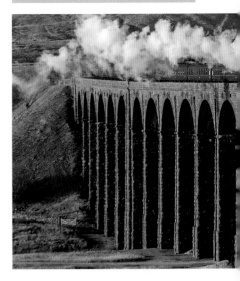

The Ribble Way falls readily into seven distinct stages, each of which can be completed in a day; no day longer than 12¼ miles (19.5km).

7 days

Start	Longton
Day 1	Penworthham Bridge *6mi / 9.5km*
Day 2	Ribchester *12¼mi / 19.5km*
Day 3	Brungerley Bridge (Clitheroe) *10¾mi / 17.25km*
Day 4	Gisburn *10¾mi / 17.25km*
Day 5	Settle *11¾mi / 18.75km*
Day 6	Horton-in-Ribblesdale *8mi / 12.75km*
Day 7	Gayle Moor (River Ribble source) *10¾mi / 17.25km*

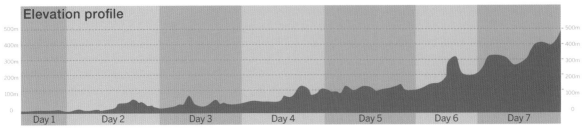

Elevation profile

Day 1 Day 2 Day 3 Day 4 Day 5 Day 6 Day 7

★ Stainforth Force

At the village of Stainforth, the Ribble Way takes briefly to the fells above, but first a visit to Stainforth Force (SD 818671) reveals a tumbling waterfall of beauty, a series of mini cascades flowing this way and that across rocky slabs. Above the force, a 17th-century packhorse bridge carries a former monastic road.

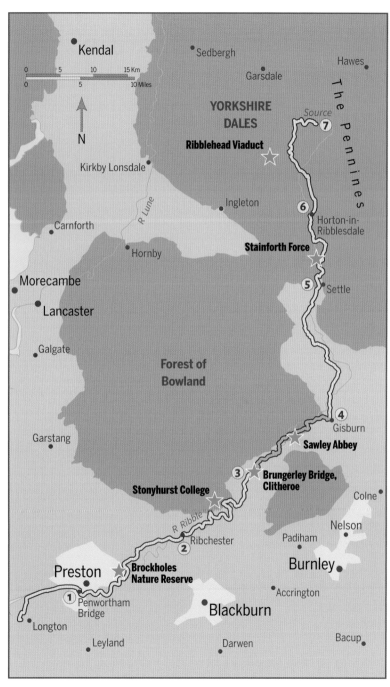

★ Ribblehead Viaduct

About a mile west of the Ribble Way, the Ribblehead Viaduct (SD 760793), used by the Settle–Carlisle railway, is one of the enduring iconic images of Yorkshire and is well worth making the time to visit. At more than 440 yards in length and with 24 arches, the viaduct stands 104 feet (32m) above the valley floor.

CLITHEROE TO GISBURN

(10¾ miles/17.25km)

The elegant stretch of the Ribble between Clitheroe, which has always been in Lancashire, and Gisburn, which hasn't, is as remarkable for its intrinsic charm as for its abundance of reasons to divert and explore adjacent villages that lie within the Forest of Bowland Area of Outstanding Natural Beauty: Waddington, frequent winner of the Best Kept Village Awards; Grindleton, which predates the Domesday survey of 1086; and Sawley for its ruined abbey (see below). The walking is easy throughout, generally following riparian field paths and minor country lanes.

★ Brockholes Nature Reserve

Based on the site of an old quarry, the Wildlife Trust has skilfully developed the Brockholes Nature Reserve (SD 585308) through which the Ribble Way passes. This 250-acre (100-hectare) reserve is increasingly popular as a place of simple recreation and the study of flora and fauna. The eco-friendly visitor centre and café is essentially a floating village built on one of the ponds.

★ Stonyhurst College

Close by the endearing village of Hurst Green, Stonyhurst College (SD 690390), a co-educational independent school, was founded in 1593 and has several notable literary associations. It provided inspiration for Gerard Manley Hopkins, whose poems feature details of the local countryside, and former pupil Sir Arthur Conan Doyle, whose 'Baskerville Hall' was modelled on Stonyhurst Hall. Tolkien wrote part of *The Lord of the Rings* during his stay at the college where his son Jonathan was a student – his 'Middle-earth' much resembling the local area.

Late Georgian in style, Brungerley Bridge (SD 738428) is a handsome structure close to Clitheroe, that replaced the medieval hipping stones, which people previously used to cross the river. As a regal crossing point, Brungerley Bridge is renowned as the place where King Henry VI (1421–1471) was captured in 1464 while retreating following defeat at the Battle of Hexham.

★ Sawley Abbey

The remains of the splendid Cistercian abbey (SD 776464), founded in 1147 and a daughter-house of Newminster abbey in Northumberland, are set against the imposing backdrop of Pendle Hill. After the abbey was dissolved in 1536, the monks briefly returned during the Pilgrimage of Grace (1536–1537), until the insurrection was suppressed and the abbot executed.

TIDAL BORES

Rising at a height of 807 feet (246m), the Ribble flows 75 miles (121km) to the Irish Sea. It is one of only 60 rivers in the world, of which 11 are in Britain, to experience a tidal bore – a surge of incoming tidal water that forms a wave against the natural seaward flow of a river's current where the shallow river with a narrow outlet empties into a flat estuary. The highest tides, during a full moon or a new moon, give rise to the biggest bore waves, and the highest of the year occur when these moon phases coincide with the spring and autumn equinox. The Ribble tidal bore can run for around 11 miles (17.5km) up to Fishwick Bottoms, and can attain a height of about 3 feet 3 inches (1m). The other ten British examples occur on the Dee (England/Wales), Eden, Great Ouse, Kent, Lune, Mersey, Nith, Parret, Severn and Trent.

WALK 14 Ridgeway 🔔

The Ridgeway is one of Britain's truly ancient tracks, part of the so-called Greater Ridgeway from Lyme Regis in West Dorset to Hunstanton in Norfolk; it is even arguably the oldest, having been in use for more than 5,000 years by drovers, traders, soldiers and invaders. For centuries, it provided a reliable trading route to the Dorset coast and The Wash in Norfolk. Scratch the surface of the Ridgeway and it bleeds history. Given that it largely sticks to high ground, the open views of undulating chalk downland are stunning. Its pedigree is given away by a preponderance of Neolithic long barrows, Bronze Age round barrows, Iron Age forts and white horses (huge stylised figures cut into the chalk).

The route is waymarked with the familiar National Trail 'acorn' symbol, but in many places waymarks are encountered highlighting intersections with other national and regional trails that criss-cross the route, such as the Chiltern Way (page 16) and the ancient Icknield Way. This is a trail to be enjoyed throughout the year, although March to November offer the best chance of seeing wildlife, appreciating the flora, and enjoying the best conditions underfoot; bluebells in particular are abundant in springtime in the Chiltern woodlands.

The Ridgeway is a tale of two contrasting trails, separated by the River Thames where it intercepts the Thames Path (page 160). The eastern part crosses the Thames at Streatley, and follows the river for a distance before diving into the Chiltern Hills, making principal use of the north-western escarpment. On this stretch, the walking is varied, using paths and tracks and crossing open downland, farms and woodland. The western part of the Ridgeway has its feet very much in history, following, as it does, the course of the prehistoric ridge track through the North Wessex Downs Area of Outstanding Natural Beauty, today a wide track.

Probably no part of Britain is more richly rooted in history; that prolific walker, Paddy Dillon, describes this as '… a ritual landscape, where Neolithic and Bronze Age peoples raised monuments, such as the enormous Avebury Stone Circle'. That heritage is difficult to ignore, and its story tells of man's long association with the land and of his journey's across it. To walk in their footsteps is both humbling and a privilege.

AMAZING BUT TRUE ...

The Beetle and Wedge Hotel at Moulsford, on the original site of the Moulsford Ferry, has several major literary connections. H G Wells (1866-1946) wrote *The History of Mr Polly* there, and the hotel features as the Potwell Inn. In *Three Men in a Boat*, Jerome K Jerome (1859-1927) used the Beetle and Wedge as his 'riverside inn' where there was an argument about a huge trout in a display case. And John Galsworthy (1867-1933) had the inn as a setting in his last book in *The Forsyte Saga* triology.

Barbury Castle, Wiltshire

The Ridgeway can comfortably be managed in six days, with no day longer than 18¼ miles (29.25km).

5 days	
Start	Overton Hill
Day 1	Ogborne St George 9¾mi / 15.75km
Day 2	Sparsholt Firs 14¼mi / 22.75km
Day 3	Streatley 18¼mi / 29.25km
Day 4	Watlington 15½mi / 24.75km
Day 5	Wendover 17mi / 27.5km
Day 6	Ivinghoe Beacon 11½mi / 18.5km

FACTS AND FIGURES

START Overton Hill, Wiltshire (SU 118680)

FINISH Ivinghoe Beacon, Buckinghamshire (SP 959168)

DISTANCE 87 miles (139km)

HEIGHT GAIN 7,115 feet (2,170m)

DIFFICULTY RATING ◆◆

IS IT FOR ME? Generally easy-going; accommodation and transport connections are mainly off route, necessitating daily detours to and from the Ridgeway.

MAPS

OS Explorer
157, 169, 170, 171, 181.

OS Landranger
165, 173, 174, 175.

PRACTICALITIES

GETTING THERE AND BACK
The most convenient railway station for the start is Swindon in Wiltshire, to which trains operate from London Paddington in under an hour. Bus services operate from Swindon to Avebury. Overton Hill is then just a short walk from Avebury. At the other end of the trail, there are good bus services from the village of Ivinghoe to Luton with onward services to London.

ACCOMMODATION
The area is popular, so it is advisable to book accommodation in advance if intending to walk the Ridgeway during the summer months. There is a good variety of accommodation, although only one youth hostel (Streatley-on-Thames). Toing and froing from the Ridgeway to reach accommodation is inevitable and calls for thoughtful planning.

CAMPING
The Ridgeway is privately owned and the right-of-way along it bestows only the right to pass and repass, not to stop or camp. But it is understood that, in general, landowners tend not to object if a tent is pitched for one night, provided no litter is left, no damage done and no fires lit. It is important to note that you should not camp in adjoining fields, woods or gallops without the consent of the landowner.

WEBSITES
www.nationaltrail.co.uk
www.chilternsaonb.org
www.ridgewayfriends.org.uk

This page: Wayland's Smithy.
Opposite page: Ivinghoe Beacon and Aylesbury Vale.

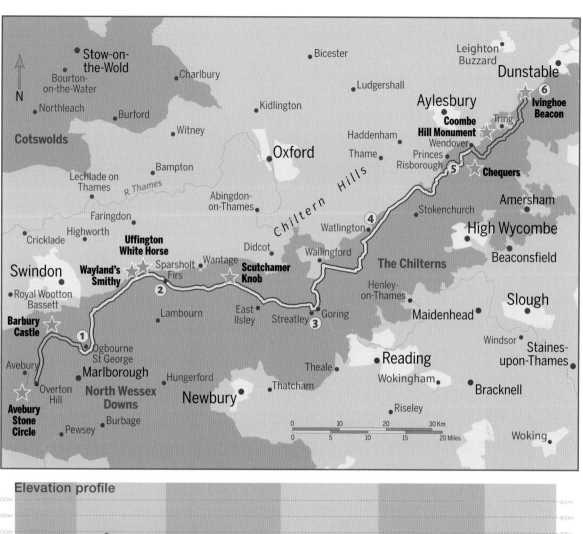

Elevation profile

| Day 1 | Day 2 | Day 3 | Day 4 | Day 5 | Day 6 |

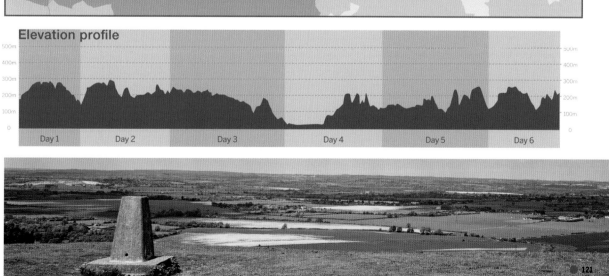

WENDOVER TO IVINGHOE BEACON

(11½ miles/18.5km)

There is a particular delight in the concluding stage of any long-distance trail, and the Ridgeway doesn't disappoint. Wendover Woods lie to the north of the trail and are worth exploring if time is available. First though, a southern loop leads through Barn Wood and Hale Wood before reaching the edge of Wendover Woods, from where the trail makes the most of the high ground en route to Wigginton. A short hiatus tackles A-roads and the Grand Union Canal before romping onwards and upwards to the top of Ivinghoe Beacon. This is the official end of the trail, although a descent is needed to reach the village from which the beacon takes its name.

A walk round the circle is an almost ceremonial way to start a walk steeped in history

★Avebury Stone Circle

One of the best-known prehistoric sites in Britain, the Avebury Stone Circle is a short distance from the start of the Ridgeway National Trail, but well worth the time to visit. It is a Neolithic henge monument containing three stone circles; it is the largest megalithic stone circle in the world, and a place of importance to modern-day pagans and the New Age Movement.

★ Barbury Castle

First occupied 2,500 years ago, Barbury Castle (SU 149762), south of Swindon, is a scheduled Iron Age hill fort, one of several along the Greater Ridgeway route. From here, as our ancestors no doubt fully recognised, there are commanding views across the Cotswolds and the River Severn.

★ Wayland's Smithy

Thought to have been constructed during the Early Neolithic period, Wayland's Smithy (SU 281853) is a chambered long barrow, which archaeologists think was built by pastoral, i.e. settled, communities shortly after the introduction of agriculture to Britain; it was agriculture that turned nomadic hunter-gatherers into resident farmers.

★ Scutchamer Knob

Also known as Cuckhamsley Hill, Scutchamer Knob (SU 455851) is an early Iron Age round barrow, and later recorded as the spot where King Edwin of Northumberland killed Cwichelm of Wessex in the 7th century. For some years it was believed to be the burial place of Cwichelm, though excavations have not proven conclusive.

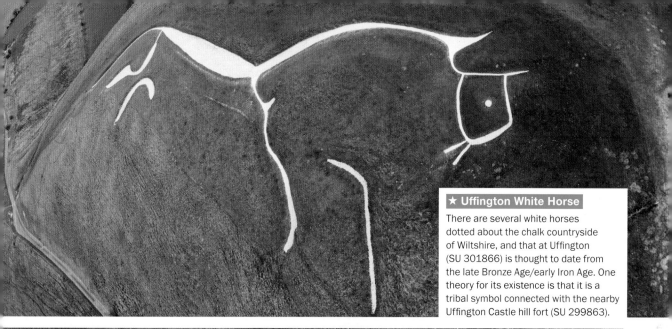

There are several white horses dotted about the chalk countryside of Wiltshire, and that at Uffington (SU 301866) is thought to date from the late Bronze Age/early Iron Age. One theory for its existence is that it is a tribal symbol connected with the nearby Uffington Castle hill fort (SU 299863).

★ Chequers

A 16th-century manor house, Chequers has been the official country residence of the British prime minister since 1921; it is a striking building and listed Grade I on the National Heritage List of England. The Ridgeway crosses the drive, so expect to be scrutinised by security personnel; the Serious Organised Crime and Police Act, 2005, criminalised trespass into the estate. You have been warned!

OVERTON HILL TO OGBOURNE ST GEORGE

(9¾ miles/15.75km)

Although the Ridgeway Trail officially starts on Overton Hill, there's no excuse for not starting in Avebury and allowing time to explore the village, surrounded as it is by a complex stone circle, ditches and embankments more than 4,000 years old. A walk round the circle, a World Heritage Site, is an almost ceremonial way to start a walk steeped in history. Thereafter, a grassy track climbs onto Overton Down, where the trail intercepts the Wessex Ridgeway. Further on, beside the trail, the curiously named Grey Wethers are sarsen stones, post-glacial remains. Barbury Castle is a fascinating hill fort dating from the Iron Age, and enjoys extensive views over the Marlborough Downs. The village of Ogbourne St George sits in the valley of the Og and features several thatched cottages, some

MAPS Day-walk taster

OS Explorer
157, Marlborough & Savernake Forest, Avebury & Devizes.

OS Landranger
173, Swindon & Devizes, Marlborough & Trowbridge.

★ Ivinghoe Beacon

This prominent hill landmark (757 feet/233m) marks the end of the Ridgeway and the starting point of the Icknield Way to the east. Like numerous others throughout Britain, the beacon was an ancient signal point used in times of crisis to send messages across the country. Its proximity to the film studios at Elstree has seen it used in no fewer than four *Harry Potter* films and in the *Star Wars* film *The Rise of Skywalker*.

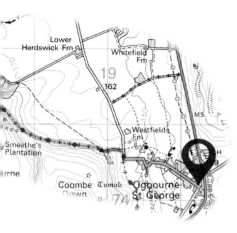

Nature on the trail
(clockwise): Stoat; small
tortoiseshell butterfly caterpillar;
redwing; milkwort.

OLD ENGLISH WORDS

Attercoppe a spider, with the literal meaning 'poison head'.

Candelstœf a candlestick.

Cuma a visitor or houseguest, a 'comer'.

Eaxle shoulder or armpit.

Insticce an 'inside-stitch', and so an apt word for an abdominal pain perhaps caused by over exertion in walking long-distance paths, or maybe it could be pins and needles.

Meolclide meaning 'milk-soft', of gentleness and mild temperament.

Selfæta used for an animal that preyed upon others of its own kind, a 'self-eater' or cannibalistic creature.

Unweder literally, un-weather, used to describe stormy conditions.

There is a particular delight in the concluding stage of any long-distance trail, and the Ridgeway doesn't disappoint

★Coombe Hill Monument

Coombe Hill Monument (SP 848 367) is significant not only due to its prominence, but because it is one of the first examples of a war memorial erected to honour the names of individual men who fell while fighting for their country as distinct from memorials commemorating victories.

Severn Way

Beginning any walk at the source of a river will always be problematic: you have to get to the source before you even begin – see also the Annandale Way (page 184) and the Ribble Way (page 112). The nearest point to the source of the Severn that is accessible by road is the Rhyd-y-benwch car park in Hafren Forest. As a consequence for most walkers the first day is occupied with getting to the start only to end the day where it began – usually Llanidloes.

But what a first day! A steady climb up through the forest on a good trail eventually ends in a squelchy trek across bog (mostly paved) to a tall post that officially declares itself to be the source of the Severn, high in the Cambrian Mountains of Powys. Then it's about retracing the upward route and continuing onward to Llanidloes. After that, theoretically, it's all downhill. Alas, the first few days will be filled with many minor undulations and circumventions, not always in company with the Severn, until the Way reaches Newtown. Here the route finally relents and stays close to the river, at least as far as Berriew where it opts for an enchanting saunter along the towpath of the Montgomery Canal. The Way stays with the Severn until it encounters Offa's Dyke Path (page 286) at Buttington; the two trails then move in harmony for a few miles

before the Severn Way diverges towards Llandrinio.

North-east of steep-sided Breidden Hill, the Severn Way bumps briefly into the Shropshire Way (page 134), and takes its leave of Wales, the two routes travelling together into Shrewsbury, where they then go their separate ways. From Shrewsbury, the Severn Way endeavours to court its river bound for Ironbridge (birthplace of the Industrial Revolution), Bridgnorth, the outskirts of Kidderminster, Bewdley, Stourport-on-Severn and Worcester.

South of the cathedral city of Worcester, the Severn Valley relaxes, leans back and, as a result, several stretches can be seasonally flooded and impassable: Upton-upon-Severn is quite often Upton-in-Severn, as are the fringes of Tewkesbury. Entering Gloucestershire, the Way passes through the city of Gloucester itself before passing Berkeley Castle and following the Severn estuary below the massive, eponymous bridge to journey's end at Severn Beach. Except, the journey doesn't have to end here: from Severn Beach a waymarked route links to the many trappings of Bristol.

From rugged, boggy, windswept uplands, the Severn Way is a largely riparian romp through history, nature, industry, heritage, architecture and just plain, fulfilling loveliness.

> **AMAZING BUT TRUE ...**
> Bewdley was described by the 16th-century antiquarian Leland as a 'most delightful town, whom Wyre's tall oaks with lofty leafage crown'. The Wyre referred to is the medieval royal hunting ground of Wyre Forest, today an area of 6,000 acres (2,425 hectares) of mixed woodland, that extends over a large tract of Shropshire and Worcestershire between Bridgnorth and Worcester, and gave its name to Worcestershire (Wyre-castra).

Near Bridgnorth

END TO END

The Severn Way falls into four 'county' stages: Powys, Shropshire, Worcestershire and Gloucestershire; these can be covered in 11 (demanding), 14 (moderate) and 21 (comfortable) days, plus the Bristol Link.

	11 days	14 days	21 days
Start	Rhyd-y-benwch	Rhyd-y-benwch	Rhyd-y-benwch
Day 1	To the Source and return to Llanidloes 22¼mi/36km	To the Source and return to Llanidloes 22¼mi/36km	To the Source and return to Llanidloes 22¼mi/36km
Day 2	Newtown 18mi/29km	Newtown 18mi/29km	Caersws 9½mi/15.25km
Day 3	Pool Quay 17¼mi/27.75km	Welshpool 13¾mi/22.25km	Newtown 18½mi/13.75km
Day 4	Shrewsbury 19¼mi/31km	Crew Green 11¼mi/18km	Welshpool 13¾mi/22.25km
Day 5	Ironbridge 15mi/24km	Shrewsbury 15½mi/24.75km	Crew Green 11¼mi/18km
Day 6	Upper Arley 19¼mi/31km	Ironbridge 19¼mi/31km	Montford Bridge 8¾mi/14km
Day 7	Worcester 20mi/29.75km	Bridgnorth 8¾mi/14.25km	Shrewsbury 6¾mi/10.75km
Day 8	Tewkesbury 18½mi/29.75km	Stourport-on-Severn 18mi/28.75km	Atcham 7¾mi/12.5km
Day 9	Upper Framilode 26mi/42km	Worcester 12½mi/20.25km	Ironbridge 11½mi/18.5km
Day 10	Berkeley 20¼mi/32.75km	Tewkesbury 18½mi/29.75km	Bridgnorth 8¾mi/14.25km
Day 11	Severn Beach 15¾mi/25.25km	Gloucester 12¾mi/20.5km	Upper Arley 10½mi/16.75km
Day 12		Upper Framilode 13¼mi/21.5km	Stourport-on-Severn 7½mi/12km
Day 13		Sharpness 16¾mi/26.75km	Worcester 12½mi/20.25km
Day 14		Severn Beach 19½mi/31.25km	Upton-upon-Severn 11¾mi/18.75km
Day 15			Tewksesbury 6¾mi/11km
Day 16			Gloucester 12¾mi/20.5km
Day 17			Upper Framilode 13¼mi/21.5km
Day 18			Frampton-on-Severn 9¼mi/14.75km
Day 19			Sharpness 7½mi/12km
Day 20			Oldbury-on-Severn 11¼mi/18km
Day 21			Severn Beach 8¼mi/13.25km

MAPS
OS Explorer
OL14, 154, 155, 167, 179, 190, 204, 214, 215, 216, 218, 219, 240, 241, 242.

OS Landranger
126, 127, 135, 136, 138, 150, 162, 172.

FACTS AND FIGURES

START Pumlumon (Plynlimon), Powys (SN 822898)

FINISH Severn Beach, South Gloucestershire (ST 539848)

DISTANCE 209 miles (336km) – excluding the Bristol Link

HEIGHT GAIN 8,330 feet (2,540m)

DIFFICULTY RATING ♦♦

IS IT FOR ME? A lengthy but not difficult, largely riparian route; with mostly good transport links and accommodation.

PRACTICALITIES

GETTING THERE AND BACK Bus services operate to Llanidloes, then either a walk or taxi ride to Rhyd-y-benwch. Severn Beach and Bristol are on rail services. All the major intermediate towns and villages are linked either by rail or bus.

ACCOMMODATION The Severn Way is well endowed with accommodation on or close to the route, including luxury and budget hotels, inns, B&Bs, and a few hostels and campsites. All start/finish points en route have some form of accommodation.

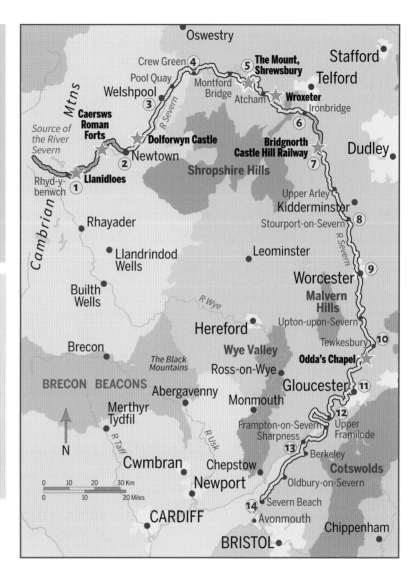

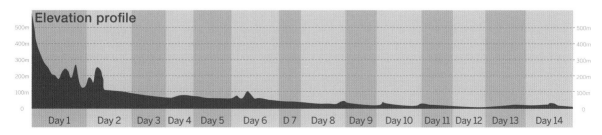

RHYD-Y-BENWCH TO SOURCE TO LLANIDLOES
(22¼ miles/36km)
AND LLANIDLOES TO NEWTOWN
(18 miles/29km)

There is much pleasure in these early stages of the Severn Way, beginning with the rise through the Hafren Forest then across heathery moorland to the source of the river at 2,034 feet (620m). The forest is a delight, generally peaceful, with just the murmur of the river burbling its way downhill, and the occasional sound of a crossbill cracking seeds high in the canopy. Several waterfalls, increasing in stature, grace the descent back to Llanidloes.

The Severn Way meets the Glyndŵr Way (page 278) in Llanidloes, and briefly travels with it until the Severn route starts heading east through pastureland, fields and meadows to Llandinam. At Llandinam, the river flows northwards to Caersws, the location of two forts from Roman Wales. Here the Severn is joined by two more rivers, the Afon Trannon and the Afon Carno, increasing its stature, but without impressing the Severn Way, which jaunts off northwards, east and south-east before the Way and the river meet up again.

★ Dolforwyn Castle

Today, the ruins of Dolforwyn Castle stand as a symbol of Welsh defiance – it was built in 1273 by Llywelyn ap Gruffydd (Llywelyn the Last), who ignored the orders of King Edward I of England forbidding him to continue working on the castle. The castle eventually fell to the Marcher Lord Roger Mortimer in 1277.

★ The Mount, Shrewsbury

As the Severn Way enters Shrewsbury, it passes through the Doctor's Field Countryside Heritage Site (SJ 485131), directly above which stands a country mansion, now offices, called The Mount. This was the birthplace in 1809 of the English naturalist, geologist and biologist, Charles Darwin.

★ Llanidloes

Taking its name from the 7th-century Celtic saint Idloes, this charming village on the banks of the Severn is said to be the centre of Wales, and received a market charter in 1280. The half-timbered market hall stands at the crossroads of four of the original medieval streets.

★ Odda's Chapel

Completed a decade before the Norman conquest by Earl Odda, a relation of Edward the Confessor, Odda's Chapel (SO 869298) is an 11th-century Anglo-Saxon building that was used for worship into the 16th century, and remains one of the most complete surviving buildings of its time.

★ Bridgnorth Castle Hill Railway

The Bridgnorth Castle Hill Railway, which opened in 1892, is the oldest and steepest inland electric funicular railway in England, and for more than 100 years has served the people of the ancient market town of Bridgnorth.

★ Wroxeter

Known in Roman times as Viriconium, Wroxeter (SJ 565087) was formerly the fourth largest city in Roman Britain. First established as a frontier post, by the middle of the 1st century it had become a garrison for the invasion of Cambria.

IRONBRIDGE TO BRIDGNORTH
(8¾ miles/14.25km)

Mellow-bricked Ironbridge, a UNESCO World Heritage Site, is renowned as the birthplace of the Industrial Revolution, its name deriving from the world's first iron bridge, a graceful structure, constructed in 1779. Between Ironbridge and the stunning market town of Bridgnorth, the Way largely follows the course of the Severn, initially on an old railway trackbed and then along riverbanks where the most notable feature is the peace and quiet where kingfishers and grey wagtails fly. Bridgnorth, when it arrives, is as dramatic as it is splendid, with roots in the days of King Alfred, when his daughter Ethelfleda built a fortified town here in a most important and strategic position.

Ironbridge

ROMANCING THE SEVERN

At a length of 220 miles (354km), the Severn is the longest river in Britain. It also has the most romantic story. The English name Severn should really be Sabrina, as it is derived from Habren or Hafren. Habren (Sabrina) was the daughter of Locrinus, the eldest son of Brutus, who gave his name to Britain after leading the Trojans to what was then called Albion. Habren's mother, Estrildis, was the mistress of Locrinus, who originally concealed his mistress in a secret cave in London. Locrinus's wife, Gwendolen, was the daughter of Corineus, the follower of Brutus who was given Cornwall because he loved fighting giants, and there were more of them in Cornwall than elsewhere. When Corineus died, Locrinus openly set aside Gwendolen to make Estrild is his queen. In response, Gwendolen summoned help from Cornwall and managed to defeat and kill Locrinus. Taking over the kingdom, she ordered the fleeing Estrildis and her daughter to be thrown into the river that now bears Habren's name. Habren became the river goddess addressed by Milton as 'Sitting under the glassy, cool translucent wave, in twisted braids of lilies knitting the loose train of thy amber-dropping hair'.

The two Roman forts at Caersws were garrisoned between the 1st and 5th centuries, when this region of Wales was part of the Roman province of Britannia Superior.

Nature on the trail
(clockwise): Grey wagtail; water vole; dunlin; may fly; willow trees; dormice.

From rugged, boggy, windswept uplands, the Severn Way is a largely riparian romp through history, Nature, industry, heritage, architecture and just plain, fulfilling loveliness

Shropshire Way 🚶

The present-day Shropshire Way is a markedly different beast from that conceived by the Ramblers Association in 1980, being now much longer and split into a 'Figure-of-Eight' centred on the county town of Shrewsbury. The southern loop is hilly, featuring the Shropshire Hills Area of Outstanding Natural Beauty and visiting several, historically important towns and villages: Bishop's Castle, Clun, Ludlow, Much Wenlock, Ironbridge and Wellington. The northern loop heads to Wem, Ellesmere and Llanymynech on the border with Wales.

Walkers who want their journeys to embrace hills, even modest ones, will be elated with the South Route which takes in the Stiperstones, a bit of Clun Forest, the Shropshire Hills, the Clee Hills, a taste of Wenlock Edge and The Wrekin. The hills are gentle and undulating, although the Stiperstones has an impressive quartzite ridge and crazy pinnacles. Some stretches, especially those bordering the River Severn, are prone to flooding and temporary impassability. The Northern Route is tame by comparison, but no less attractive and appealing.

Of the two loops, the southern is the longer. It departs Shrewsbury bound for the village of Bridges, to the west of the Long Mynd – a large and long plateau, the western aspect of which is much less fearsome than the east. Gradually, the trail climbs into the Stiperstones National Nature Reserve, a splendid ridge of Ordovician quartzite rocks that are more than 480 million years old. This is a wild, rugged and atmospheric landscape, which was torn apart during the last Ice Age.

Ancient Bishop's Castle, at one time the smallest 'borough' in England, dates from the late 8th century, and is the start of the southernmost stretch of the Way, which leads first to the village of Clun, arguably one of the most peaceful villages in Britain. To the east, the extended village of Craven Arms feeds into Ludlow and the Clee Hills, before striking north to rejoin the River Severn in Ironbridge, the so-called cradle of the Industrial Revolution.

On its route out of the Ironbridge gorge, the Way deviates to gather in the graceful form of The Wrekin, before heading for Telford and back to Shrewsbury to begin the northern loop. Here, the going is much less demanding, the walking becoming easier as the Way heads north to Wem and Whitchurch, before striking south-west to Ellesmere. It touches the border with Wales where it briefly encounters the Offa's Dyke Path (page 286) and follows the border river – the Afon Efyrnwy – to a meeting with the Severn Way (page 126) at Melverley. Thereafter, the Shropshire Way heads back to Shrewsbury, but does so in a dallying, meandering best way as if to to postpone the inevitable.

AMAZING BUT TRUE ...

Whixall Moss is one of Britain's largest and last remaining lowland raised bogs. It saw use as a rifle range last century between 1914 and 1918 and 1939 and 1945. In the Second World War, peat piled over the Moss was set ablaze in an attempt to divert night-time Luftwaffe bombers from their intended target at Liverpool docks. Today, it is internationally important for its wetland wildflowers, birds and insects, including 29 species of dragonfly and damselfly.

The Wrekin

END TO END

The Shropshire Way falls into two loops and 15 distinct stages, and readily allows the walk to be completed in day sections, as well as in one or two continuous treks. No stage is greater than 15 miles (24km) and even those involving hills should be within the abilities of any reasonably fit and regular walker.

15 stages

South Route	
Start	Shrewsbury
Stage 1	Bridges *15mi/24km*
Stage 2	Bishop's Castle *12mi/19.25km*
Stage 3	Clun *12mi/19.25km*
Stage 4	Craven Arms *11mi/17.75km*
Stage 5	Ludlow *10½mi/17km*
Stage 6	Wheathill *10½mi/17km*
Stage 7	Wilderhope *11mi/17.75km*
Stage 8	Ironbridge *12½mi/20km*
Stage 9	Wellington *11mi/17.75km*
Stage 10a	Haughmond *12mi/19.25km*
Stage 10b	Shrewsbury *5mi/8km*

North Route	
Start	Haughmond
Stage 10b	Shrewsbury *5mi/8km*
Stage 11	Wem *11½mi/18.5km*
Stage 12	Ellesmere/Whitchurch *14mi/22.5km*
Stage 13	Llanymynech *14mi/22.5km*
Stage 14	Nesscliffe *14mi/22.5km*
Stage 15	Shrewsbury *12mi/19.25km*

Stiperstones

Elevation profile

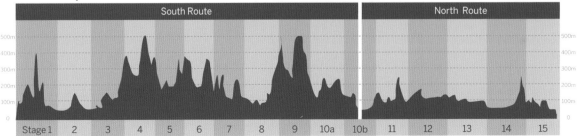

FACTS AND FIGURES

START / FINISH Kingsland Bridge, Shrewsbury, Shropshire (SJ 488121)

DISTANCE 203 miles (327km) – North Loop, 82 miles (132km); South Loop, 121 miles (195km)

HEIGHT GAIN 18,565 feet (5,660 metres) – North Loop, 2,920 feet (890m); South Loop, 15,645 feet (4,770m)

DIFFICULTY RATING ♦♦♦

IS IT FOR ME? North Route – relatively gentle; South Route – undulating with some strenuous parts; good transport planning essential to make piecemeal completion successful.

PRACTICALITIES

GETTING THERE AND BACK There are bus and rail services to Shrewsbury, the conventional start and finish point.

ACCOMMODATION There is a good choice of accommodation throughout Shropshire, including campsites and hostels.

WEBSITE https://shropshireway.org.uk.

MAPS

OS Explorer 201, 203, 216, 217, 241, 242, 257.

OS Landranger 117, 126, 127, 137, 138, 148.

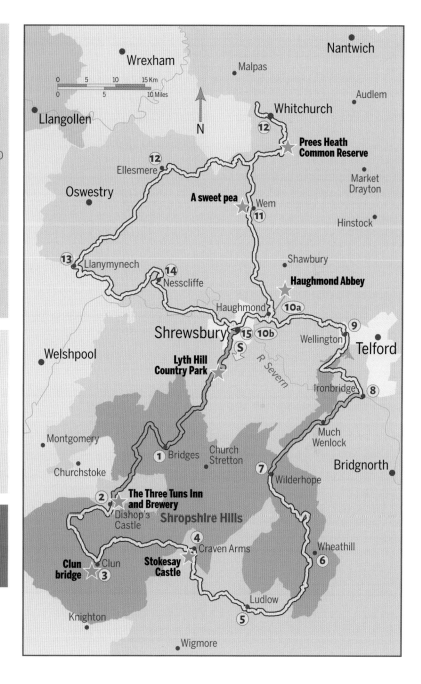

SHREWSBURY TO BRIDGES
(15 miles/24km)

The Shropshire Way hastens out of Shrewsbury, dashing across Kingsland Bridge, bound for the village of Meole Brace from where its wooded way climbs through the Reabrook valley and on to the narrow confines of Lyth Hill Country Park, where A E Housman's 'Blue-remembered' Shropshire Hills, his 'land of lost content', first come into view.

BRIDGES TO BISHOP'S CASTLE
(12 miles/19km)

The onward route from Bridges, after a network of quiet lanes, could not be more different, taking as it does to paths and tracks travelled for thousands of years. Gradually it climbs up onto the Stiperstones ridge, turning south over ancient quartzite rocks and across rough terrain. Even once this fine section is completed, the Way is reluctant to abandon high ground, and diverts to gather in Linley Hill before finally capitulating and traversing farmland meadows and lanes to Bishop's Castle, which stands on an ancient trackway, the Kerry Ridgeway.

★ Lyth Hill Country Park

Lyth Hill offers a superb panoramic view of the south Shropshire Hills, from The Wrekin in the east to Wenlock Edge in the south-east and the Stiperstones in the south-west. The site has areas of woodland, scrub and open grassland providing a wildlife refuge on the outskirts of Shrewsbury. Historically, rope making was carried out on the site. The author Mary Webb, author of *Precious Bane* and *The Golden Arrow*, lived in Spring Cottage on the edge of Lyth Hill.

★ Prees Heath Common Reserve

To the south of Whitchurch, Prees Heath (SJ 558380) is the only remaining sanctuary for the silver-studded blue butterfly in the Midlands, a feature much at odds with the common's use as a military training site during both World Wars.

★ Clun bridge

Dating from 1450, and one of the oldest structures in Shropshire, the limestone rubble humped packhorse bridge (SO 300807) at the heart of this historic village is still an important bridging point over the River Clun, around which each May bank holiday, the Green Man Festival is held. Although commonly regarded as a village, Clun has the distinction of having been granted a town charter, in the 14th century.

★ Stokesay Castle

One of the best-preserved medieval fortified manor houses in England, Stokesay Castle (SO 436816) was built, substantially in its present form, in the 13th century for Laurence of Ludlow, one of the richest men in the country.

★ Haughmond Abbey

The remains of the Augustinian Haughmond Abbey (SJ 541152) include the abbot's quarters, the cloister, refectory and chapter house, which is hallmarked by several 12th- and 14th-century carvings and statuary.

★ A sweet pea

Unlikely as it may seem, the town of Wem, virtually destroyed during the Wars of the Roses and the Civil War is today the home of the modern sweet pea, developed by Henry Eckford, a 19th-century nurseryman.

WILDERHOPE TO IRONBRIDGE
(12½ miles/20km)

Wilderhope Manor, an Elizabethan-period manor house built of local limestone and dating from 1585, has been used as a hostel since 1937. From here, the Shropshire Way climbs onto the limestone escarpment of Wenlock Edge, a Site of Special Scientific Interest, its north-western edges fringed with deciduous woodland. The edge inspired A E Housman, whose poem, XXXI, from *A Shropshire Lad* began 'On Wenlock Edge the Wood's in Trouble'; and, a few years later, Ralph Vaughan Williams composed a song cycle called *On Wenlock Edge*, to great acclaim.

The adorable village of Much Wenlock, which featured in the 1986 comedy film, *Clockwise*, starring John Cleese and Alison Steadman, might also be hailed as the birthplace of the modern Olympic Games, the Wenlock Olympian Games being established here in 1850. From Much Wenlock, the Way runs into the Ironbridge Gorge, where it encounters the Severn Way and a wealth of industrial history and a UNESCO world heritage site (see www.ironbridge.org.uk).

Wenlock Edge

'LOVELIEST OF TREES, THE CHERRY NOW'
A SHROPSHIRE LAD BY A E HOUSMAN

Loveliest of trees, the cherry now
Is hung with bloom along the bough,
And stands about the woodland ride
Wearing white for Eastertide.

Now, of my three score years and ten,
Twenty will not come again,
And take from seventy springs a score,
It only leaves me fifty more.

And since to look at things in bloom
Fifty springs are little room,
About the woodlands I will go
To see the cherry hung with snow.

In the ancient town of Bishop's Castle, the Three Tuns Inn is associated with its nearby brewery, the oldest licensed brewery in Britain, established when King Charles I gave it a brewing licence in 1642 to raise funds for his army fighting the Civil War.

The Shropshire Way is heading back to Shrewsbury, but does its dallying, meandering best to postpone the inevitable

Nature on the trail (clockwise): Common toad; wild cranberry; black-headed gulls; great crested newt; Whixall Moss; banded demoiselle.

South Downs Way

The South Downs Way is a remarkably peaceful, elongated oasis in an otherwise busy neck of the woods, the only national trail to be entirely within a National Park. Paradoxically, it contrives to be far from the brouhaha of modern living and yet always close to civilisation. The Way was opened as a National Trail in 1972, and initially ran almost entirely within Sussex from Buriton to Beachy Head, but it was later decided to extend the route westwards to Winchester. The Way follows a range of chalk hills characterised by rolling downland, close-cropped turf and dry valleys; they form a long escarpment rising from the Itchen valley near Winchester to Eastbourne, their high points punctuated in places with stands of trees that often mark the location of hill forts or burial places.

The trail visits flora-rich downland, bird-loud woodlands, lush river valleys and pleasing villages. The South Downs Way was the first *bridleway* national trail, meaning that it was suitable also for horse riders and cyclists; so expect to encounter those on your travels. Anyone with a reasonable level of fitness can manage the South Downs Way, which is graded as 'moderate'; it involves straightforward, undulating walking on farm tracks and chalk down, albeit with several ups and downs. There are very few habitations along the line of the Way itself, which seeks to avoid villages, preferring high ground and open spaces, with commendable good reason.

The Way extends from the time-worn cathedral city of Winchester – the Saxon capital of England, until the Norman Conquest in the 11th century – to the white chalk cliffs of the Seven Sisters and Beachy Head at Eastbourne. For much of its length, the South Downs Way is part of the E9 European Coastal Path from Cabo de São Vicente in Portugal to north-east Estonia; it is also part of the network of routes that form the International Appalachian Trail.

As in much of southern Britain, people have been using the high-ground tracks that network the South Downs for more than 8,000 years; in the Mesolithic period these elevated trails were safer and drier than the low-level valley alternatives.

The journey along the Way traverses a varied landscape with many protected habitats, including internationally important chalk rivers, rich chalk grasslands and ancient woodland. No fewer than five National Nature Reserves and dozens of Sites of Special Scientific Interest are on or close to the route, offering plentiful scope to enjoy wildlife at close quarters and adding to the joys of this journey through time.

AMAZING BUT TRUE ...
The unimproved chalk grassland of the South Downs is a butterfly utopia with, typically, 35 species recorded on the most favourable sites. Stand out among these are the blues, but in common, adonis and chalk hill blues only the males are in fact blue, the females being brown, while with the brown argus, (also in the blues family) both sexes are brown.

Beachy Head

END TO END

Proximity to transport and accommodation makes the South Downs Way a perfect candidate for completing over several weekends rather than in one continuous journey. As a multi-day trek it can be wrapped up in six days, which involves several long days. An eight-day option is less demanding and allows more time to explore.

	6 days	8 days	9 days
Start	Winchester	Winchester	Winchester
Day 1	Exton 12½mi/20km	East Meon 17½mi/28km	Exton 12½mi/20km
Day 2	South Harting 15¾mi/25.5km	Cocking 18¾mi/30km	Buriton 12½mi/20km
Day 3	Amberley 19mi/30.5km	Amberley 11¼mi/18km	Cocking 11¼mi/18km
Day 4	Upper Beeding 14mi/22.5km	Steyning 10¼mi/16.5km	Amberley 11¼mi/18km
Day 5	Rodmell 20½mi/33km	Pyecombe 11mi/17.5km	Steyning 10¼mi/16.5km
Day 6	Eastbourne 19½mi/31.25km	Rodmell 13½mi/21.5km	Pyecombe 11mi/17.5km
Day 7		Alfriston 8¾mi/14km	Kingston 10½mi/16.75km
Day 8		Eastbourne 10¾mi/17.25km	Alfriston 11¾mi/18.75km
Day 9			Eastbourne 10¾mi/17.25km

Bignor Hill

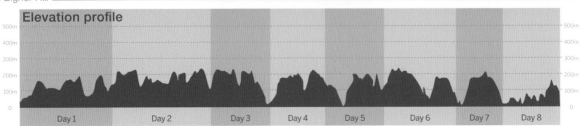

Elevation profile

Day 1 · Day 2 · Day 3 · Day 4 · Day 5 · Day 6 · Day 7 · Day 8

FACTS AND FIGURES

START Winchester, Hampshire (SU 483293)

FINISH Eastbourne, East Sussex (TV 600972)

DISTANCE 101 miles (163km)

HEIGHT GAIN 13,185 feet (4,020m)

DIFFICULTY RATING ♦♦♦

IS IT FOR ME? A well-waymarked route favourable for year-round walking with some energetic parts; good access to facilities and reasonable transport connections.

MAPS

OS Explorer OL3, OL8, OL10, OL11, OL25, OL32.

OS Landranger 185, 197, 198, 199.

PRACTICALITIES

GETTING THERE AND BACK The proximity to London and the south coast make it easy to get to the start of the Way. Regular trains from London Waterloo and Victoria take between 60 and 90 minutes to get to Winchester.

GETTING AROUND There is a good network of buses that link railway stations and villages, enabling a multi-visit approach to completing the Way.

ACCOMMODATION Some careful planning will be needed to find somewhere to stay and eat throughout the walk, frequently requiring the walker to deviate off-route in search of it. There are two youth hostels – one in Southease, near Lewes, and one at Truleigh Hill – along with many opportunities to camp and glamp (see www.campsites.co.uk).

WEBSITES
www.nationaltrail.co.uk
www.southdownsway.co.uk
www.southdowns.gov.uk/south-downs-way

CHALK

The chalk forming the South Downs was laid down in the warm seas of the Cretaceous Period, 100–65 million years ago. It's a form of limestone composed of calcite: a soft, porous sedimentary rock formed in deep marine environments over millennia through the accumulation of shells of microorganisms on the seabed.

Chalk pits and evidence of quarrying are widespread throughout the South Downs. Chalk is spread as an agricultural lime to raise the pH levels of acidic soils. Chalk – CaCO3, calcium carbonate – is high in calcium which is essential for good plant growth. Chalk is also used in cement manufacturing; and over the years has been an ingredient in toothpaste, mixed as a pigment to mark out playing pitches and tennis courts, and compressed into rods for blackboard chalk.

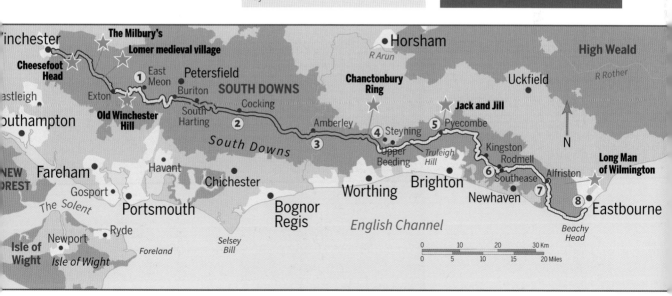

BURITON TO STEYNING

(32¾ miles/52.5km – 3 days)

The comparatively gentle nature of this stretch of the Way and the proximity of 'civilisation' renders it ideal for a bank holiday weekend, spread over three days.

BURITON TO COCKING HILL

(11¼ miles/18km)

From Buriton, the Way gains the ridge of the Downs and provides views of the Weald of Sussex and the Channel. There is the opportunity to visit Uppark House and Garden, a peaceful 17th-century house in relaxing gardens and woodland a short distance off the trail to the south. Although the Way passes round Beacon Hill, it is worth deviating to its summit for a truly splendid view before descending to Cocking.

COCKING HILL TO AMBERLEY

(11¼ miles/18km)

Beyond Cocking, the Way is a delight, a coming together of pasturelands, woodland and wild flower interludes; indeed, this is the most wooded part of the entire route. En route, Bronze Age burial mounds are encountered; as is a splendid example of a Roman road on Bignor Hill, with a Roman villa a short distance off route.

AMBERLEY TO STEYNING

(10¼ miles/16.5km)

Moving into Day 3, the route finds itself in mixed farmland, beginning with a steep climb to Amberley Mount before dropping to Washington. From here, the route rises again, to Chanctonbury Ring, a gathering of beech trees steeped in myth and legend and sited on an Iron Age fort. The Way then heads for Steyning, but is remarkably reluctant to quit the high ground.

★ Long Man of Wilmington

On the steep slopes of Windover Hill near Wilmington, the Long Man (TQ 542034) is one of two major extant human hill figures in England; and, like the Cerne Abba Giant, near Dorchester, is a Scheduled Ancient Monument. Once thought to date from Neolithic times, recent investigation suggests that it may be as contemporary a construction as the 16th or 17th century.

★ Cheesefoot Head

This large, natural amphitheatre (SU 528281) is where General Eisenhower is said to have addressed troops prior to D-Day – many of whom stayed locally. This steep, sloping area of chalk grassland is actually the site of three bowl barrows, now contained within a biological Site of Special Scientific Interest. . Those of an ornithological bent will be pleased to discover that this is a stronghold of the elusive corn bunting and a regular site for quail.

★ Jack and Jill

The Clayton windmills (TQ 304135), known locally as Jack and Jill, comprise a post mill and a tower mill and the roundhouse of a former post mill. Dating from the 19th century, all three structures are listed buildings.

★ Chanctonbury Ring

This prehistoric hill fort (TQ 139120), crowned by a ring of ancient beeches, is one of several historical features dating back more than 2,000 years. The ring sits in a strategic position overlooking the Sussex Weald, and on the edge of a steep natural escarpment.

★ Lomer medieval village

With little more to see on the ground than earthworks, a few small bumps in a field and a pond, it is nevertheless worth pausing just after passing Lomer Farm, north-west of Beacon Hill. Here (SU 592233) is the site of a medieval village, last occupied in 1550, though its decline may have begun with the plague in the 14th century. There were also settlements and areas of cultivation on this plateau in prehistoric times, and groups of Neolithic and Bronze Age barrows lie in and around the area.

★ Old Winchester Hill

To the east of Meonstoke, Old Winchester Hill (SU 642208), has a summit Iron Age hill fort that embraces several Bronze Age barrows dating from between 6,500 and 5,500 years ago. As well as being a Site of Special Scientific Interest, the hill is a National Nature Reserve featuring unimproved chalk downland that is the perfect habitat for a wide range of butterfly species: Adonis blue, dark green fritillary, Essex skipper, marbled white, silver-spotted skipper, small skipper and the speckled wood.

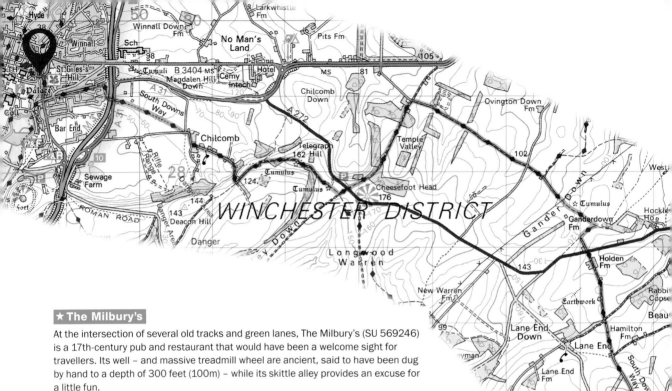

★ The Milbury's

At the intersection of several old tracks and green lanes, The Milbury's (SU 569246) is a 17th-century pub and restaurant that would have been a welcome sight for travellers. Its well – and massive treadmill wheel are ancient, said to have been dug by hand to a depth of 300 feet (100m) – while its skittle alley provides an excuse for a little fun.

Best section for
Day-walk taster

WINCHESTER TO EXTON
(12½ miles/20km)

The exploration of the cathedral city of Winchester, the first capital of England, before setting off along the South Downs Way will prove to be an aid to understanding much about the region through which the Way passes. Linked forever with King Alfred the Great, king of the West Saxons (871–c.886) and king of the Anglo-Saxons (c.886–899), Winchester holds such an important place in England's history that it should not be missed.

   On leaving the city, once the Way has dealt with the M3 and A31, it gets into its stride, heading first for the village of Chilcomb and its Norman church, before climbing gently to Telegraph Hill and on to Cheesefoot Head (see page 146) and its bowl barrows. Undulating tracks and paths follow, leading to The Milbury's, a 17th-century pub at the top of Millbarrow Down (see above). Onward, the Way makes for Beacon Hill National Nature Reserve, an excellent habitat for butterflies such as the chalk hill blue, silver-spotted skipper, brown argus and grizzled skipper, as well as for declining farmland bird species like the linnet and yellowhammer. Beyond Beacon Hill, an easy descent leads down to the tiny village of Exton – 1,000 years ago known as East Seaxena Tun – and its Shoe Inn pub in the heart of the Meon Valley.

MAPS Day-walk taster
OS Explorer
OL32, Winchester.
OS Landranger
185, Winchester & Basingstoke, Andover & Romsey.

Nature on the trail (clockwise): Common blue butterfly; horseshoe vetch; common linnet; blackthorn in autumn; essex skipper butterfly; green woodpecker; blackthorn in spring.

Paradoxically, at one and the same time it contrives to be far from the brouhaha of modern living and yet always close to civilisation

South West Coast Path

Rooted in the anti-smuggling endeavours of the 19th century, the South West Coast Path is England's longest waymarked trail, running from Minehead on the edge of Exmoor to Poole Harbour in Dorset. Unquestionably, it is the ultimate challenge for the multi-day walker, and it can be quite tough on those who do it in short stages, involving steep cliff tops and wooded combes from the outset.

Along its length, the path bonds visitors with a geological and geographical wonderland of coastal scenery, and boasts an Order of Merit that includes several National Nature Reserves, five Areas of Outstanding Natural Beauty, two World Heritage Sites, a UNESCO-designated Biosphere Reserve, a UNESCO Geopark and a National Park, Exmoor. Today, the Path, following ancient footfall, is an encounter with wildlife, heritage, geology and culture that can overpower the senses, and inspire and invigorate anyone who touches on it, whether for a day, a week … or two months.

Mining for copper and tin was a key feature of the industry of Devon and Cornwall, and its importance is reflected in the Cornwall and West Devon Mining Landscape World Heritage Site, inaugurated in 2006, and spread across ten different locations passed by the Coastal Path. Further into the trail, the Jurassic Coast of Dorset and East Devon comprises wild beaches, white cliffs and some amazing rock formations that tell of life on Earth 185 million years ago; collectively, they make this England's first 'Natural' World Heritage Site.

With so much stunning scenery to hand, the highlights come thick and fast, through *Poldark* country in Cornwall, where the television series was filmed, along with that stunning Jurassic Coast and England's highest sea cliff, Great Hangman in Devon. But it is important not to be beguiled into complacency by the extravagant landscapes; this is coastal walking, subject to the ravages of maritime assault and that means deviations and closures to bypass unstable cliffs.

There is a noteworthy synergy about the South West Coast Path; the whole is greater than the sum of its parts. That might suggest a 'do or die' invitation to tackle the whole thing, but you have only to stand on any of the remote headlands, walk the coves, peer down into dry valleys or meander the moorland expanses and the message soon comes across that small is also beautiful. A bit at a time is an aid to a satisfying digestion of the menu on offer, with time to reflect, ponder, amble and consume the detail; for it is in the detail that the full picture emerges.

AMAZING BUT TRUE …

Westward Ho!, the only place name in Britain to contain an exclamation mark, derives its name from the novel by Charles Kingsley, a tale of swashbuckling high-seas adventure published in 1855. The story was set in Bideford and was such a popular read that it brought tourists to the north Devon coast. Subsequently, a hotel was built, called the Westward Ho!, and soon a small village developed and took on the name of the hotel.

Mayon Cliff Old Coastguard Lookout, Land's End

END TO END

With time and inclination, the South West Coast Path can be completed in between six and eight weeks, but few people will have the time or the inclination … or the stamina for such an undertaking. It is usually walked in an anti-clockwise direction, but is signposted in both directions. For lesser mortals, one itinerary, featuring week-long stages with days of either six or seven days of walking, with no day longer than 16 miles (25.5km) and some short days thrown in, is shown in the attached table. There is a more detailed breakdown on the website of the South West Coast Path Association (www.southwestcoastpath.org). This is a dedicated charitable organisation that maintains a constant overview of the Path, and protects and improves it.

8 weeks

Week 1	Minehead to Westward Ho! 87½mi / 141km
Week 2	Westward Ho! to Padstow 78¾mi / 126.75km
Week 3	Padstow to St Ives 66½mi / 107km
Week 4	St Ives to Lizard 69mi / 110.5km
Week 5	Lizard to Par 69¾mi / 112km
Week 6	Par to Torcross 94½mi / 152km
Week 7	Torcross to Seaton 71½mi / 115km
Week 8	Seaton to South Haven Point 93¾mi / 150km

FACTS AND FIGURES

START Minehead, Somerset (SS 971467)

FINISH South Haven Point, Dorset (SZ 036867)

DISTANCE 631 miles (1,016km)

HEIGHT GAIN 108,595 feet (33,110m)

DIFFICULTY RATING ◆◆◆◆◆

IS IT FOR ME? Rugged, strenuous paths in many places, typically with distances taking longer to cover than you'd think; a popular trail in a busy region for tourism, making accommodation forward planning essential.

PRACTICALITIES

GETTING THERE AND BACK
Both the start and finish of the Path can be reached by combining rail and bus services. Frequent rail services from London and the north of England go through to Penzance, via Plymouth, while many intermediate coastal towns are accessible on branch lines or by transferring to a bus for the final leg. Long-distance coach services link with local services to make many of the towns en route accessible.

ACCOMMODATION The South West Coast Path has a good range of accommodation, including, B&Bs, guest houses, pubs and inns, boutique and luxury hotels, farmhouses, camping and glamping sites and hostels. You can expect many places that are 'South West Coast Path Walker Friendly', offering drying facilities, flexible breakfast times and packed lunches. Bear in mind that during the summer months accommodation will be competed for with conventional tourists, while in winter some of it may close down altogether.

GETTING AROUND Most towns and villages are connected by local bus services, and 15 towns also tap into the rail network.

WEBSITE
www.southwestcoastpath.org.uk

Elevation profile

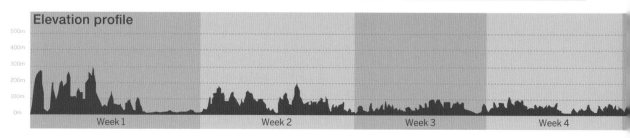

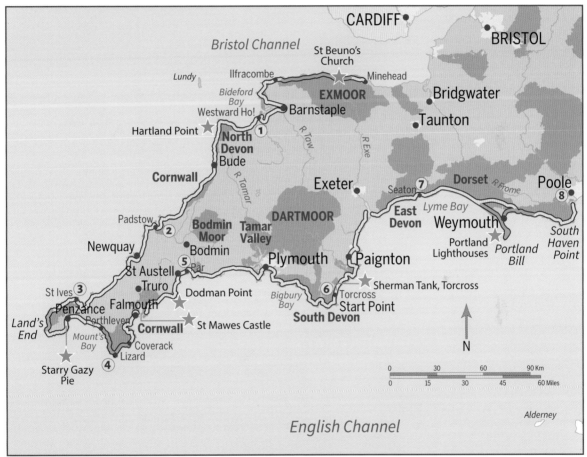

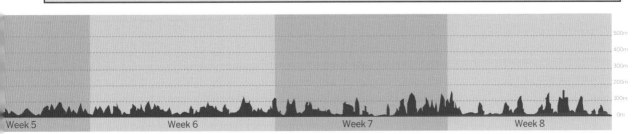

★Hartland Point

Lying at the edge of the known world, the remote Hartland peninsula was Ptolemy's "Promontory of Hercules" and is Devon's most north-westerly point. Here, the cliff edge-hugging South West Coast Path probably has its toughest section – dramatically rising and falling and sharply twisting and turning, encountering a succession of steep-sided combes, rocky bays and coastal waterfalls. The scenery is magnificent and there's a wonderful feeling of space.

★St Beuno's Church, Culbone

Located in a quiet combe looking out to sea, the mystical atmosphere of St Beuno's (SS 842482) is said to have inspired the images of Xanadu depicted by poet Samuel Taylor Coleridge in 'Kubla Khan'. With room for only 30 or so parishioners, this Saxon church has a simple font and a 14th-century chancel screen. At a mere 35 feet (10.7m) long, it is believed to be the smallest parish church in England.

★St Mawes Castle

The best-preserved of Henry VIII's coastal defensive fortresses, and by far the most elaborately decorated, St Mawes Castle (SW 841327) is just one of a chain of forts built in the early to mid-16th century to counter the constant invasion threat from Catholic France and Spain, a task it shared with Pendennis Castle on the opposite side of the Fal estuary. There is a ferry from St Anthony.

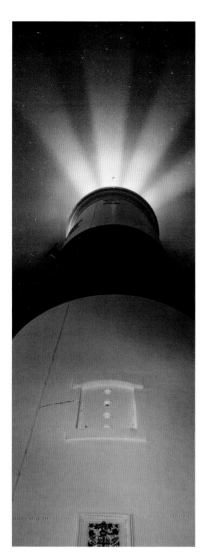

★Portland lighthouses

The shape of the seabed off Portland Bill gives rise to a tidal race that can run to 8 knots (9.2mph) and is a notorious hazard to coastal shipping. Beacon fires warned of the danger from Roman times until 1716, when the upper and lower lighthouses were built to operate as a pair. The present light came into service in 1906, and has been fully automated since 1996.

★Sherman tank, Torcross

The black Sherman tank at Torcross was recovered from the seabed in 1984 and placed here as a memorial to over 700 US servicemen killed by a surprise German attack in April 1944 while rehearsing for the D-Day landings. News of the tragedy was suppressed at the time and it remained largely unknown until a local man, Ken Small, wrote about it and helped arrange the tank memorial.

★Dodman Point

Topped by a large granite cross, Dodman's Point (SX 001394) is the highest headland on the south Cornwall Coast (374 feet/114m) and boasts the remains of an Iron Age promontory fort.

★Starry Gazy Pie

The traditional fishing village of Mousehole (SW 469263) is in the Cornwall Area of Outstanding Natural Beauty and was acclaimed by Dylan Thomas as the prettiest in England, but its claim to fame is more culinary than poetic. Because of gales, so the story goes, the people of Mousehole were unable to fish, and were close to starving until a man called Tom Bawcock braved the storm and brought back a massive haul of seven different types of fish. His heroic acts are celebrated every 23 December, Tom Bawcock's Eve, when all of Mousehole gather to eat 'Starry Gazy Pie' – a fish pie with several fish heads poking upwards through the crust. In 2007, contestant Mark Hix won the BBC's *Great British Menu* with a variant of the dish.

PORLOCK TO LYNMOUTH
(13 miles/21km)
LYNMOUTH TO COMBE MARTIN
(13 miles/21km)

Leaving Porlock, the Coast Path offers a choice of ways: one takes to the wooded slopes above the sea, the other using paths and farm tracks at a higher level. The two routes unite on Sugarloaf Hill (SS 806492). The ensuing mix of broad-leaved and conifer woodland makes for comparatively sheltered going. There is a temptation to deviate round The Foreland to the lighthouse, which the Coastal Path shuns – it would add just over ½ mile (1km) to the walk should you opt for that. There is another temptation, too, to divert to the Blue Ball Inn in Countisbury, easily accessed from the Path; and then it is all downhill to Lynmouth, a village

that straddles the confluence of the West Lyn and East Lyn rivers in a gorge 700 feet (more than 200m) below Lynton. Thomas Gainsborough, who spent his honeymoon in Lynton with his bride Margaret Burr, described the area as 'the most delightful place for a landscape painter this country can boast'.

After climbing out from Lynmouth, the Coast Path crosses a steep slope to reach the distinctive Castle Rock (SS 704497) set amid the so-called Valley of Rocks, a popular tourist spot. A minor road leads on from Lee Abbey. After traversing steep slopes around Woody Bay, a brief diversion can be made to The Beacon, a Roman fortlet; following which, the Path eases on above steep sea cliffs to Holdstone Down and Girt Down, linking the two small hills of Great Hangman and Little Hangman. A swift descent

then leads to Combe Martin, a popular long-street seaside resort in a sheltered cove. The unusual dedication of the parish church – St Peter ad Vincula (St. Peter in Chains) – is said to be derived from the ancient Basilica of San Pietro in Vincoli in Rome.

PORTHLEVEN TO LIZARD
(13 miles/21km)
LIZARD TO COVERACK
(11 miles/17.5km)

On a walk already laden with temptations it is difficult to resist a visit to mainland Britain's most southerly point, but there is far more than pure geography on this two-day stretch round the coast. In spite of the proximity of civilisation, there remains around this peninsula a keen sense of seclusion and rugged wildness, notably within the Lizard National Nature Reserve where the Mullion and Predannack cliffs command everyone's attention. Here is a great place for birdwatchers to seek out the red-billed chough, while everyone will delight in the fishing villages and the palette of colours brought in season by the rare heathers and wild flowers, especially the pink and yellow of the Hottentot fig.

Once beyond Lizard Point, the route passes through one of the Path's Areas of Outstanding Natural Beauty. This stretch is shorter, but more strenuous, involving steep ascents and descents, relatively short in themselves, but enough to get the heart racing, until beyond Cadgwith. Geology is very much to the fore here, the way crossing outcroppings of granite, schist and serpentine, a beautiful dark green rock veined with red and white that has historically been used as decorative stone and is said to hold healing properties. With a reputation for gathering-in ships to wreck, Kennack Sands, a beach and sand dune system, are today part of a National Nature Reserve.

ISLE OF PORTLAND CIRCULAR
(15½ miles/25km)
FERRY BRIDGE TO LULWORTH COVE
(14 miles/23km)

The original course of the South West Coast Path ignored the Isle of Portland, heading straight for Weymouth instead. But a circuit of the island is an interesting amendment to the route. The island is renowned for its limestone, and the Path makes use of old quarry tracks along the western side to reach Portland Bill, the southernmost point, where the sea stack, Pulpit Rock, impresses. The eastern side of the island seems beset with a plethora of quarries and prisons of one sort or another, but no less interesting for all that. Portland Castle (SY 684743) is one of Henry VIII's finest coastal forts, built in the 1540s. The island, also renowned for its birdlife, is left where it was joined, at Ferry Bridge.

King George III went sea bathing at Weymouth, among other places, but the Coast Path is keen to move on to Bowleaze, where some semblance of less busyness prevails. Landslips divert the Path inland from time to time. At Osmington, the Smuggler's Inn, originally built in the 13th century, was the sometime base of French smuggler Pierre Latour, and one of the main landing places for smuggled goods in the 17th century.

Just as Ringstead is approached, the site of the medieval village of West Ringstead, mentioned in the Domesday Book, is encountered. East of Ringstead, the path becomes markedly undulating, passing the renowned Durdle Door (SY 805802) before finally crossing Hambury Tout and descending to shapely Lulworth Cove, a distinctive landform and a World Heritage Site on that account.

The Path makes use of old quarry tracks along the western side to reach Portland Bill, the southernmost point, where the sea stack, Pulpit Rock, impresses

This page: Chesil Beach looking towards the Isle of Portland, Dorset.
Opposite page (top): Mullion Cove, The Lizard, Cornwall; **(bottom)**: Valley of Rocks, Lynmouth, Devon.

PENDEEN TO LAND'S END

(10½ miles/16.5km)

From the lighthouse at Pendeen, the Coast Path soars above craggy granite cliffs to the curve of golden sand at Sennen Cove. It takes in part of Cornwall's mining legacy, and visits one of only two 'capes' in Britain, Cape Cornwall (the other is Cape Wrath in northern Scotland). High cliffs and heath lead to Land's End, which, in spite of its renown as a tourist hot spot, can be remarkably peaceful and secluded. From here, there are views to Wolf Rock lighthouse and the distant Isles of Scilly. There are rock stacks, cliffs and the natural land bridge of Tol-Pedn-Penwith at Gwennap Head to take in that contribute to this stretch standing alongside the best on the Coast Path. Keep an eye out for soaring fulmars, dashing rock pipits and dark green shags.

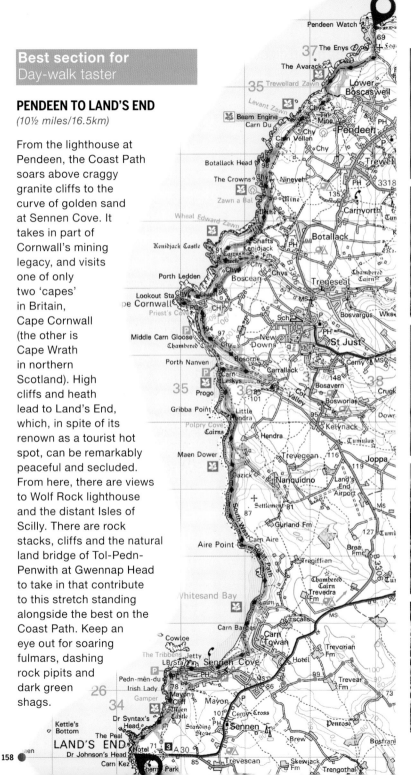

From the lighthouse at Pendeen, the Coast Path soars above craggy granite cliffs to the curve of golden sand at Sennen Cove

Nature on the trail With over 500 miles of coastal habitats, there is much to look out for and admire. **This page (clockwise)**: Grey seal, St Clement's Isle; marram grass, Saunton Sands; goose barnacles; adder, Isle of Purbeck; thrift and typical Cornish wall. **Opposite page (from top)**: Fulmar; rock pipit; chough; thrift; stonecrop.

FLAGS

The South West Coast Path explores four counties: **Somerset** (top left), **Devon** (top right), **Cornwall** (bottom left) and **Dorset** (bottom right).

Of these, the Cornish flag is the most well-known, and there are moves to promote the Cornish language as well as calls for greater legislative autonomy.

Thames Path

WALK 19

The Thames Path is unique in being the only National Trail that does its best to closely follow a river. The journey it takes is one through history, often Royal history. Meandering from its Cotswolds source through the rich countryside of several counties at a leisurely pace, the force of its story grows as the path moves downstream. Trade unionist and politician John Elliott Burns (1858–1943) described the river as 'liquid history', accountable for London's very existence. Throughout that history, the Thames has inspired artists and poets, people with the capacity to be at one with riparian beauty whether that be found in serene country ways or majestic cities and Royal palaces.

Overall, the Thames Path is an easy riverside trail using paths, tracks and some roads as it descends with few undulations gently with the river to the sea. There is something to be said for starting the Thames Path at the London barrier, penetrating inland just as the early settlers and invaders did to conclude amid the mellow, honey-coloured warmth of the Cotswolds; to do so, leads from the dramatic to the dreamy, from bustle and brouhaha to the clean, gentle breath of rurality. But source to sea seems to be the more favoured direction.

The source of the Thames may be elusive, springing (or not, according to season) from the shadow of an ancient ash tree in a Cotswold meadow. But its conclusion is never in doubt: the huge, gleaming Thames Barrier is one of the largest movable flood barriers in the world, spanning 1,700 feet (520 metres) across the river. When raised, the gates of the barrier, each weighing 3,300 tonnes, are five storeys high.

Once under way, the trail visits several cities, towns and villages of note, all of which can introduce delightful delay into planned days: Cricklade, Lechlade, Oxford, Abingdon-on-Thames, Reading, Henley-on-Thames, Marlow and Maidenhead, and passing Windsor Castle and the palaces of Hampton Court, Richmond and Kew. The trail then tackles central London, following options on either bank of the river to reach the Thames Barrier. Along this stretch, Kew Gardens, Westminster, the Tower of London and Maritime Greenwich are all close to the route, and all enjoy World Heritage Site status.

To walk any river from source to sea is a satisfying journey for many, often intangible, inexplicable, reasons – it just feels good. The Severn Way (page 126) is another fine example; but no other National Trail is quite so varied as the Thames Path, which tackles towns and villages steeped in heritage, history and prehistory and combines those with rural landscapes that will gladden the heart.

AMAZING BUT TRUE ...

From its source to the Thames Barrier, there are more than 200 bridges across England's longest river. There are two surviving toll bridges across the Thames: linking Eynsham and Swinford; and between Whitchurch-on-Thames and Pangbourne. The only surviving ford is at Duxford, where the original channel may be forded to reach what is now an island at Shifford Lock.

Marlow

The Thames Path National Trail is rarely far from public transport links or civilisation, and lends itself to completion over several weekends, or as a continuous journey with days of variable length.

	11 days	15 days
Start	Source	Source
Day 1	Cricklade *12mi/19.5km*	Cricklade *12mi/19.5km*
Day 2	Lechlade *10¾mi/17.25km*	Lechlade *10¾mi/17.25km*
Day 3	Bablock Hythe *20mi/32.25km*	Newbridge *16¼mi/26.25km*
Day 4	Abingdon *19¾mi/31.75km*	Oxford *15mi/24km*
Day 5	Wallingford *13¼mi/21.5km*	Abingdon *8½mi/13.75km*
Day 6	Reading *15mi/24km*	Wallingford *13¼mi/21.5km*
Day 7	Marlow *20¼mi/32.75km*	Pangbourne *11mi/17.75km*
Day 8	Windsor *10¼mi/16.5km*	Henley-on-Thames *13½mi/21.75km*
Day 9	Kingston *22¼mi/36km*	Marlow *10¾mi/17.25km*
Day 10	Putney *11½mi/18.5km*	Windsor *10¼mi/16.5km*
Day 11	Thames Barrier *27½mi/44km*	Shepperton *14½mi/23.25km*
Day 12		Teddington *9½mi/15.5km*
Day 13		Putney *9¾mi/15.75km*
Day 14		Tower Bridge *12½mi/20km*
Day 15		Thames Barrier *15mi/24km*

FACTS AND FIGURES

START Thames source, Kemble, Gloucestershire (ST 980995)

FINISH Thames Barrier, Woolwich (TQ 415792)

DISTANCE 183 miles (294km)

HEIGHT GAIN 3,525 feet (1,075m)

DIFFICULTY RATING ♦

IS IT FOR ME? Relatively gentle, easy-going, riparian walking, never too far from habitation and facilities with good transport connections.

Source of the Thames

Old Father Thames

PRACTICALITIES

GETTING THERE AND BACK

Rail and bus services operate to Kemble from London, and it is but a short evening stroll to the source of the river before heading downstream the next morning. A greater range of transport options focus on Cirencester, making it feasible to begin there, taking the Monarch's Way south-west to reach the source. At the other end, many train and bus services run close to the Thames Barrier.

ACCOMMODATION

There is a good choice of accommodation along the whole of the Thames Path, from B&Bs and guest houses, to inns, hotels and rural pubs with rooms. Once within the urban sprawl of London, it is worth seeking out budget hotel accommodation, which is widespread though often lacking in atmosphere.

WEBSITES

www.nationaltrail.co.uk
tfl.gov.uk: this Transport for London link gives detailed information about the Thames Path through London.

MAPS

OS Explorer
OL45, 159, 160, 161, 162, 168, 169, 170, 171, 172, 173, 180.

OS Landranger
163, 164, 173, 175, 176, 177.

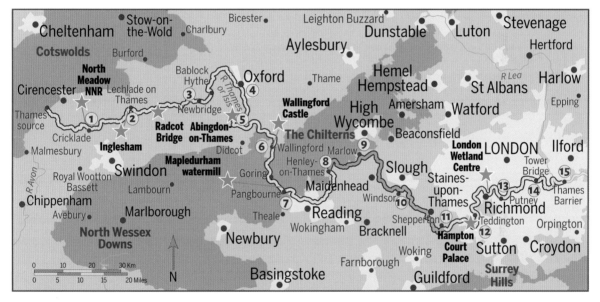

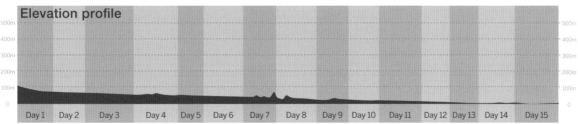

Elevation profile

HENLEY-ON-THAMES TO WINDSOR
(21 miles/33.75km)

Easily split into two days at Marlow, there is much to enjoy as the day begins, very briefly, in harmony with the Chiltern Way (page 16). It follows the length of the famous Henley Regatta course to Temple Island, built as a fishing lodge to enhance the view from nearby Fawley Court country house, a Grade I Listed Building. Onward, the path passes Hurley and Temple locks before arriving in the lovely Georgian town of Marlow set between the meadows of the river valley and the woodlands of the Chiltern Hills.

After Marlow, tranquil river paths ensue, leading by several places of historic significance and with connections to the world of literature: in the 1920s, Bourne End became home to Enid Blyton, the popular children's writer, and to Edgar Wallace, a prolific crime author and dramatist. Gradually, the outline of Windsor Castle eases into view. Founded by William the Conqueror, the castle has since been the home of 39 monarchs. Windsor is an historic market town, immediately south of the River Thames, which forms the boundary with the smaller town of Eton, famed for its college.

The outline of Windsor Castle eases into view. Founded by William the Conqueror, the castle has since been the home of 39 monarchs

★ Abingdon-on-Thames

Known simply as Abingdon between 1974 and 2012 (when it successfully sought to revert to its full title), Abingdon is one of the most important of all the historic towns on the Thames, with a magnificent town hall and a Benedictine abbey established in 676. The town gained its first royal charter in 1556, following the dissolution of the abbey. Of an earlier date, Abingdon Bridge offers a fine view of the town and perpendicular spire of St Helen's church, which was built around 1100 and is the second widest church in England.

★North Meadow National Nature Reserve

Lying between the River Churn and the Thames, the North Meadow National Nature Reserve is of international importance as one of the best examples of a lowland hay meadow in Europe, supporting Britain's largest population of the lovely snake's head fritillary. The meadow enjoys a special status as 'Lammas Land', i.e. lands over which there is a 'several' right of either arable or meadow crop growing, but as soon as the crop has been taken a 'common' right of pasturage arises generally from about Lammas (1 August) (reaping time), until 25 March (sowing time).

★ Inglesham

The Inglesham village Round House, built in the late 18th century, was the unusual residence of the lock-keeper – horses were stabled on the ground floor and living accommodation above. The unassuming, 13th-century Church of St John the Baptist is Anglo-Saxon in origin, and not much of the present building has changed since 1205. The English textile designer, artist, writer and socialist, William Morris, long associated with the Pre-Raphaelite Brotherhood and the English Arts and Crafts Movement, lived 10 miles (16km) away at Kelmscott and campaigned to save the church without unsympathetic alterations.

★ Mapledurham watermill

Built in the 15th century, Mapledurham (SU 669767) is an historic watermill, and preserved in an operational state. The mill is located in the grounds of Mapledurham House, an Elizabethan stately home. The house and watermill are open to visitors on weekend and bank holiday afternoons from April to September.

★ Radcot Bridge

Often claimed as the oldest bridge on the Thames, having been built in 1200, Radcot Bridge (SU 285994) has had a chequered history. The Cistercian monks of Cîteaux in Normandy were granted land on which to build the bridge by King John. Much of their structure was broken down during the Battle of Radcot Bridge in 1387 between troops loyal to Richard II and an army captained by Henry Bolingbroke, Earl of Derby (the future Henry IV). Radcot Bridge was reconstructed six years later, suffered again during the Wars of the Roses, but then was largely rebuilt as it appears today.

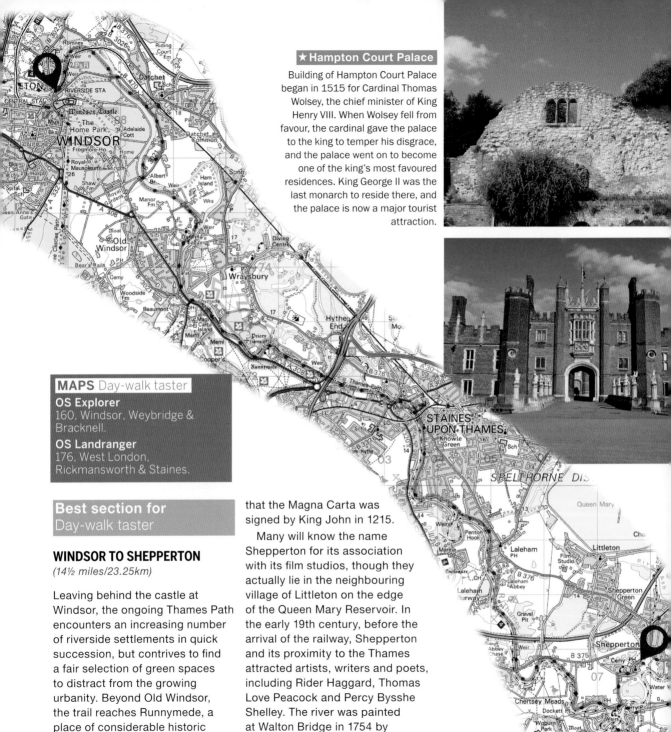

Building of Hampton Court Palace began in 1515 for Cardinal Thomas Wolsey, the chief minister of King Henry VIII. When Wolsey fell from favour, the cardinal gave the palace to the king to temper his disgrace, and the palace went on to become one of the king's most favoured residences. King George II was the last monarch to reside there, and the palace is now a major tourist attraction.

MAPS Day-walk taster

OS Explorer
160, Windsor, Weybridge & Bracknell.

OS Landranger
176, West London, Rickmansworth & Staines.

Best section for
Day-walk taster

WINDSOR TO SHEPPERTON
(14½ miles/23.25km)

Leaving behind the castle at Windsor, the ongoing Thames Path encounters an increasing number of riverside settlements in quick succession, but contrives to find a fair selection of green spaces to distract from the growing urbanity. Beyond Old Windsor, the trail reaches Runnymede, a place of considerable historic significance, for it was here that the Magna Carta was signed by King John in 1215.

Many will know the name Shepperton for its association with its film studios, though they actually lie in the neighbouring village of Littleton on the edge of the Queen Mary Reservoir. In the early 19th century, before the arrival of the railway, Shepperton and its proximity to the Thames attracted artists, writers and poets, including Rider Haggard, Thomas Love Peacock and Percy Bysshe Shelley. The river was painted at Walton Bridge in 1754 by Canaletto, and in 1805 by Turner.

★ Wallingford Castle

Now in ruins, Wallingford Castle was established in the 11th century as a motte-and-bailey design, and grew to become one of the most powerful royal castles of the 12th and 13th centuries. The castle fell into decline in the 16th century, and the structure was stripped for its lead and other building materials, which found their way to Windsor Castle. The castle grounds are open to the public.

★ London Wetland Centre

Managed by the Wildfowl and Wetlands Trust, the centre (TQ 226768) is formed from disused Victorian reservoirs in a loop in the Thames. Given its city location, it is surprising, perhaps, to find many wild birds here that cannot be found elsewhere in London, including bittern, pintail, sand martin, kingfisher and the raucous ring-necked parakeet.

Windsor Castle

RATTY

'As he sat on the grass and looked across the river, a dark hole in the bank opposite, just above the water's edge, caught his eye, and dreamily he fell to considering what a nice snug dwelling-place it would make for an animal with few wants and fond of a bijou riverside residence, above flood level and remote from noise and dust. As he gazed, something bright and small seemed to twinkle down in the heart of it, vanished, then twinkled once more like a tiny star. But it could hardly be a star in such an unlikely situation; and it was too glittering and small for a glow-worm. Then, as he looked, it winked at him, and so declared itself to be an eye; and a small face began gradually to grow up round it, like a frame round a picture.

'A brown little face, with whiskers.

'A grave round face, with the same twinkle in its eye that had first attracted his notice.

'Small neat ears and thick silky hair.

It was the Water Rat!

Then the two animals stood and regarded each other cautiously.

'"Hullo, Mole!" said the Water Rat.

'"Hullo, Rat!" said the Mole.'

An extract from *The Wind in the Willows* by Kenneth Grahame, first published 1908.

WALK 20

Two Moors Way

Suitable for long-distance and day walkers, the Two Moors Way is a delightful coast-to-coast romp across the moorlands and landscapes of Dartmoor and Exmoor national parks. The trail is, infact, a combined trek made up of the Two Moors Way from Ivybridge to Lynmouth and the short Erme-Plym Trail from the coast at Wembury to Ivybridge. The route is usually followed south to north, and falls into four distinct sections: South Devon, Dartmoor, Mid-Devon and Exmoor, and gives a focused introduction to essential Devon.

The southern section is a gentle introduction to the trail, making use of clearly signed public footpaths through the rolling pastures and copses of South Hams, a gentle, undemanding landscape. Dartmoor, however, is another matter, featuring barren, isolated moorland stretches dotted with weird outcroppings of granite tors, the high point of which is Hamel Down (1,745 feet/532m). But Dartmoor has a more benevolent character, too; not without good reason is it encompassed in a national park. There are colourful and appealing hamlets and villages, wooded river valleys and walled fields that betray Dartmoor's gentler side.

The central part of Devon is surprisingly less well known, and here hills and a network of hedgerowed lanes and farmsteads are a recurring feature that hint at a timelessness, of 'other'. The northern part of the trail – some in Devon, some in Somerset – has different geology that yields a moorland plateau dominated by rounded, smooth-sided slopes and riven by steep-sided valleys, or 'combes' as they call them here. And all of that is in stark contrast to the weather-beaten sea cliffs that mark the end of the trail.

Both the start and finish points feature as part of the greater South West Coast Path (page 150). The entire route is prominently waymarked (in both directions), and there is a low-level, bad-weather alternative should it be needed, but that does not erase the need for the ability to navigate across remote moorland terrain in poor weather. The juxtaposition of pastoral stretches, river valleys and high moorland is a combination that brings pleasure and quality to the whole ensemble, moments of reflection and oases of gritty grandeur, silken ways and breezy heights.

> ## AMAZING BUT TRUE ...
> Amid the fine Mid Devon countryside surrounding the hamlet of Morchard Road, the Two Moors Way intersects the Exeter to Barnstaple railway line, splendidly known as the Tarka Line. Morchard Road's tiny station served the village of Morchard Bishop some 2½ miles (4km) to the north-east. The footsteps of those villagers too poor for the pony and trap ride home can be followed on the Two Moors Way on the 'walk up from the station'.

Tarr Steps

END TO END

The Two Moors Way can be accomplished in seven days (strenuous), 10 or 11 days (moderate/demanding) or 12 days (moderate).

	7 days		10 days		12 days	
Start	Wembury		Wembury		Wembury	
Day 1	Ivybridge	16mi/25.75km	Ivybridge	16mi/25.75km	Yealmpton	7mi/11.25km
Day 2	Scorriton	12½mi/20km	Scorriton	12½mi/20km	Ivybridge	9mi/14.5km
Day 3	Chagford	19mi/30.5km	Widecombe-in-the-Moor	8¼mi/13.25km	Scorriton	12½mi/20km
Day 4	Morchard Bishop	19¾mi/32km	Chagford	10¾mi/17.25km	Widecombe-in-the-Moor	8¼mi/13.25km
Day 5	Withypool	16mi/26km	Colebrooke	12mi/19.5km	Chagford	10¾mi/17.25km
Day 6	Knowstone	14mi/22.5km	Morchard Bishop	7¾mi/12.5km	Colebrooke	12mi/19.5km
Day 7	Lynmouth	19mi/30.5km	Knowstone	16mi/26km	Morchard Bishop	7¾mi/12.5km
Day 8			Withypool	14mi/22.5km	Witheridge	8mi/13km
Day 9			Simonsbath	7mi/11.25km	Knowstone	8mi/13km
Day 10			Lynmouth	12mi/19.25km	Withypool	14mi/22.5km
Day 11					Simonsbath	7mi/11.25km
Day 12					Lynmouth	12mi/19.5km

★ Pupers Hill

Lying along the extensive ridge overlooking Buckfastleigh, Pupers Hill (SX 672673) is marked by three distinct rock piles – Inner, Middle and Outer – said to be the embodiment of the Dartmoor tradition that anyone who 'piped', or danced, on the Sabbath would be turned to stone.

The moor above Buckfastleigh

★ Knowstone Moor

Linked to Rackenford Moor to the east, Knowestone Moor (SS 851211) is a rare habitat of culm grassland that hosts distinctive, acid-clay loving plants, such as saw wort and meadow thistle in the drier parts, and meadowsweet and angelica in the wetter area.

Elevation profile

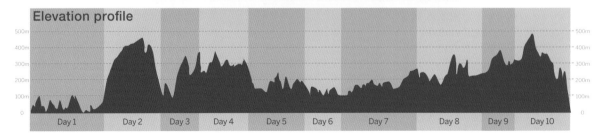

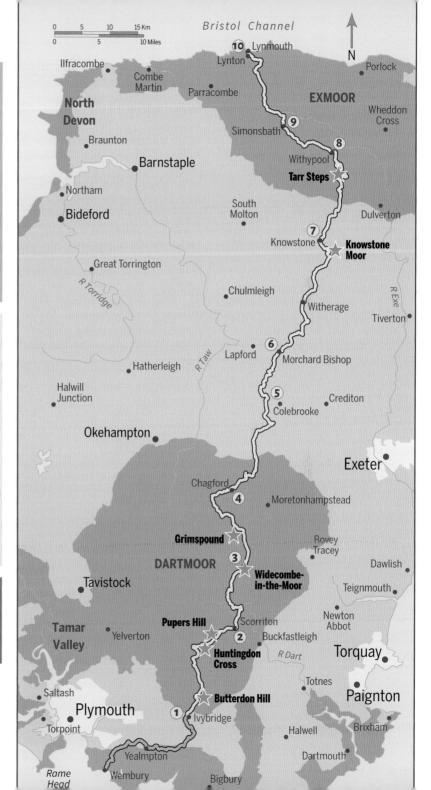

FACTS AND FIGURES

START Wembury, Devon
(SX 517485)

FINISH Lynmouth, Devon
(SS 722496)

DISTANCE 117 miles (187km)

HEIGHT GAIN 15,825 feet
(4,825m)

DIFFICULTY RATING ◆◆◆◆

IS IT FOR ME? Rugged and
remote moorland sections linked by
rolling low-level field paths; good
fitness and forward planning is
needed.

PRACTICALITIES

GETTING THERE AND BACK
Wembury is served by local bus
services from Plymouth (except on
Sundays), which has a direct main
line railway service from London
Paddington. Lynmouth is served by
local bus services.

ACCOMMODATION The
south-west of England is popular
with conventional tourists and
well supplied with all types of
accommodation. But it is a busy
place in the summer months, and
advance planning is vital to success.

WEBSITE
https://twomoorsway.org

MAPS

OS Explorer
OL9, OL20, OL28, 113, 114.

OS Landranger
180, 181, 191, 202.

WEMBURY TO IVYBRIDGE
(16 miles/25.75km)

South Devon makes a gentle introduction to the Two Moors Way, offering a relaxed tour of the undulating fields and woodland valleys of South Hams. Wembury is a popular resort on the coast; while equally popular Ivybridge sits at the southern edge of the Dartmoor National Park.

From Wembury, the trail, which here is generally referred to as the Erme-Plym Trail, has to contend with the River Yealm; it does so by taking a looping route via Spriddlestone, crossing a finger of Cofflete Creek, before heading for Brixton and Yealmpton, the latter reveals itself to be the location of Kitley House, the housekeeper of which was the model for 'Mother Hubbard' in the children's nursery rhyme.

More easy-going countryside ensues, leading roughly east to reach the River Erme south of the Saxon village of Ermington, renowned for its crooked church spire. From the village, the trail tries to maintain faith with the river, sticking to riverside meadows as far as Ivybridge. Dating from the 13th century, Ivybridge's status rests on its location as a crossing point of the River Erme, by a hump-backed bridge.

More easy-going countryside ensues leading roughly east to reach the River Erme south of the Saxon village of Ermington, renowned for its crooked church spire

★ Huntingdon Cross
Believed to have originally been a waymarker for the Abbot's Way, linking the abbeys at Tavistock and Buckland with Buckfast Abbey, Huntingdon Cross (SX 664662) was later usurped and used as a boundary marker for the Manor of Brent.

★ Butterdon Hill
At the southern edge of Dartmoor National Park, Butterdon Hill (SX 655586) is crowned by the remains of a small stone circle and a stone row.

★ Tarr Steps
Located in a National Nature Reserve, Tarr Steps (SS 867321) is a clapper bridge, an ancient form of river crossing found in Devon and in several other upland areas of England, and formed by placing large flat slabs of stone on stone piers.

★ Grimspound

Consisting of 24 hut circles surrounded by a stone wall, Grimspound (SX 700809) is a late Bronze Age settlement, first settled about 4,000 years ago.

★ Widecombe-in-the-Moor

Popularised by the song 'Widecombe Fair' featuring 'Old Uncle Tom Cobley and All', the village is also known for its tall church, known locally as the 'Cathedral of the Moors'. The actual Widecombe Fair is held annually, and was originally a cattle fair.

'WIDECOMBE FAIR'
(THE FIRST TWO VERSES)

Tom Pearce, Tom Pearce,
    lend me your grey mare.

All along, down along,
    out along lea.
For I want for to go to
    Widecombe Fair,
With Bill Brewer, Jan
    Stewer, Peter Gurney,
Peter Davy, Dan'l Whiddon,
    Harry Hawke,
Old Uncle Tom Cobley and all,
Old Uncle Tom Cobley and all.

And when shall I see
    again my grey mare?
All along, down along,
    out along lea.
By Friday soon, or
    Saturday noon,
With Bill Brewer, Jan
    Stewer, Peter Gurney,
Peter Davy, Dan'l Whiddon,
    Harry Hawke,
Old Uncle Tom Cobley and all,
Old Uncle Tom Cobley and all.

Yorkshire Wolds Way

The Yorkshire Wolds Way is a gentle meander through the undulating chalk uplands of the Yorkshire Wolds, from the Humber estuary to the Cleveland coastline. Making the most of typical downland landscapes, which are bright red in spring and early summer with rafts of poppies, the Way, like so many trails, was initiated by the Ramblers' Association and originally known simply as the 'Wolds Way'.

From the Humber estuary, the Way heads around the edge of the Wolds, through woodland and across arable farmland, and then along the northern escarpment of the Wolds, where it reaches its highest point (712 feet/217m) on Toisland Wold. On the journey, the Way tackles wooded slopes, dry valleys, sheep pastures and climbs steadily onto the breezy tops of the rolling hills. At Filey, the Way meets the Cleveland Way (page 24), offering a chance to continue the journey through the Cleveland Hills … or call a halt on the headland of Filey Brigg.

The Yorkshire Wolds are a range of low hills rippling across East and North Yorkshire, on the western edge of which they rise to an escarpment which then falls steeply to the Vale of York, 'fold upon fold of … encircling hills, piled rich and golden', according to writer Winifred Holtby who lived in the area. To the north, across the Vale of Pickering, lie the North York Moors.

Geologically, the Wold hills are formed from marine limestones and take the form of an elevated, gently rolling plateau incised by numerous deep and steep-sided, flat-bottomed valleys, glacial in origin. The predominance of chalk means good drainage; as a result, most valleys are dry, but the complexities of the landscape have resulted in an inverse system of farming, with cattle and sheep in the valley and crops being grown on the hills above.

Along with Wessex and Orkney, the Yorkshire Wolds comprise a vital domain for the study of the Neolithic period in Britain. A wealth of archaeological remains, notably a profusion of Neolithic, Bronze Age and Romano-British sites extend across the entire Wolds area.

Mention 'wolds' and thoughts may first turn to the Cotswolds, and many will be surprised to learn that Yorkshire, too, has its wolds, every bit as tranquil, full of charm and allure as their southern counterpart. The Yorkshire Wolds Way reveals their secrets and delights.

AMAZING BUT TRUE …

Fridaythorpe is the highest village in the Yorkshire Wolds. Its unusual name has nothing to do with the anticipation of an approaching weekend, but instead betrays the settlement's 9th-century Scandinavian origins as the homestead of Frigda. The tiny village church has an unusual clock, styled on one found in a French château, and bearing the inscription 'Time is short, eternity is long'.

Londesborough Park

The Yorkshire Wolds Way can comfortably be completed over a period of six days, whether spread over several weeks or months, or done as one complete exercise.

6 days

Start	Hessle	
Day 1	South Cove	12½mi / 20km
Day 2	Market Weighton	11¾mi / 19km
Day 3	Millington	9¼mi / 14.75km
Day 4	Thixendale	11mi / 17.75km
Day 5	Sherburn	18¾mi / 30.35km
Day 6	Filey	15mi / 24.25km

PRACTICALITIES

GETTING THERE AND BACK
Rail services operate to Hull, with a frequent bus service between Hull and Hessle, while Filey is well supplied by rail and bus services.

ACCOMMODATION
There is a wide choice of accommodation along the Yorkshire Wolds Way, and only at the height of the tourist season is finding somewhere to stay likely to be a problem. There is a stage-by-stage accommodation list on the National Trails website. Campsites are found along the Way, but wild camping, as such, is illegal in England. It is worth bearing in mind that if you plan your journey from mid-week to mid-week you will be out of sync with wayfarers who start on a weekend, and that accommodation is then more likely to be available.

WEBSITE
www.nationaltrail.co.uk

FACTS AND FIGURES

START Hessle Haven, East Yorkshire (TA 034256)

FINISH Filey Brigg, North Yorkshire (TA 130815)

DISTANCE 79 miles (126km)

HEIGHT GAIN 8,265 feet (2,520m)

DIFFICULTY RATING ♦♦

IS IT FOR ME? A good route favourable for year-round walking, but with limited public transport on some sections.

MAPS

OS Explorer 281, 293, 294, 300, 301.

OS Landranger 100, 101, 106, 107.

Glacial in origin, these chalk valleys are dry

Millington Pastures

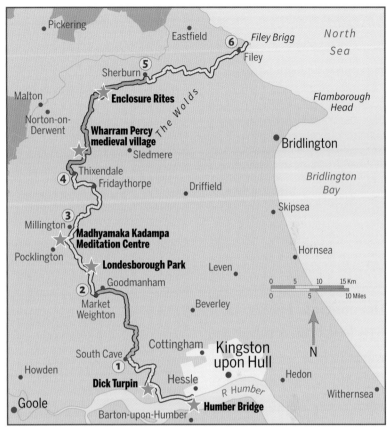

Pickering

Eastfield

Filey Brigg

⑥

Filey

North Sea

Sherburn

⑤

Malton

Enclosure Rites

The Wolds

Flamborough Head

Norton-on-Derwent

Wharram Percy medieval village

Sledmere

Bridlington

Thixendale

④

Fridaythorpe

Driffield

Bridlington Bay

Millington

③

Skipsea

Pocklington

Madhyamaka Kadampa Meditation Centre

Londesborough Park

Leven

Hornsea

Goodmanham

②

Market Weighton

Beverley

South Cave

Cottingham

Kingston upon Hull

①

Hessle

Hedon

Howden

Dick Turpin

N

Goole

Barton-upon-Humber

Humber Bridge

R Humber

Withernsea

| 0 | 5 | 10 | 15 Km |
| 0 | 5 | 10 Miles |

They rise to an escarpment which then falls steeply to the Vale of York, 'fold upon fold of … encircling hills, piled rich and golden', according to writer Winifred Holtby

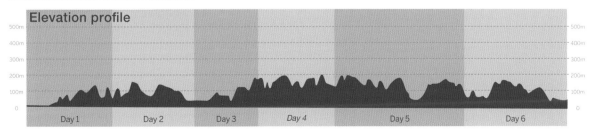

Elevation profile

Day 1 Day 2 Day 3 Day 4 Day 5 Day 6

THIXENDALE TO SHERBURN

(18¾ miles/30.35km)

On the climb out of Vessey Pasture Dale, the Way reaches its highest point before descending into Deepdale and the deserted village of Wharram Percy (see opposite). Today, little remains other than the walls of St Martin's Church, which continued to be used for 400 years after the village was deserted. The mixed woodland around Settrington makes for pleasant walking, beyond which there is a fine view of the Vale of Pickering as the route changes direction once Wintringham is reached. To the north of the village, before the Way heads east for Sherburn, it encounters a unique artwork in the corner of a field, 'Enclosure Rites' (see page 181).

★Dick Turpin

Not far from its start, the Way reaches the ancient village of Welton, where, in 1519, the first instance of an accidental fatal shooting was recorded when a woman was killed by a handgun; it was a new-fangled conundrum for the Coroners' Court. It was here, too, that highwayman Dick Turpin was charged with horse theft in 1739 and later tried and hanged in York. Local legend attests that he was arrested at the 17th-century coaching inn, the Green Dragon in Welton, a favoured haunt of his.

The concrete towers are 510 feet (155.5m) tall and were built to be 1.4 inches (36mm) further apart from each other at the top than at the bottom, to allow for the curvature of the Earth

★ Humber Bridge

The Way passes directly beneath the Humber Bridge (TA 023253), which, when it opened in 1981, was the longest single span suspension bridge in the world, a distinction it still holds for the UK. The concrete towers are 510 feet (155.5m) tall and were built to be 1.4 inches (36mm) further apart from each other at the top than at the bottom, to allow for the curvature of the Earth.

★ Londesborough Park

Londesborough Hall (SE 870457) was built by Frances Clifford in 1589, and enlarged during the late 17th century for the first Lord Burlington, commanding impressive views over the sloping land to the south. Today, this is a landscaped park, woodland and gardens with avenues, a lake, cascades and a 1730s kitchen garden.

★ Madhyamaka Kadampa Meditation Centre

Historic Kilnwick Percy Hall (SE 825498) is a Grade II listed building set in 42 acres (17 hectares) of grounds with woodland walks, parkland and a lake. It has been home to the Madhyamaka Kadampa Meditation Centre for over 25 years, a relaxing place of peace and tranquillity to rest and reflect. There is open access across the grounds and around the lake.

★ Wharram Percy medieval village

Wharram Percy (SE 858643) is the most famous of more than 100 deserted medieval villages in the Yorkshire Wolds. It is exciting first and foremost for its beautiful location, but also because it is the best-preserved uninhabited village in England. The Black Death, sheep farming and its very isolation gradually reduced the population until the last house was abandoned in 1500.

SOUTH CAVE TO MARKET WEIGHTON
(11¾ miles/19km)

The easy walking and wealth of interesting villages and historic locations make the stretch from South Cave to Market Weighton a reassuring and inviting introduction to the Way. Not long after leaving South Cave there are extensive views of the Humber. On leaving Wind Dale, east of North Newbald, you might be forgiven for thinking the Way has no intention of ever heading for the market town of Market Weighton, keeping as it does resolutely to the high ground of the Wolds. But there is good reason: the high ground is full of interest, and you will pass the site of a Roman amphitheatre and several tumuli around Arras Farm that date from the Iron Age.

In Market Weighton you encounter several mentions of William Bradley, the Yorkshire Giant born here in 1787 who reached a height of 7 feet 9 inches (2.36m). He was the fourth son in a family of 13 and at birth weighed 14lbs (6.4kg).

SUSPENSION BRIDGES

When it comes to ranking suspension bridges, the determining factor is the length of the span supported between the principal towers. In the Humber Bridge, this distance is 4,625 feet (1,410m), currently making it the world's 11th longest. The record holder is Akashi Kaikyo Bridge, in Kobe, Japan, with a span of 6,530 feet (1,991m), opened in 1998. However, the Çanakkale 1915 Bridge, due to open by 2023, and crossing the Dardenelles Strait in Turkey, has a span 105 feet (32m) longer at 6,635 feet (2,023m).

Filey Brigg

Whiting Chalk Mill, Hessle

MAPS Day-walk taster
OS Explorer
293, Kingston upon Hull & Beverley; 294, Market Weighton & Yorkshire Wolds Central, Pocklington.

OS Landranger
106, Market Weighton, Goole & Stamford Bridge.

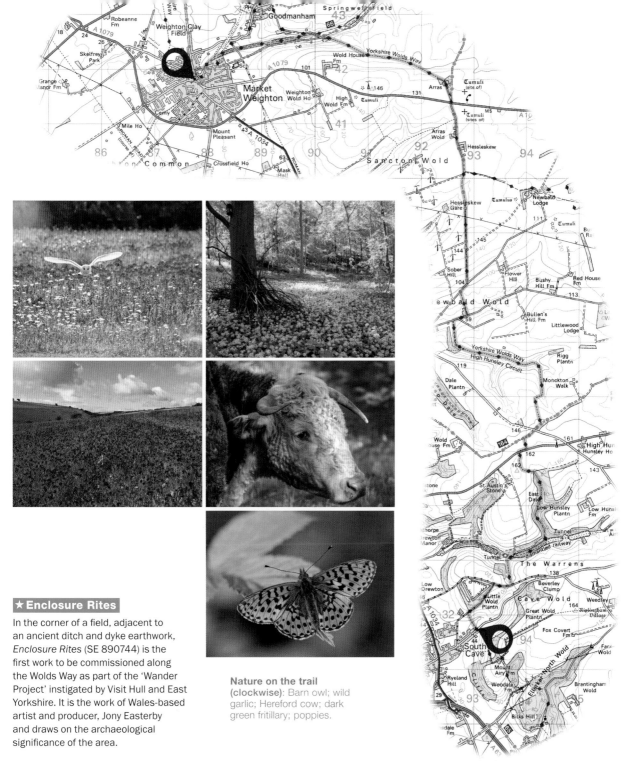

★ Enclosure Rites

In the corner of a field, adjacent to an ancient ditch and dyke earthwork, *Enclosure Rites* (SE 890744) is the first work to be commissioned along the Wolds Way as part of the 'Wander Project' instigated by Visit Hull and East Yorkshire. It is the work of Wales-based artist and producer, Jony Easterby and draws on the archaeological significance of the area.

Nature on the trail (clockwise): Barn owl; wild garlic; Hereford cow; dark green fritillary; poppies.

SCOTLAND

Loch Lomond

Annandale Way 🕭

Only just a teenager, being developed only in 2009 by the landscape partnership Sulwath Connections and the community in association with local estates and farmers, the Annandale Way is a delightful but curious creature. The Way is constrained by the course of the River Annan, but in a way that gives the impression it wants to make much more of the hills above. Following the River Annan from source to sea, the Way wants to start, with commendable intention, on Annandale Head, high above the notorious Devil's Beef Tub – where Border reivers (gangs of marauders and thieves) used to conceal their rustled cattle – but that is only accessible by car and then an uphill walk. So, by way of compromise, it begins in the market town of Moffat and performs a loop that takes it up the valley to Annandale Head, then east to the head of Tweedhope Burn before descending all the way back to Moffat.

Once in Moffat, things settle down as the route strikes south through farmland, forest and moorland, passing under the M74 motorway and over the West Coast rail line, briefly saying 'Hello' to the Southern Upland Way (page 236). Then, as if uncertain of its intentions, at Corncockle the route divides: one branch stays in the valley and passes close by Lockerbie, while the other, the more demanding of the two, heads for Lochmaben and climbs onto the hills above. The two routes rejoin on Sorrysike Moor and continue southwards in company with the river to the town of Annan and on to the Solway Firth.

Apart, from that first loop onto the hills, which is invigorating and the only stage with significant altitude gain (the highest point is 1,649 feet/500m on Chalk Rig Edge), the Annandale Way mostly pursues footpaths, country lanes, forest and farm tracks, and is generally well waymarked. The terrain throughout is mixed and this adds to the quality of the walk, especially in terms of flora and fauna: there are some fine stands of woodland and a diverse range of birdlife from moorland golden plover to the geese and waders that love coastal mudflats. The River Annan itself has clear water that supports a diverse range of wildlife, including otters.

Any walk that follows a river from source to sea threads a diverse wonderland of geology, geography, flora and fauna. The Annandale Way is no exception, and short enough to encourage you to turn round and head back the way you came … possibly.

AMAZING BUT TRUE …

Moffat's attractive location in Upper Annandale and its assortment of hotels, shops, inns and cafés makes the town an excellent walking and touring base. The fountain surmounted by a ram in the middle of Moffat's unusually wide high street symbolises the town's history as an important wool centre. In the 18th and 19th centuries, Moffat became a popular spa, and the town hall once housed the baths and pump room.

Solway Firth

The Annandale Way falls into five distinct stages.

5 days

Start	Moffat
Stage 1	Annandale Head – Moffat *14 mi / 22.5km*
Stage 2	St Ann's *9¾ mi / 15.5km*
Stage 3	Lochmaben *8½ mi / 13.5km*
Stage 4	Hoddom Castle *13¼ mi / 21.5km*
Stage 5	Solway Firth *10½ mi / 17km*

FACTS AND FIGURES

START Annan Bridge, Moffat (NT 083048)

FINISH Solway Firth, near Newbiebarns (NY 180644)

DISTANCE 56 miles (90km)

HEIGHT GAIN 4,970 feet (1,515m)

DIFFICULTY RATING ♦♦

IS IT FOR ME? Largely riparian paths through a good mix of countryside; best tackled as an end-to-end route where public transport options make this feasible.

PRACTICALITIES

GETTING THERE AND BACK
Moffat has bus links from Carlisle and Glasgow. Lockerbie and Annan both have rail and bus links.

GETTING AROUND
Anyone intending to do the Way over several individual visits may have logistical considerations to take into account. Not all stages have public transport, but details of those that do can be found at www.travelinescotland.com.

ACCOMMODATION
There are hotels and B&B accommodation in Moffat, Lochmaben, Lockerbie and Annan, though the other stages can be problematic. There are campsites at Moffat, Lochmaben, Hoddom Castle and Annan, but if not intending to camp, it is worth asking your accommodation provider if they are able pick you up and drop you off at the end points of stages.

WEBSITES
www.scotlandsgreattrails.com
http://annandaleway.org

★ Annan

Annan is a medieval red sandstone town, dating from the 13th century. It was sometime home of the Bruce family, the lords of Annandale, the most famous of whom was Robert the Bruce, the Scottish king who won independence from England at the Battle of Bannockburn in 1314.

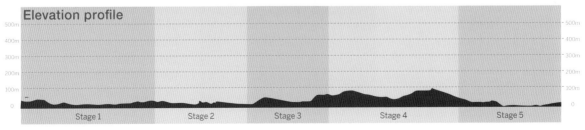

Elevation profile

| | Stage 1 | Stage 2 | Stage 3 | Stage 4 | Stage 5 |

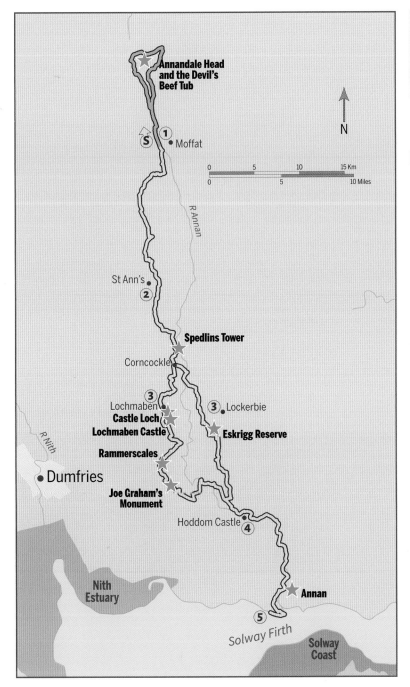

Annandale Head
and the Devil's
Beef Tub

S **1** • Moffat

R Annan

0 5 10 15 Km
0 5 10 Miles

N

St Ann's
2

Spedlins Tower
Corncockle
3 Lochmaben
Castle Loch
Lochmaben Castle
3 • Lockerbie
Eskrigg Reserve
Rammerscales
R Nith
• Dumfries
Joe Graham's
Monument
Hoddom Castle **4**

Nith
Estuary

5
Solway Firth
Solway
Coast

Annan

MAPS
OS Explorer
314, 322, 330.
OS Landranger
78, 85.

★ **Rammerscales**

Commissioned in around 1760, during the reign of George III, Rammerscales (NY 081775) is a classic Scottish mansion and open to the public. Like nearby Spedlins Tower (page 189), the mansion is said to be haunted.

CLAN BRUCE TARTAN

Robert the Bruce (1274–1329), was Robert I of Scotland from 1306 until his death. He was the eighth 'Robert' in a direct lineage descended from Robert de Bruce, a Norman knight who crossed the English Channel with William the Conqueror. The second Robert de Bruce (d. 1141) was granted the lordship of Annandale by Scotland's King David I. The Bruce family's royal connection began when the fourth Robert married Isabel, daughter of King William I of Scotland.

MOFFAT – ANNANDALE HEAD – MOFFAT
(14 miles/22.5km)

This first stage of the Annandale Way is a fine walk in its own right, and while its upland moors and undulating terrain may not hold the tang of the seaside, it stands out as a rugged and pleasing high-level circuit. From the town of Moffat, the stage follows a mix of riverbanks, farmland, moorland, footpaths, tracks and quiet lanes, with just one steep climb. A short stretch runs along the upland edge before descending and returning to Moffat by a different route.

★ Annandale Head and the Devil's Beef Tub

Directly below the edge of Annanhead Hill, the Devil's Beef Tub is a deep and dramatic hollow from which the River Annan flows. It was renowned as a hideaway for cattle stolen during the notorious period in Border history when this area was a lawless no-man's land. Novelist Walter Scott, writing in his novel *Redgauntlet*, said that '... it looks as if four hills were laying their heads together, to shut out daylight from the dark hollow space between them. A damned deep, black, blackguard-looking abyss of a hole', although, to be fair, such a bleak description is rarely valid.

★ Lochmaben Castle

The ruined Lochmaben Castle (NY 088811), on a thumb of land poking into the southern shore of Castle Loch (opposite), was built by King Edward I in the 13th and 14th centuries, and later rebuilt by James IV of Scotland. King Edward used a site to the south of an earlier motte-and-bailey castle built in the 12th century by the Bruce family, lords of Annandale. Lochmaben Castle was a key outpost for the English, and they made tremendous efforts to keep it in their possession throughout the 1300s. It withstood several sieges and attacks, before falling to the Scots in 1385. Mary, Queen of Scots visited Lochmaben in 1565 with her second husband, Lord Darnley.

★ Castle Loch

South of Lochmaben, Castle Loch (NY 085819) is the largest and shallowest of the Lochmaben lochs. It was one of the first nature reserves in Scotland, and is a site of international importance for its birdlife, which includes for wintering pink-footed geese from Iceland and Greenland, along with greylag geese and goosanders.

★ Spedlins Tower

This strong fortress (NY 097875) on the south bank of the River Annan was built in Tudor times for the Jardine family. Today, the tower is of considerable architectural interest and, since the 1980s, in a good state of preservation. It is said to be haunted by the ghost of the local miller, a quarrelsome character, whom the laird imprisoned in his dungeon and then went away to Edinburgh and forgot about.

★ Eskrigg Reserve

Located just outside Lockerbie, Eskrigg Reserve occupies the site of an old curling pond, and contains a mix of habitats including woodland, grassland, heathland, willow carr and reed bed. There is coniferous woodland to the north and west, grassland to the east and marshland to the south.

★ Joe Graham's Monument

A prominent obelisk on Almagill Hill, Joe Graham's Monument (NY 089757) commemorates a local Master of Fox Hounds who died in 1893. The monument is a great vantage point from which to spot deer and other mammals.

Renowned as a hideaway for cattle stolen when Border Reivers ruled a lawless no-man's land

Arran Coastal Way ⬡

For generations of Glaswegians, Arran was a popular trip 'Doon the Watter'. With an area of just 165 square miles (427sqkm), the island continues to shoulder a disproportionate burden of tourism, testimony to its capacity to provide something for everyone. Viewed from afar, Arran doesn't seem like an island at all, set as it is against the backdrop of Kintyre. Nor can you make out the diversity of its land forms. Only as the island is approached by sea does it become apparent that there is a marked distinction between the craggy upthrusts of the north and the fertile farmlands of the south. Between the two lies that great geological signature, the Highland Boundary Fault, but you would need to be high on the slopes of Goat Fell to see the distinction at its best, a characteristic that eluded Robert Burns, constrained as he doubtless seems to have been by the minutiae of his Ayrshire homeland.

The Coastal Way, usually taken in an anti-clockwise direction, encircles the island, for the most part at or near sea level with just two excursions inland: one to visit Goat Fell, at 2,867 feet (874m) the highest point on the island, the other to take in a loop that visits Glenashdale Falls, south of Whiting Bay. It is a challenging and rewarding circling of the island, often described as 'Scotland in Miniature', with good cause because it hosts many typical Highland and Lowland landscapes, wildlife and culture. Offshore from Lamlash, Holy Island is a temptation, accessible in summer by boat.

The circuit leads round the coastal fringe of the island's mountainous north, then down its western flank to visit sandy beaches, rocky shores and gentler landscapes. The east coast offers forest and woodland walking and passes Iron Age hill forts and burial cairns. Many of the coastal paths have been upgraded in recent years, but overall the Way demands a good level of fitness, even though much of it is low level: there are several areas where it passes through slippery and ankle-testing boulder fields. The stretch along the south coast from Bennan Head to Dippin Head can be problematic, but there is a high tide alternative that makes use of the road for a while.

Being coastal, the chances of seeing wildlife are good, notably otters, seals, a wide range of seabirds and possibly eagles, minke whale, dolphins, porpoises and basking sharks; it's that kind of place.

> ## AMAZING BUT TRUE ...
> Arran's population rose during the 18th and into the 19th century, reaching a high of around 6,600 in 1821, thereafter gradually declining to almost half that number at the 1971 census. Over the past 50 years, the population has risen slowly, with 4,600 recorded in 2011. However. the density of population on Arran is still only 28 per square mile, compared to approximately 952 per square mile on the Isle of Wight, which is slightly smaller in terms of area but has 140,000 inhabitants.

Blackwaterfoot

The Arran Coastal Way falls into seven distinct stages and, as such, provides an ideal way of getting to know the island over the course of a week or so. None of those stages is more than 10 miles (16km), and strong walkers could accomplish the walk in as few as five days. Some of the terrain is demanding, while some stretches between Kingscross and Lamlash can be affected by high tides and become impassable. The first day out from Brodick should not be underestimated. There is a choice of routes: one climbing high onto Goat Fell, the other taking an easier line along forest trails. Both routes meet at High Corrie, followed by coastal road walking to Sannox.

FACTS AND FIGURES

START / FINISH Brodick (NS 014361)

DISTANCE 65 miles (104km)

HEIGHT GAIN 6,295 feet (1,920m)

DIFFICULTY RATING ◆◆◆

IS IT FOR ME? A trail that is tougher than it looks, with some pathless parts and rugged terrain; general proximity to the coast road bus services permit piecemeal completion.

MAPS

OS Explorer 361.

OS Landranger 69.

PRACTICALITIES

GETTING THERE AND BACK
Ferry crossing (55 minutes) from Ardrossan to Brodick (www.calmac.co.uk). Ardrossan is 45 minutes by train from Glasgow Central.

GETTING AROUND
Bus services operate along the entire coastal road (www.spt.co.uk).

ACCOMMODATION
There is a good selection of accommodation – hotels, guests houses, B&Bs, bunkhouses, a youth hostel and campsites – all around the island, notably at Sannox, Lochranza, Pirnmill, Blackwaterfoot, Lagg, Whiting Bay and Lamlash, but availability should not be taken for granted during the summer season (see www.visitarran.com)

WEBSITES
www.coastalway.co.uk
www.scotlandsgreattrails.com

	5 days		7 days	
Start	Brodick		Brodick	
Day 1	Sannox	10 mi / 16.25km	Sannox	10 mi / 16.25km
Day 2	Imachar	18¾ mi / 30.25km	Lochranza	9¾ mi / 15.75km
Day 3	Lagg	16½ mi / 26.5km	Imachar	9 mi / 14.5km
Day 4	Whiting Bay	9½ mi / 15.5km	Blackwaterfoot	9¼ mi / 15km
Day 5	Brodick	9½ mi / 15.5km	Lagg	7¼ mi / 11.5km
Day 6			Whiting Bay	9½ mi / 15.5km
Day 7			Brodick	9½ mi / 15.5km

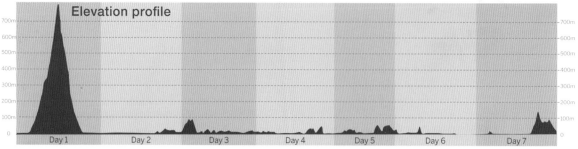

Elevation profile

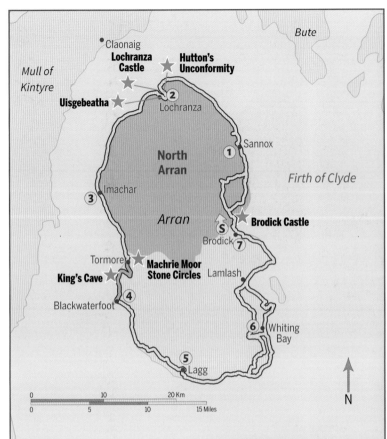

This page (top left): Basking shark;
(top right): sea otter; (middle): Goat Fell;
(bottom): Lochranza.
Opposite page: Sannox.

★ Brodick Castle

The former seat of the Dukes of Hamilton, Brodick Castle (NS 016379) is not to be ignored, the Way passing through its extended grounds. There has been a fortress on this spot since the 5th century, as raiders from Antrim sought to extend this Dál Riata kingdom. The castle is now owned by the National Trust for Scotland and is open to the public.

TORMORE, STANDING STONES TO BLACKWATERFOOT
(7 miles/11.5km)

The Machrie standing stones are not on the line of the coastal path, but they have a delightful skill in waylaying good intentions; hours can be spent exploring the circles, standing stones and other prehistoric remains. Onward, after a short stretch of road walking, the Way skirts the Torr Righ Beag plantation to the coast, paralleling the shoreline south to King's Cave (see opposite) to the viewpoint of Drumadoon Point, not only a peaceful place from which to sea watch, but a place of interest for geologists. Thereafter, it is an agreeable saunter out along a fine beach to Blackwaterfoot, which faces out into Drumadoon Bay and across to the Kintyre peninsula.

★ Hutton's Unconformity

Hutton's Unconformity is a name given to geological sites in Scotland identified by the 18th-century Scottish geologist, James Hutton, as places where the junction between two types of rock formations created at different times and by different forces can be seen. For Hutton, this was evidence that the Earth was unimaginably older than Biblical timescales claimed. There is a clear example of the rock distinction at Lochranza (see www.castlekirk.co.uk/geology.html).

★ Lochranza Castle

At the north-west edge of the island, Lochranza Castle (NR 933506) is an L-shaped tower house built on a promontory poking out into Loch Ranza. The castle dates from the 13th century, and is thought to have been used as a hunting lodge. In the 15th century, James IV of Scotland used the castle as a base from which to campaign against the Lords of the Isles, Clan MacDonald.

OFFSHORE ISLANDS

Of all the offshore islands around the British coastline Arran is the ninth largest, the top ten being:

1. **Lewis and Harris**
   841 sq mi (2,179sqkm)
2. **Skye** 639 sq mi (1,656sqkm)
3. **Shetland – Mainland**
   374 sq mi (969sqkm)
4. **Mull** 338 sq mi (875sqkm)
5. **Anglesey** 276 sq mi (714sqkm)
6. **Islay** 239 sq mi (620sqkm)
7. **Isle of Man**
   221 sq mi (572sqkm)
8. **Orkney – Mainland**
   202 sq mi (523sqkm)
9. **Arran** 165 sq mis (427sqkm)
10. **Isle of Wight**
    147 sq mi (381sqkm)

★ King's Cave

This huge cave is said to have been a refuge in 1307 for Robert the Bruce en route from Ireland to the Scottish mainland. Here, so legend relates, the king watched a spider's repeated attempts to build a web, and from it drew the determination never to cease in his struggles against the English. Of equal interest is its geological significance, having been created when isostatic uplift brought about by the melting of glaciers resulted in a raised beach, effectively elevating what was previously a coastal feature.

★ Uisgebeatha

Meaning the 'Water of Life', *uisgebeatha* (pronounced oosh-keh bay-ah, with many variations) was the name used by Irish monks during the Middle Ages for distilled alcohol. A distillery at Lochranza began production around 1995, close to Loch na Davie in Gleann Easan Biorach to the south. A second island distillery was opened in 2019 at Laggs on the south coast (NR 946216). Both are passed by the Arran Coastal Way, and both are open to the public for visits and tastings (www.arranwhisky.com).

This is a challenging and rewarding circling of the island, often described as 'Scotland in Miniature'

★ Machrie Moor Stone Circles

A short way inland from the settlement of Tormore are six stone circles (NR 909324); some formed from granite boulders, others from tall red sandstone pillars. There are several hut circles here, too, distinguished as low rings of turf-covered stone.

Borders Abbeys Way ⬡

Making use of riverside paths, tracks, forest rides, farm fields, country lanes, old railway lines and old drove roads, the Borders Abbeys Way is a circular route linking the historic border towns and villages of Jedburgh, Denholm, Hawick, Selkirk, Melrose, St Boswells and Kelso. The Way connects the ruined Borders abbeys (established by David I of Scotland, 1124–1153) at Kelso, Jedburgh, Melrose and Dryburgh, homes to the monks who lived there between the 12th and, 16th centuries. For good measure, the route passes close to Abbotsford House, the home of Sir Walter Scott (see page 201). Opened in 2006, the Way intercepts four more of Scotland's Great Trails: the Cross Borders Drove Road, the Romans and Reivers Route, St Cuthbert's Way and the Southern Upland Way (page 236), which offer even more opportunity to lose oneself in the lush landscapes of the Scottish Borders region.

Lowland farmland, meadows and pastures feature throughout the route and provide an agreeable opportunity to spend time in an active rural landscape and to observe flora and fauna. There is particular riparian delight as the Way leads you beside Jed Water and the rivers Teviot and Tweed, as well as crossing the Ale Water near, Ashkirk and the Rule Water at Bedrule. Riverside trees include alder and willow, around which you will also find plentiful aromatic ramsons (wild garlic) and the bright yellow marsh marigold.

Nor is the Way committed exclusively to low-level pathways. There are several crossings of high ground, including Black Law, Drinkstone Hill, Wollrig and between Selkirk Hill and the outskirts of Melrose, all of which reward the modest effort needed with inspiring views of rippling landscapes. Woodland appears in abundance and features Sitka spruce, Scots pine and larch in forestry plantations, along with small stands of rowan, cherry and oak. Native and semi-natural woodland – oak, ash and alder – put in appearances throughout the route, and provide shelter for roe deer, foxes and badgers, as well as wood sorrel (an ancient woodland indicator species), campion and primrose.

But it is with abbeys that the Way is primarily concerned. King David was one of medieval Scotland's great monastic patrons, founding more than a dozen new monasteries, notably establishing Selkirk Abbey in c.1119 (later moved to Kelso); Melrose Abbey, 1136; Jedburgh Abbey, 1138; and Dryburgh Abbey in 1150. All of these are visited by the Way. Not only were they an expression of the king's piety, but through their influence functioned to transform Scottish society.

AMAZING BUT TRUE ...

Despite centuries of cross-border strife and conflict, the abbey at Kelso, around which the ancient town has grown, became the wealthiest monastery in Scotland. In 1547, English forces acting upon the orders of Henry VIII largely destroyed the abbey and following the Reformation in 1560, it fell derelict, with much of the stone plundered for reuse in the town's buildings.

Melrose Abbey

The Borders Abbeys Way has been completed in under 24 hours, but lesser mortals will find that a five-day itinerary imposes no greater day walk than (17¾ miles/28.5km).

5 days

Start	Melrose	
Day 1	Kelso	17¾ mi / 28.5km
Day 2	Jedburgh	13½ mi / 21.5km
Day 3	Hawick	13 mi / 20.75km
Day 4	Selkirk	12½ mi / 20km
Day 5	Melrose	10½ mi / 17km

FACTS AND FIGURES

START / FINISH Melrose, Scottish Borders (NT 547339)

DISTANCE 68 miles (109km)

HEIGHT GAIN 6,595 feet (2,010m)

DIFFICULTY RATING ◆◆

IS IT FOR ME? Mostly a low-level route but it does include some rough moorland walking; well served with accommodation and public transport.

PRACTICALITIES

GETTING THERE AND BACK Melrose is accessible from Edinburgh Waverley to the Borders Railway terminus at Tweedbank (NT 522349), and the route is well provided for throughout by buses operated by several providers.

GETTING AROUND Because of the good bus links between them, it is possible to do the entire route from one base. By car it's even easier: drive to a start point, take the walk at a leisurely pace, and then take a bus back to your day's start.

ACCOMMODATION There is a wide range of accommodation in all the towns and villages visited en route, although some are closed outside the main tourist season. There are several camping options, both at commercial and at free campsites (i.e. with basic or no facilities). Wild camping is legal in Scotland subject to the Scottish Outdoor Access Code.

WEBSITES
www.scotborders.gov.uk/ bordersabbeysway
www.bordersabbeysway.com

MAPS

OS Explorer
OL16, 331, 338, 339.
OS Landranger
73, 74, 79, 80.

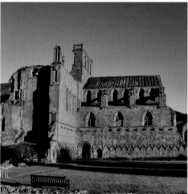

This page (clockwise): Melrose Abbey; Dryburgh Abbey; Jedburgh Abbey; Kelso Abbey.

★ Rhymer's Stone

South-east of Melrose stands the Rhymer's Stone (NT 565335), erected in 1929 by the Melrose Literary Society to mark the spot on which the fabled Eildon Tree once grew. Under this tree, Sir Thomas de Ercildoun, better known as Thomas the Rhymer or Thomas Learmont, a Scottish laird with a reputation as a prophet, took a fateful nap while out hunting. He was awakened by the Queen of Elfland, whom he kissed and then spent seven years with in the Land of the Elves before returning having acquired the gift of prophesy ... as well, it is said, the inability to tell a lie. The man went on to predict several key events in Scotland's history: the death of King Alexander III in 1296; the succession of Robert the Bruce; the defeats at Flodden in 1513 and of Mary, Queen of Scots' forces at the Battle of Pinkie in 1567; and the Union of the Crowns in 1603.

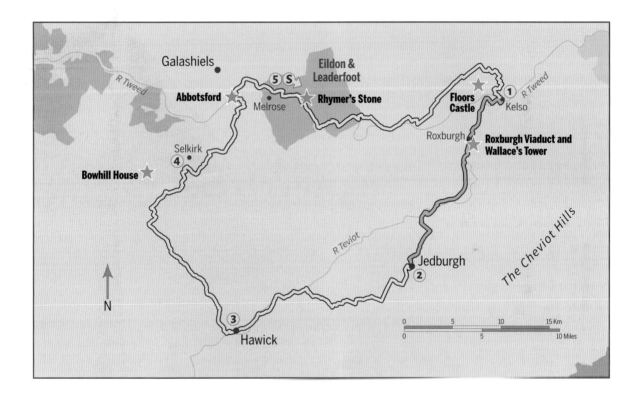

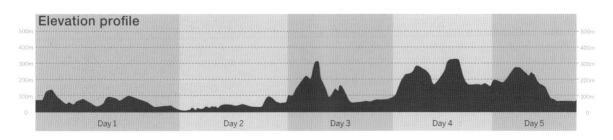

Elevation profile

KELSO TO JEDBURGH

(13½ miles/21.5km)

The stretch of the Way between Kelso and Jedburgh is relatively easy, largely following the course of the River Teviot but concluding with a gentle climb along the Roman road, Dere Street, built by Agricola in the 1st century. There is a regular bus service between the two towns. Kelso's abbey was the first of King David's to be built and is closely linked with the town, which has a cobbled centre, several fine buildings and a square that was once used as a cattle market.

Soon after leaving Kelso, the Way encounters the remains of Roxburgh Castle, one of the most important strongholds in Scotland and one of the four principal Royal burghs in Scotland alongside Edinburgh, Stirling and Berwick. For some distance then, the Way follows the bank of the Teviot, passing beneath Roxburgh viaduct (see opposite) and running on to join an old railway track.

There is much that is relaxing and pleasing about this stretch: one of a number of caves along the Teviot is said to have served as a stable for Bonnie Prince Charlie's horses during the Jacobite rebellion of 1745. Near Nisbet, the Way abandons the old railway line, and does its best to stay faithful to the river as far as Jedfoot Bridge, from where it rises gently before finally dropping into Jedburgh.

★ Bowhill House

A little off-route to the west of Selkirk, Bowhill House (NT 425277), built in 1708, is one of the homes of the Duke of Buccleuch. Today, it houses one of the world's greatest private art collections, featuring works by Canaletto, Gainsborough and Reynolds. The house sits at the heart of a huge woodland, Ettrick Forest, that once covered all the surrounding hills, valleys and riversides. In 1322, King Robert the Bruce gave it to the Scott clan, the ancestors of today's Buccleuch family, in recognition of their loyalty.

One of a number of caves along the Teviot is said to have served as a stable for Bonnie Prince Charlie's horses

★ Floors Castle

Just outside Kelso, Floors Castle (NT 711346) is the largest inhabited castle in Scotland, home to the 11th Duke of Roxburgh, and built for the 1st Duke in 1721. In spite of its name, it is less of a fortress than a country house, albeit a large one. The garden is listed among the most significant in Scotland, and is open to the public. The castle was a film location for the 1984 movie *Greystoke: The Legend of Tarzan, Lord of the Apes.*

★ Roxburgh Viaduct and Wallace's Tower

Built in 1847 by the North British Railway, the 13-arch Roxburgh viaduct is typical of Victorian imagination and engineering. It crosses the river Teviot and is unusual in its construction, being built on a curve. A pedestrian suspension bridge hanging from one side allows residents of Heiton to get to Roxburgh. The remains of Wallace's Tower, a 16th-century tower-house (NT 700304), stand in a field north-west of the disused Roxburgh viaduct. The tower is thought to have been founded by Walter Ker of Cessford, and has no apparent connection with the legendary William Wallace.

★ Abbotsford

On the south bank of the River Tweed, Abbotsford (NT 508342) was the home of the novelist and poet, Walter Scott, and was occupied by his descendants until 2004. The house is a prime example of 19th-century Scottish Baronial style, and remains a key site in the history of European Romanticism.

FIVE QUOTES BY SIR WALTER SCOTT

1 *Oh, what a tangled web we weave ... when first we practice to deceive.*

2 *Love rules the court, the camp, the grove, and men below, and the saints above, for love is heaven, and heaven is love.*

3 *Blessed be his name, who hath appointed the quiet night to follow the busy day, and the calm sleep to refresh the wearied limbs and to compose the troubled spirit.*

4 *When true friends meet in adverse hour; 'Tis like a sunbeam through a shower. A watery way an instant seen, The darkly closing clouds between.*

5 *The seat of the Celtic Muse is in the mist of the secret and solitary hill, and her voice in the murmur of the mountain stream.*

Fife Coastal Path ◊

Tying into one walk many of Scotland's former fishing villages and the so-called home of golf, the university town of St Andrews, the Fife Coastal Path links the mighty estuaries of the Tay and the Forth. Along the way there are miles of award-winning sandy beaches, woodlands and nature reserves; there is much to please industrial archaeologists and historians, too, from the remains of the many coal mines that once populated central Fife to castles, and Pictish and prehistoric cave carvings. The path will appeal to all standards of walker, offering something for everyone, from easy, family-friendly stretches to more demanding sections that favour the more experienced walker.

The path, which is managed and maintained by Fife Coast and Countryside Trust, was extended ten years ago to give a complete circuit of the coast from Kincardine to Newburgh, and is consistently waymarked, offering for the most part straightforward walking. Two stretches, between Craig and St Andrews and from Balmerino to Newburgh are unavoidably long, quite remote and more taxing than the rest of the trail. The usual direction of travel is anti-clockwise, to keep the prevailing wind behind you for most of the way.

There is a short optional section between Kincraig Point and Earlsferry, known as the Elie Chain Walk, which should only be used at low tide. With chains fixed to the rocks in often precarious positions, it is described as 'Scotland's Via Ferrata', and it's not for everyone. Thankfully, the main route passes safely above this section.

There is much of interest along the coast, not least the historic Tay Bridge, which first opened in 1878 but suffered a catastrophic collapse only 19 months later, arguably the worst bridge disaster in Britain. A second bridge was opened in 1887 and has remained in use to the present day. Several castles – Aberdour, Macduff's, Pitmilly and Wemyss – appear along the route. Offshore there is a diverse range of wildlife that not infrequently includes porpoise and dolphin, while the Harbourmaster's House in claustrophobic Dysart will intrigue film buffs, having been used as a location in the historical drama, *Outlander*. The three Forth bridges are iconic, but so too is the village of Culross, famed for its many unique historic buildings and with a history said to date from the 6th century.

The Fife Coastal Path is undoubtedly and deservedly one of Scotland's Great Trails, part of Fife's Core Path network and one of central Scotland's most attractive and fascinating treks.

> **AMAZING BUT TRUE ...**
> Elie Ness is made of a volcanic rock called tuff, which comprises blocks of basalt embedded in layers of volcanic ash. These rocks contain rare crystals of garnet, known locally as 'Elie rubies'. Further round the coast, near St Andrews, is a basalt formation called the Rock and Spindle, the radial pattern of columnar jointing on the 'spindle' caused by magma cooling within a pipe-like conduit.

Lady's Tower, Sauchar Point

The Fife Coastal Path can be completed in eight days of fairly straightforward walking.

8 days

Start	Kincardine
Day 1	Limekilns *11 mi / 17.75km*
Day 2	Burntisland *17 mi / 27.5km*
Day 3	Buckhaven *14 mi / 22.5km*
Day 4	Elie *13 mi / 21km*
Day 5	Cambo Sands *16 mi / 15.75km*
Day 6	Leuchars *14 mi / 22.5km*
Day 7	Wormit Bay *16 mi / 15.75km*
Day 8	Newburgh *15 mi / 24.25km*

FACTS AND FIGURES

START Kincardine (NS 930874)

FINISH Newburgh (NO 235186)

DISTANCE 117 miles (187km)

HEIGHT GAIN 8,330 feet (2,540m)

DIFFICULTY RATING ◆◆

IS IT FOR ME? The Firth of Tay length is trickier in terms of terrain, hard to reach by public transport and short on accommodation, otherwise the route is straightforward and well served.

PRACTICALITIES

GETTING THERE AND BACK There are good bus services throughout Fife, although it is difficult to reach the Path between Balmerino and Newburgh by public transport. The section between Kincardine and Kirkcaldy is served by mainline railway.

ACCOMMODATION Hotel and B&B accommodation is plentiful in all locations except from Balmerino to Newburgh, but you are recommended to book early wherever you intend to stay. There are hostels at Anstruther and St Andrews. Wild camping is legally allowed in Scotland if practised responsibly under the Scottish Outdoor Access Code.

WEBSITES
www.scotlandsgreattrails.com
https://fifecoastandcountrysidetrust.co.uk

MAPS

OS Explorer
349, 350, 366, 367, 370, 371, 380.

OS Landranger
59, 65, 66.

★ Culross

Scotland's most complete example of a burgh dating from the 17th and 18th centuries, Culross's white-harled houses line steep, cobbled streets that radiate from the central ochre-coloured palace replete with a period garden. Culross Palace is a late 16th-/early 17th-century merchant's house constructed between 1597 and 1611 by Sir George Bruce, the Laird of Carnock and a successful merchant who had a thriving trade with other Forth ports and across the North Sea.

Seafield Tower, Kirkcaldy

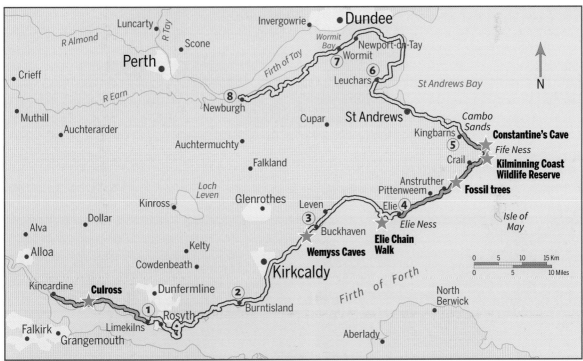

Luncarty

R Almond

R Tay

Scone

Perth

Crieff

R Earn

Muthill

Auchterarder

Auchtermuchty

Newburgh (8)

Cupar

Falkland

Loch Leven

Kinross

Glenrothes

Alva

Dollar

Alloa

Kelty

Cowdenbeath

Kincardine

Culross

Dunfermline

Limekilns

Rosyth

(1)

Falkirk

Grangemouth

Invergowrie

Dundee

Wormit Bay

Newport-on-Tay

Firth of Tay

Wormit (7)

Leuchars (6)

St Andrews Bay

St Andrews

Cambo Sands

Kingbarns

Constantine's Cave

Fife Ness

Crail

(5)

Kilminning Coast Wildlife Reserve

Anstruther

Pittenweem

Fossil trees

Leven (3)

Elie (4)

Buckhaven

Elie Ness

Wemyss Caves

Elie Chain Walk

Kirkcaldy

Burntisland (2)

Firth of Forth

North Berwick

Aberlady

Isle of May

N

0   5   10   15 Km
0   5   10 Miles

Elevation profile

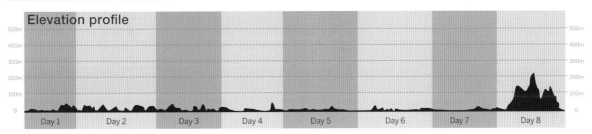

500m								500m
400m								400m
300m								300m
200m								200m
100m								100m
0								0

Day 1 | Day 2 | Day 3 | Day 4 | Day 5 | Day 6 | Day 7 | Day 8

Best section for
Weekends/Short breaks

ELIE TO KINGBARNS (CAMBO SANDS)
(16 miles/25.75km)

This stretch turns the corner of Fife at its most easterly point, and is full of wildlife, geological and historical interest. The Path passes several time-worn fishing villages and, in its early stages, the sites of two ancient castles, Ardross and Newark. Even before reaching the first of these it is worth deviating to Sauchar Point and Lady's Tower, built for

Lady Janet Anstruther as a summer house in the 1760s; the view is inspiring. Beyond the castles, a high tide variant may be brought into play, before pressing on to St Monan's and its 14th- century church. Pittenweem is Fife's only working fishing harbour, and the site of a cave said to have been used by St Fillan in the 7th century. The Path around Fife Ness is narrower and more irregular, and passes through the Kilminning Coast Wildlife Reserve (see below), before dashing north-westwards to the expanse of Cambo Sands.

Devil's cave

★ Constantine's Caves

This natural cave (NO 632101) at Fife Ness contains occupation deposits dating from the Iron Age into the 2nd century, and was later used as an Early Christian chapel or hermitage. The eponymous name conventionally associated with the cave is that of Constantine II, King of Alba (903-943).

★ Elie Chain Walk

A unique feature of the Fife coast, the Elie Chain Walk (NT 466997) is a section of the cliff west of Elie village towards Kincraig Point and Shell Bay, where chains are built into the cliff. This is a challenging part of the coastline, a unique scramble across hazardous close-water terrain, but does not form part of the Fife Coastal Path – unless you want it to (see www.fife.gov.uk).

MAPS Day-walk taster

OS Explorer
367, Dunfermline, Kirkcaldy & Glenrothes South, Methil & Culross.

OS Landranger
65, Falkirk & Linlithgow, Dunfermline.

★ Kilminning Coast Wildlife Reserve

The stretch of coastline embraced within the wildlife reserve at Kilminning (NO 634091) has species-rich grassland, coastal scrub and salt marsh, amid which the northern marsh orchid flourishes alongside flocks of linnets and the more solitary stonechat and whitethroat.

KINCARDINE TO LIMEKILNS
(11 miles/17.75km)

Start as you mean to go on: the themes of heritage, natural history and iconic bridges are the leitmotif on this opening stage of the walk. The dramatically appealing village of Culross and its abbey and palace (see page 204) come quite early. Soon after Culross, the Torry Bay Nature Reserve and its rare salt marsh plants and wildlife can occasion delay. At the end of the day, the village of Limekilns is an intriguing terminus, throughout its history involved in shipbuilding and soap manufacture; the oldest building, the King's Cellar, dates from the 16th century.

★ Fossil trees

Observant walkers may well notice the petrified trunks of primitive tree ferns (NO 590050) from the Carboniferous era on the shore just off the Path at Caiplie farm, between Anstruther and Crail.

★ Wemyss Caves

Located near the village of East Wemyss, these caves, thought to have been the product of wave action, are historically important for their many wall inscriptions. The earliest are thought to date from the Bronze Age, though the majority are Pictish, making this the most potent concentration of Pictish carvings in Britain. The caves featured in the archaeological television programme, *Time Team*, ITV's *Off the Beaten Track* and in Scottish crime author, Val McDermid's novel, *A Darker Domain*.

THE HOME OF GOLF

To many, the town of St Andrews is synonymous with golf because it is the home of the game's ruling authority, the Royal and Ancient Club. The Old Course at St Andrews is considered to be the oldest and most iconic of golf courses, its illustrious history extending back, it is claimed, almost 600 years. It was in 1552 that Archbishop Hamilton's charter formally granted the right of locals to play golf on the links at St Andrews. The Open has been held at St Andrews a record 29 times, the first being in 1873. The infamous Road Hole, the par-4 17th, is considered one of the hardest to play in the world, while the fairway on the ensuing closing hole is the widest in golf. The popularity of the game and of the Open Championship is such that St Andrews holds the record attendance, when 239,000 spectators watched the tournament in 2000.Ma,

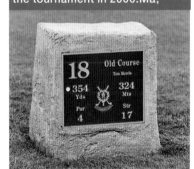

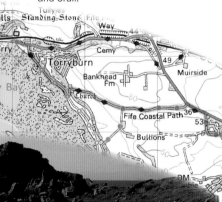

Great Glen Way

There is a remarkable directness about the Great Glen Way, not least because the Great Glen is itself an arrow-straight line linking Fort William at the head of Loch Linnhe with Inverness on the edge of the Moray Firth. The entire route of this coast-to-coast walk passes through a landscape of extravagant, wild beauty, flanked as it is by high, heather-rich hills and open moors and waterways. Mostly an uncomplicated low-level walk, the trail pursues tracks, forest trails, quiet road and hill paths, often close to the Caledonian Canal or running beside the great lochs of Loch Lochy, Loch Oich and Loch Ness.

The 'great glen' in question follows a geological fault known as the Great Glen Fault, a gift of tectonic misbehaviour that bisects the Highlands into the Grampian Mountains to the south-east and the North-West Highlands. The fault is much greater than the stretch followed by this trail, extending south-west through Loch Linnhe and the Firth of Lorne and on into north-western Ireland. In the opposite direction, linking in with other fault lines, it continues all the way to Shetland. The fault is mostly inactive today, although minor tremors have been recorded over the last 150 years. Not surprisingly, the glen has been an important thoroughfare for centuries, and was particularly strategically important during the times of the Jacobite rebellions.

Heading out from Fort William, the first stages of the Great Glen Way are not unduly demanding and, of necessity, loop round the village of Caol before reaching the Caledonian Canal. Thereafter it follows this man-made stretch of water to the southern edge of Loch Lochy. There is a long, delightful romp through the South Laggan forest to Laggan Locks where the route divides – the original line takes a military road along the eastern flank of Loch Oich, while a higher variant finds a way to Invergarry and on above the loch as far as Aberchalder, where the two recombine. Beyond Fort Augustus, there are again high- and low-level options, the higher route being favoured until it descends to Invermoriston.

Ahead lies Loch Ness, of monstrous fame; it is best viewed from the high-level route, and while time spent in search of ancient monsters is permitted, it is perhaps not the best use of time on such a fine trail that concludes, faithful to the end to the Caledonian Canal, at the city of Inverness. Given its simplicity, the Great Glen Way could be of interest to walkers as a continuation of the West Highland Way (page 250), which it meets at Fort William.

AMAZING BUT TRUE ...

At Dores (pronounced 'doors') on the north-eastern edge of Loch Ness, across the loch from the Great Glen Way, the long gravel beach is a popular tourist spot. It is also the base for Steve Feltham, the 'Nessie Hunter', who has been maintaining his vigil over the loch for monster sightings since 1991. www.nessiehunter.co.uk

Loch Linnhe

The Great Glen Way can be completed comfortably in six or seven days, a mix of short days and one long day. North of Fort Augustus there are options to take high- and low-level variants onward towards Invermoriston and Drumnadrochit.

	6 days		7 days	
Start	Fort William		Fort William	
Day 1	Gairlochy	10½ mi / 17km	Gairlochy	10½ mi / 17km
Day 2	North Laggan	14¼ mi / 22.75km	North Laggan	14¼ mi / 22.75km
Day 3	Fort Augustus	9½ mi / 15.25km	Fort Augustus	9½ mi / 15.25km
Day 4	Invermoriston	9¼ mi / 14.75km	Invermoriston	9¼ mi / 14.75km
Day 5	Drumnadrochit 14¼ mi / 23km		Drumnadrochit 14¼ mi / 23km	
Day 6	Inverness	19¾ mi / 31.75km	Blackfold	12¼ mi / 19.75km
Day 7			Inverness	7½ mi / 12km

FACTS AND FIGURES

START The Old Fort, Fort William (NN 104742)

FINISH Inverness (NH 666448)

DISTANCE 78 miles (125km)

HEIGHT GAIN 7,920 feet (2,415m)

DIFFICULTY RATING ♦♦

IS IT FOR ME? A relatively undemanding, low-level route with, on two stages, higher-level forest trail alternatives; reasonable public transport connections and accommodation options.

★ Urquhart Castle

On Strone Point, near Drumnadrochit, Urquhart Castle (NH 530285) was captured in 1296 by King Edward I of England in an invasion that marked the beginning of the Wars of Scottish Independence. The castle was ultimately retaken by Robert the Bruce in 1307, and became a Royal castle. Once renowned as one of Scotland's largest castles, Urquhart saw constant conflict during its 500 years as a medieval fortress.

★ Well of the Seven Heads

As grisly as it sounds, by the side of the A82, just north of the Laggan crossing, Tobar nan Crean (Well of the Seven Heads) is a monument erected in 1812, close by an ancient well. Its gory carving is that of a hand holding a dagger and seven severed heads, and it commemorates an incident that took place in 1665. The well is said to have been the one in which the decapitated heads of seven murderers were washed – they had been killed in revenge for the murder of two of the Keppoch family, members of the powerful MacDonald clan.

GETTING THERE AND BACK Rail services link Glasgow (Queen Street) with Fort William, and Edinburgh with Inverness. There is a bus service between Fort William and Inverness, which stops at settlements along the Great Glen.

ACCOMMODATION There is a good choice of hotel, B&B and guest house accommodation as well as hostels, bunkhouses and wigwams along the trail, although limited in Gairlochy and South Laggan, where Spean Bridge and Invergarry are workable alternatives. Wild camping is legally allowed in Scotland if practised responsibly under the Scottish Outdoor Access Code.

WEBSITE
www.scotlandsgreattrails.com/trail/great-glen-way

MAPS

OS Explorer
OL55, 392, 399, 400, 415, 416, 431.

OS Landranger
26, 34, 35, 41.

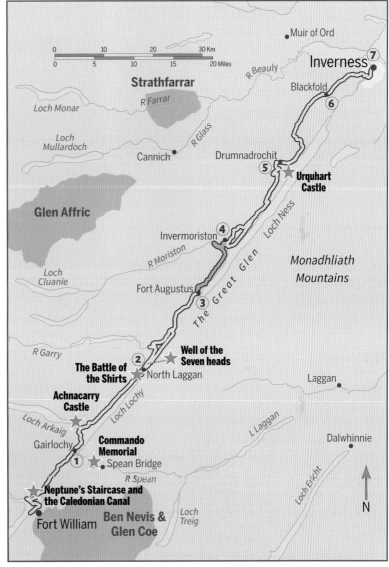

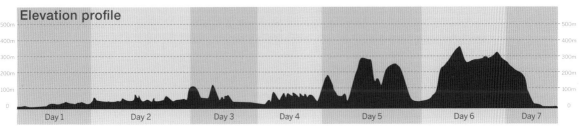

Elevation profile

FORT AUGUSTUS TO INVERMORISTON (HIGH-LEVEL)
(9¼ miles/14.75km)

The high-level option between Fort Augustus and Invermoriston soon heads up into forest. On a good, dry trail it traverses rugged moorland slopes and waterfalls, especially those thrown down by the Allt na Criche. The high point is achieved on Carn an Doire Mhoir, from where there are stunning views of Loch Ness. Several more burns are passed en route to Portclair Burn, after which the trail drops back into the forest and rejoins the low-level option, sidling along above the River Moriston before giving in and heading for the village.

★ Commando Memorial

Off-route via Gairlochy, the Commando Memorial above Spean Bridge is dedicated to the British Commando Forces raised during the Second World War. It is one of Scotland's most-renowned monuments, and overlooks the training areas established in 1942 at Achnacarry Castle. The memorial is unavoidable should anyone be branching out from Gairlochy for overnight accommodation in Spean Bridge. What isn't obvious is that there is a fine path from just north-west of the memorial down to and then along the River Spean, which loops round to rejoin the road close to the village.

★ Neptune's Staircase and the Caledonian Canal

At the village of Banavie, north of Fort William, Neptune's Staircase is an amazing feat of engineering that raises the level of the Caledonian Canal by almost 65 feet (20m) over the distance of a quarter of a mile. Built by the man-about-everywhere, Thomas Telford, between 1803 and 1822, at a time when the government was considering means of stemming emigration from the Highlands by providing local employment, this historic work is the longest staircase lock in Britain.

PLACE NAMES

Many of the place names in Scotland are Gaelic in origin, and some of the more common of these are listed here to illustrate the relationship between place names and landscape features.

aber *mouth of loch, river*
abhainn *river*
allt *stream*
auch, ach *field*
bal, bail,
  baile *town,*
  homestead
bàn *white,*
  fair, pale
bealach *hill pass*
beg, beag *small*
ben, beinn *hill*
bhuidhe *yellow*
brae, braigh *upper*
  slope, steepening
breac *speckled*
cairn *pile of*
  stones, often
  marking a summit
cam *crooked*
càrn cairn, cairn-
  shaped hill
caol, kyle *strait*
ceann, ken,
  kin *head*
cil, kil *church, cell*
clach *stone*
clachan *small*
  village
cnoc *hill, knoll,*
  knock
coille, killie *wood*
corrie, coire,
  choire *mountain*
  hollow
craig, creag *cliff,*
  crag
crannog,
  crannag *man-*
  made island
dàl, dail *field, flat*
damh *stag*
dearg *red*
druim, drum *long*
  ridge
dubh, dhu *black,*
  dark
dùn *hill fort*
eas *waterfall*
eilean *island*

eilidh *hind*
eòin, eun *bird*
fionn *white*
fraoch *heather*
gabhar, ghabhar,
  gobhar *goat*
garbh *rough*
geal *white*
ghlas, glas *grey*
gleann,
  glen *narrow,*
  valley
gorm *blue, green*
inbhir,
  inver *confluence*
inch, inis,
  innis *island,*
  meadow by river
lag, laggan *hollow*
làrach *old site*
làirig *pass*
leac *slab*
liath *grey*
loch *lake*
lochan *small loch*
màm *pass, rise*
maol *bald-*
  shaped top
monadh *upland,*
  moor
mór, mor(e) *big*
odhar, odhair *dun-*
  coloured
rhu, rubha *point*
ruadh *red, brown*
sgòr, sgòrr,
  sgùrr *pointed*
sron *nose*
stob *pointed*
strath *valley*
  (broader
  than glen)
tarsuinn *traverse,*
  across
tom *hillock*
  (rounded)
tòrr *hillock (more*
  rugged)
tulloch,
  tulach *knoll*
uisge *water, river*

★ The Battle of the Shirts

Said to be named the Battle of the Shirts because it was so hot the combatants removed their chain mail and fought in their long shirts, this Scottish clan conflict took place on 15 July, 1544 in a swampy field at South Laggan. The brutal contest was between John of Moidart, Chief of Clan Ranald, supported by the MacDonalds and Camerons, and Hugh, 3rd Lord Lovat, the MacShimi Chief of Clan Fraser of Lovat. The battle, in which the MacDonalds triumphed, was said to be so bloody that of the 800 fighters involved only a dozen or so survived.

★ Achnacarry Castle

Found on a narrow neck of land between Loch Lochy and Loch Arkaig, Achnacarry Castle was burned to the ground in 1746 after the Battle of Culloden, but rebuilt 50 years later by Donald Cameron, the 22nd Chief of Clan Cameron. The castle and its estate became the Commando Training Depot for the Allied Forces between 1942 and 1945; in all, some 25,000 commandos are said to have completed their training here. There is a clan museum nearby (NN 175877), which is open to the public.

MAPS Day-walk taster

OS Explorer
416, Inverness, Loch Ness & Culloden, Fort Augustus & Drumnadrochit.

OS Landranger
34, Fort Augustus, Glen Roy & Glen Moriston.

John Muir Way

Best known as 'The Father of National Parks' in America, John Muir (1838–1914) was one of the world's most influential conservationists. He was born in the small town of Dunbar, near the mouth of the Firth of Forth, where the rolling Lammermuir Hills formed his southern horizon. This coast-to-coast trail across the heart of Scotland, celebrates his life and work, as it takes in mountains, lochs, canals and coastline from the shores of the Clyde to the North Sea.

The Way, which also accommodates cyclists, traverses the heart of Scotland, exploring places that enshrine the nation's natural, cultural and industrial heritage, and takes in Scotland's first National Park around Loch Lomond and The Trossachs. There is a fine repertoire of scenery and landscapes from upland trails, undulating farmland, canal towpaths, woodlands, beaches, clifftops and country parks.

Once the Clyde and the urbanity of Helensburgh is left behind, the Way enters the southern edges of the Loch Lomond and The Trossachs National Park, with lush green, island-studded views up the loch, hemmed in by the heights of Ben Lomond and the more distant Ben Ime and Ben Vorlich. At Carbeth Loch, the Way briefly greets the West Highland Way (page 250).

There are close encounters with the Antonine Wall, the outer limits of the Roman Empire; and easy-going strolls along peaceful towpaths accompanied by wildlife on the canals. The Forth and Clyde Canal, the Falkirk Wheel, Linlithgow Palace, Blackness Castle, the Forth bridges all draw the walker across Scotland to the coastal scenery of East Lothian and, ultimately, to John Muir's birthplace museum in Dunbar.

Waymarking, which differentiates between walkers and cyclists where their routes diverge or converge, is consistent throughout the route, achieving its highest point in the Kilpatrick Hills (892 feet/272m) near Burncrooks Reservoir. Gradients are mostly undemanding and facilities/towns and villages are well spaced, making this an ideal route for the novice multi-day walker, in spite of its length.

As a route of inspiration, the John Muir Way endeavours to commemorate the spirit of the man who made it his lifelong mission to protect nature and the world's wild places. When you reach the trail's end and the terraced house that was his birthplace, now a visitor centre, it is not difficult to imagine the young boy gazing out of the window, developing escapades of delight that would one day draw him away, far from his home, to raise a cry for conservation years before its time. The trail opened in 2014 to commemorate the 100th anniversary of John Muir's death.

AMAZING BUT TRUE ...
Evidence of Scotland's volcanic past is clearly visible along the John Muir Way as it passes the foot of two remarkable landmarks, Arthur's Seat in Edinburgh (823 feet/251m) and North Berwick Law (613 feet/187m). These are both cores of ancient volcanoes, and both make supreme viewpoints with short but steep detours to their respective summits. Islands in the Firth of Forth, such as Inchkeith and Bass Rock, are also remnant volcanic plugs.

Falkirk Wheel

The John Muir Way can be comfortably completed in ten days, and has plenty of places at which the walk can be fragmented, to be completed in discontinuous day-walk stages.

10 days

Start	Helensburgh
Day 1	Balloch 9 mi / 14.5km
Day 2	Strathblane 18½ mi / 29.5km
Day 3	Kilsyth 13 mi / 20.75km
Day 4	Falkirk 13 mi / 20.75km
Day 5	Linlithgow 8½ mi / 13.5km
Day 6	South Queensferry 14 mi / 22.5km
Day 7	Edinburgh 15½ mi / 24.75km
Day 8	Prestonpans 10 mi / 16km
Day 9	North Berwick 16½ mi / 26.5km
Day 10	Dunbar 15 mi / 24km

FACTS AND FIGURES

START Helensburgh, Argyll and Bute (NS 294822)

FINISH Dunbar, East Lothian (NT 678790)

DISTANCE 134 miles (215km)

HEIGHT GAIN 8,855 feet (2,700m)

DIFFICULTY RATING ♦♦

IS IT FOR ME? Covering a diverse mix of terrain, the route passes through countryside, town and along the coast, generally with good public transport links and a range of accommodation.

MAPS

OS Explorer
OL38, 342, 348, 349, 350, 351, 367.

OS Landranger
56, 63, 64, 65, 66, 67.

PRACTICALITIES

GETTING THERE AND BACK
Public transport is good across Scotland's central belt, although is at its most sparse in the west. Trains serve Helensburgh from Glasgow Queen Street; those from Edinburgh Waverley operate out to Dunbar. Where rail stations are fewer, bus services plug the gap.

ACCOMMODATION
There is no shortage of accommodation along the John Muir Way from luxury nights in castles, B&Bs, hotels and inns to places to pitch a tent. But there are no hostels or bunkhouses outside Edinburgh. Wild camping is permitted in Scotland, but in accordance with the Scottish Access Code. Seasonal byelaws apply in the Loch Lomond and Trossachs National Park which mean that camping in certain areas of the National Park is permitted only within campsites or with a camping permit (see the National Park website, below).

WEBSITES
https://johnmuirway.org
www.lochlomond-trossachs.org

★ Carbeth Huts

Near Carbeth Loch are the Carbeth Huts (NS 525791), the home of the most famous Scottish hutting community. Originally it was formed when the landowner granted camping rights so that soldiers returning from the First World War could enjoy the healthy air and activities of the countryside. During the Second World War, the huts housed evacuees from bombed-out homes. Today, most of the huts are used as holiday cottages.

★ Balloch Castle Country Park

On the south-eastern shores of Loch Lomond, the Balloch Castle Country Park developed as a park from a 19th-century private estate, and comprises semi-natural and ornamental woodland, parkland, gardens, meadows and loch shoreline. Pass this way in July, and you may get roped into the Loch Lomond Highland Games.

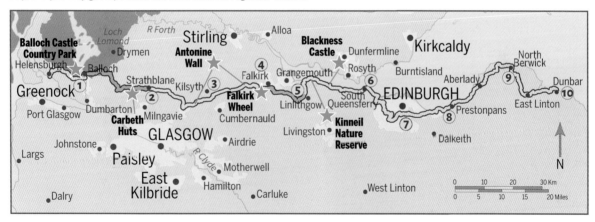

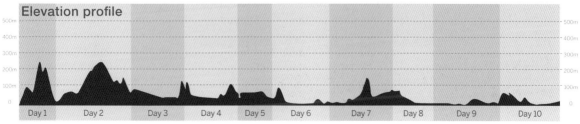

BALLOCH TO STRATHBLANE
(18½ miles/29.5km)

Beauty begins this stretch, with a walk through Balloch Castle Country Park, adorned by views from the shores of Loch Lomond. Onward, the trail leads through the Kilpatrick Hills, crossing the highest point of the entire route and the most remote stretch of the route, providing an invigorating upland experience regaled by the scents and sounds of wild places especially around the Burncrooks Reservoir. At Carbeth the route intercepts the West Highland Way on its first stage north to Fort William, and almost in the shadow of the Campsie Fells, before tumbling on easily to Strathblane.

Antonine Wall

★ Antonine Wall

In several places, the John Muir Way encounters the Roman Antonine Wall, a turf fortification on stone foundations representing the northernmost frontier of the Roman Empire, although there were several outposts further north. Begun in the year 142, the wall took 12 years to complete and was protected by 16 forts, but it was occupied by Roman forces for only eight years before they retreated south to the more substantial Hadrian's Wall. What sections remain are in the care of Historic Environment Scotland and are part of the 'Frontiers of the Roman Empire' World Heritage Site.

Opposite page (top left): Kirkpatrick Hills; **(top right):** John Muir's birthplace, Dunbar.
Opposite page Ducks (clockwise): Shelduck, teal, wigeon, pintail.

★ Falkirk Wheel

This rotating boat lift (NS 852801) which links the Forth and Clyde and Union Canals might well have been a giant see-saw, an overhead monorail, tilting tanks or even rolling eggs, such were the concepts put forward for dealing with the need to connect the two canals (see www.scottishcanals.co.uk/falkirk-wheel).

Gradients are mostly undemanding and facilities/towns and villages are well spaced, making this an ideal route for the novice multi-day walker, in spite of its length

★ Kinneil Nature Reserve

This important nature reserve sits on the site of the former Kinneil Colliery and is part of the Firth of Forth Special Protected Area. It is especially important for over-wintering wildfowl and waders, such as shelduck, wigeon, teal, goldeneye and pintail.

FALKIRK TO LINLITHGOW
(8½ miles/13.5km)

This is a relatively simple stretch of the trail, following the Union Canal towpath once beyond Callendar Park, and therefore an ideal taster. In the park, Callendar House was originally a 14th-century tower house, which has since been given a French Renaissance chateau-style makeover, and is today one of the most important historic houses in the area having hosted Mary Queen of Scots, Oliver Cromwell, Bonnie Prince Charlie and Queen Victoria.

Back on the canal, the towpath crosses the huge Avon Aqueduct, the longest and tallest aqueduct in Scotland, surpassed in Britain only by the Pontcysyllte Viaduct on Offa's Dyke Path (page 286) in Wales. The trail opts to bypass Linlithgow and head north instead for another section of the Antonine Wall and the coast at Bo'ness, but as a day's end there can be no better conclusion than taking in the light and shade of lovely Linlithgow Loch.

★ Blackness Castle

A 15th-century fortress in a commanding position jutting out into the firth, Blackness Castle (NT 055802) probably stands on the site of an earlier castle; in time it became the avant-garde of contemporary artillery fortifications. In spite of its strength, it was overwhelmed in 1650 by the forces of Oliver Cromwell. It is now a Scheduled Ancient Monument in the care of Historic Environment Scotland.

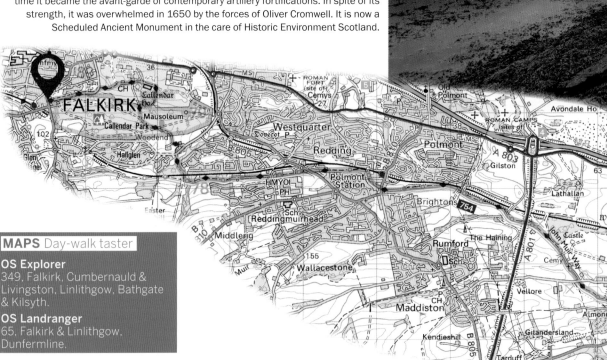

MAPS Day-walk taster

OS Explorer
349, Falkirk, Cumbernauld & Livingston, Linlithgow, Bathgate & Kilsyth.

OS Landranger
65, Falkirk & Linlithgow, Dunfermline.

FIVE QUOTES BY JOHN MUIR

John Muir was a prolific walker, writer, naturalist and environmental philosopher who made many noteworthy remarks on travelling and finding a sense of wellbeing in nature. Here are five John Muir quotations:

1 *In every walk with nature one receives far more than he seeks.*
2 *When one tugs at a single thing in nature, he finds it attached to the rest of the world.*
3 *Everybody needs beauty ... places to play in and pray in where nature may heal and cheer and give strength to the body and soul alike.*
4 *Climb the mountains and get their good tidings, nature's peace will flow into you as sunshine flows into trees. The winds will blow their own freshness into you and the storms their energy, while cares will drop off like autumn leaves.*
5 *Going to the mountains is going home.*

Forth and Clyde Canal

WALK 28

Loch Lomond and Cowal Way ⬦

Formerly known simply as the Cowal Way, the trail enjoys an abundance of the most scenic walking country in the central part of Scotland, extending from Portavadie, ferry port for Kintyre in the south-west, to Inveruglas on the 'bonnie' banks of Loch Lomond. The route traverses forestry land, slips by waterfalls, heads along the shore of sea-lochs and over hill passes – rugged, earthy countryside rich in wildlife.

The Cowal peninsula lies west of Glasgow and offers up a menu of moorland, deep glens and sea lochs that typically characterise the sea-fashioned west coast of Scotland. From Portavadie, the Way strikes across the peninsula to Tighnabruaich on the Kyles of Bute, following the shoreline of Loch Riddon/Ruel and heading through tranquil scenery north with the River Ruel and into Strath nan Lub to Strachur. Striking east, the Way heads for Lochgoilhead, then tackles high ground into the Ardgartan Forest to Arrochar, a strung-out village directly below the rugged crags of Ben Arthur, better known as The Cobbler. Now, just a short stretch through Glen Loin awaits before crossing Inveruglas Water to reach the end of the trail.

Given the proximity of the urban sprawl of Glasgow and its industrious past, the Way has a richness of history and heritage, and wildlife, too. Half of the Way lies within the Loch Lomond and The Trossachs National Park. Enjoying fine views over Bute and the Firth of Clyde, the Way engages surprisingly remote and rugged countryside, a mix of woodland and waterside walking and some quiet minor roads. The northern section of the Way has three significant hill climbs: across Sròn Criche (985 feet/300m); Bealach an Lochain (1,148 feet/350m); and north of Cnoc Coinnich (1,607 feet/490m). The route is well waymarked throughout, but is robust and walkers must contend with several exposed stretches.

Walkers wanting to lose themselves along Scotland's trails will find that a ferry from Portavadie to Kintyre will link with the enthralling Kintyre Way, while a trip on the seasonal waterbus across Loch Lomond from Inveruglas to Inversnaid will connect with the ever-popular West Highland Way (page 250), north to Fort William and onward via the Great Glen Way (page 208) to Inverness – expect to be gone for some time.

As much as anything else, on the Way it is the range of interest and terrain that especially pleases – from wildlife sightings, through lands steeped in clan history and prehistoric sites to the peace and isolation that are the essence and joy of multi-day walks. And this is all crammed into such a short distance – 'Scotland in 57 miles', as they say.

> **AMAZING BUT TRUE ...**
> The old right of way followed by the Cowal Way between Millhouse and the quayside at Kames was used to transport gunpowder from its site of manufacture to its point of shipping. This route was known as the 'Green Road' because a top layer of turf was put on the surface to avoid any sparks caused by horses' shoes hitting the road stone. At the peak of production, some 70 cart loads of gunpowder were hauled along the road daily.

Kyles of Bute

The Loch Lomond and Cowal Way falls into six distinct day stages, none greater than 16 miles (25.75km); it can also be readily accomplished in five days; strong walkers could do it in less, but should not underestimate the ruggedness of the terrain.

	5 days	6 days
Start	Portavadie	Portavadie
Day 1	Tighnabruaich 6¼ mi / 10km	Tighnabruaich 6¼ mi / 10km
Day 2	Glendaruel 11¼ mi / 18km	Glendaruel 11¼ mi / 18km
Day 3	Strachur 16 mi / 25.75km	Strachur 16 mi / 25.75km
Day 4	Lochgoilhead 8¾ mi / 14km	Lochgoilhead 8¾ mi / 14km
Day 5	Inveruglas 15 mi / 24km	Arrochar 10 mi / 16.25km
Day 6		Inveruglas 5 mi / 7.75km

FACTS AND FIGURES

START Portavadie, Loch Fyne, Argyll and Bute (NR 929698)

FINISH Inveruglas, Argyll and Bute (NN 322099)

DISTANCE 57 miles (92km)

HEIGHT GAIN 8,595 feet (2,620m)

DIFFICULTY RATING ◆◆◆

IS IT FOR ME? There's a mix of terrain, some surprisingly rugged, not to be underestimated, and forward planning is needed to make the best of public transport and accommodation options.

MAPS

OS Explorer
OL37, OL39, 362.
OS Landranger
55, 56, 62.

★ Asgog Castle

Once home to Clan Lamont, Asgog Castle (NR 946704), is a ruinous 15th-century tower house. It was besieged by the Campbells during the Civil Wars in 1646 who, after a month-long siege, massacred the garrison and burned the castle down.

PRACTICALITIES

GETTING THERE AND BACK
There is a bus service from Dunoon that serves Tighnabruaich and Portavadie, and infrequent links along the A886 through Glendaruel. Dunoon on the eastern side of the peninsula can be reached via ferry across the Clyde, linking with trains and buses to Glasgow. Inveruglas at the end of the way is on the bus route between Glasgow, Fort William and the north.

GETTING AROUND
Strachur has bus links to Dunoon, Inveraray and Lochgoilhead. Arrochar shares a rail station with nearby Tarbet on Loch Lomond, and is also accessible by bus.

ACCOMMODATION
There is a good choice of hotels, B&Bs, caravan and campsites and areas for wild camping: Portavadie, Tighnabruaich, Glendaruel, Strachur, Lochgoilhead, Arrochar, Inveruglas. Wild camping is legally permitted in Scotland if practised responsibly and in accordance the Scottish Outdoor Access Code.

WEBSITES
www.lochlomondandcowalway.org
www.scotlandsgreattrails.com/trail/loch-lomond-cowal-way

'Scotland in 57 miles', as they say

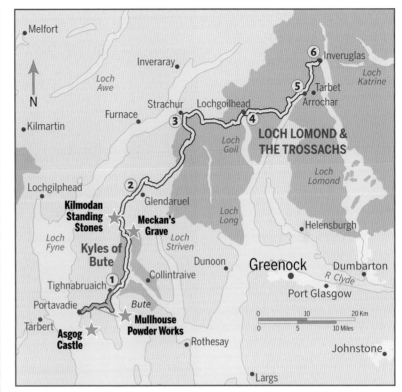

Inveruglas, Loch Lomond

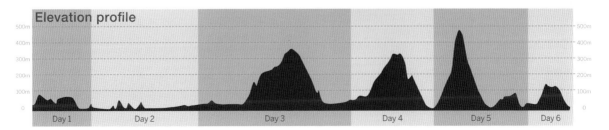

Elevation profile

Day 1 · Day 2 · Day 3 · Day 4 · Day 5 · Day 6

PORTAVADIE TO TIGHNABRUAICH

(6¼ miles/10km)

In spite of its brevity, this first stage of the Way, a gentle climb, provides varied cross-country walking, spanning the southernmost point of the peninsular. There are pleasing views of Loch Fyne and the Kyles of Bute. From Portavadie, the route passes Asgog Loch and its ruined castle, and passes on to the village where gunpowder was manufactured for more than 80 years; a gentle descent leads to the lochside village of Kames before taking the B-road north to Tighnabruaich.

★ Meckan's Grave

At the northern end of Loch Riddon, Meckan's Grave (NS 008807) is said to be that of Meckan, son of Magnus, King of Norway, who was killed in battle at Crudail.

This page (above): Ardgartan; **(left)**: Inverglas; **(right)**: *Waverley* paddle steamer on Loch Lomond.
Opposite page: Loch Goil.

★ Millhouse Powder Works

Arguably an unlikely spot, but Millhouse (NR 957705) is the place where the manufacture of gunpowder began in 1839, continuing until the inter-war years of the 20th century, despite several accidents. The remains of the mill are visible in the woods to the right of the road, as is a memorial to those who lost their lives.

There are pleasing views of Loch Fyne and the Kyles of Bute

★ Kilmodan Standing Stones

In the graveyard of Kilmodan church (NR 994841), built in 1783 and dedicated to the Celtic saint, Modan, are a number of carved stones dating from the 14th and 15th centuries. The church is also notable for having three separate entrances, each leading to its own gallery so that the three local Campbell families could speak to God without having to speak to one another.

THE LURE OF THE COBBLER

Around Arrochar, the surrounding mountainous upland has long been known as the 'Arrochar Alps'. The alpine-like shape of Ben Arthur, now seldom referred to by this name, was christened 'The Cobbler' by Dorothy Wordsworth when she and William passed by in 1803, describing the summit rocks to be 'like castles or watchtowers'. As soon as the railways provided easy access, The Cobbler was adopted by many Glaswegians as a favourite excursion, and the peak has attracted rock climbers and ramblers ever since.

Professor George Ramsay of the University of Glasgow founded Scotland's first climbing club, The Cobbler Club, in 1866. It had just three members, but by 1889, mountaineering in Scotland was becoming a popular pastime, attracting experienced Alpinists, and the Scottish Mountaineering Club was formed. William Naismith, who formulated Naismith's Rule as a means of estimating the time needed to complete a hill walk, instigated the idea for the club. Among its original members was Hugh Munro, author of the list of all Scotland's 3,000-foot peaks, ever since known as Munros.

Rob Roy Way

Branded as Scotland's most notorious outlaw-cum-folk hero, Rob Roy MacGregor (1671–1734) was born at Glengyle near Loch Katrine, and died at Inverlochlarig Beag on the braes of Balquhidder, having lived most of his life among the Lomond and Trossach hills and glens. The Rob Roy Way from Drymen to Pitlochry was created in 2002 and named in his honour. Not only did the man *become* the 'stuff of legend', he was a legend in his own lifetime, moving George I of England to issue a pardon for his crimes just as he was about to Burns transported to the colonies.

In Drymen, the Rob Roy Way shares its start with the en passant West Highland Way (page 250) with the two soon crossing swords in Garadhban Forest – the West Highland Way takes a longer but more satisfying route to the place where the two meet again. The Rob Roy Way then diverges through the Trossachs, visiting Aberfoyle and the bustling town of Callander and enjoying the company of lochs – Venachar, Lubnaig and Earn – and several lochans on the way to Killin. From Killin, after a skirmish with the uplands of Lochan Breaclaich, Creag Gharbh and Meall Odhar,

it plunges to a minor road at Ardeonaig, following the length of Loch Tay.

At Ardtalnaig an upland loop is introduced as a variant heading into the delights of Glen Almond and squeezing between Meall nan Fuaran and Beinnna Gainimh to finally strike down to the shores of Loch Freuchie and Glen Quaich. This optional and demanding variant adds (31½ miles/50.5km) to the route, with the two re-joining south of Aberfeldy. The River Tay leads the route onward until the Way scampers through the Tay Forest Park and down to its end in Pitlochry.

The association with Rob Roy, who spent his life in this region in the 17th and 18th centuries, gives the trail a *raison d'être* and adds colour and substance to its character. But the reality is that this is a stunning trail in its own right, rich in history and romance, passing through rugged glens, beside rivers and burns, and by mountains and remote upland lochs; it makes use of forest trails, farm tracks, railway trackbed, cycle paths and minor roads. This memorable trail was designated as one of Scotland's Great Trails by NatureScot in 2012, and deservedly so.

AMAZING BUT TRUE ...

Just 1¼ miles (2km) south of Aberfeldy, the Moness Burn winds its way through a gorge that was called the Den of Moness until Robert Burns visited it in August 1787. Burns was inspired by the splendid birch trees overhanging the gorge, so sat down and wrote *The Birks o' Aberfeldy*:

The braes ascend
like lofty wa's.
The foaming stream
deep-roaring fa's
O'erhung wi' fragrant
spreading shaws
The Birks of Aberfeldy.

It was an excellent piece of public relations for Aberfeldy, even then, and it has continued to bring visitors ever since, some now following the Rob Roy Way.

Ardtalnaig, Loch Tay

The Rob Roy Way falls into seven distinct stages, and is usually tackled over seven days (or eight if the Amulree/Glen Quaich variant is taken).

7 days

Start	Drymen	
Day 1	Aberfoyle	11 mi / 17.5km
Day 2	Callander	9 mi / 14.5km
Day 3	Strathyre	9 mi / 14.5km
Day 4	Killin	13¼ mi / 21.5km
Day 5	Ardtalnaig	11¾ mi / 19km
Day 6	Aberfeldy	14½ mi / 23.5km
Day 7	Pitlochry	10¼ mi / 16.5km

FACTS AND FIGURES

START Drymen, Stirling (NS 474886)

FINISH Pitlochry, Perth and Kinross (NN 939580)

DISTANCE 79 miles (127km), plus a variant of (31½ miles/50.5km)

HEIGHT GAIN 9,675 feet (2,950m) (variant 3,380 feet / 1,030m)

DIFFICULTY RATING ◆◆◆◆

IS IT FOR ME? Mostly on rough forest and moorland tracks, where good navigation skills are essential, with some minor road sections; parts of the route are not accessible by public transport and have no accommodation.

PRACTICALITIES

GETTING THERE AND BACK
Drymen is linked by bus to Glasgow. Pitlochry has excellent bus and rail links. Along the way, Aberfoyle, Callander, Strathyre and Killin all have good services, but there is no public transport to Ardtalnaig. Amulree has an infrequent bus on weekdays only, while the town of Aberfeldy has regular links. For more details, see www.travelinescotland.com.

ACCOMMODATION
Hotels and B&Bs are plentiful in all locations along the main route except for Ardtalnaig. Wild camping is legally allowed in Scotland if practised responsibly under the Scottish Outdoor Access Code.

WEBSITES
https://robroyway.com
www.scotlandsgreattrails.com/trail/rob-roy-way

MAPS

OS Explorer
OL38, OL46, OL47, OL48, OL49, 348, 379.

OS Landranger
51, 52, 57.

★ Falls of Leny

On the course of the Garbh Uisge, aka the River Leny, the Falls of Leny (NN 591087), near the village of Kilmahog, mark a spot where the river crosses the Highland Boundary Fault, a dramatic fault line that traverses Scotland from Arran in the Firth of Clyde to Stonehaven on the east coast.

The map contains the following labels:

Rannoch Station

Grampian Mountains

Loch Rannoch

R Tummel

Blair Atholl

Loch Tummel

Pitlochry (7)

Fonab Stone Circle

Loch Rannoch & Glen Lyon

R Lyon

R Tay

(6b)

Aberfeldy

Kenmore

Birks of Aberfeldy

R Tay

Dunkeld

L Lyon

R Lochay

Killin and the Falls of Dochart

Loch Tay

Ardtalnaig

(5)

Amulree

(6a)

Killin

(4)

R Dochart

R Almond

Crianlarich

Glen Ogle Viaduct

Lochearnhead

R Earn

LOCH LOMOND & THE TROSSACHS

L Earn

Crieff

Muthill

R Earn

(3) Strathyre

Loch Katrine

Auchterarder

Falls of Leny

Callander (2)

R Teith

Aberfoyle

(1)

Thornhill

Dunblane

N

Dollar

Loch Lomond

R Forth

Alva

Alloa

Drymen

Stirling

0 10 20 30 Km
0 5 10 15 20 Miles

This page (below): Rob Roy MacGregor; (bottom): Glen Almond.
Opposite page (left): Falls of Leny; (right): Pitlochry suspension bridge crosses the River Tummel.

Elevation profile

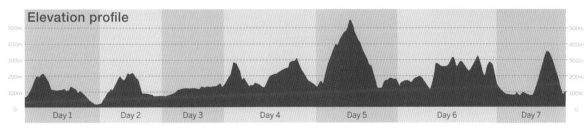

Day 1   Day 2   Day 3   Day 4   Day 5   Day 6   Day 7

Best sections for
Weekends/Short breaks

ARDTALNAIG TO AMULREE
(16¼ miles/26km)

AND AMULREE TO ABERFELDY
(15¼ miles/24.5km)

This is very much a weekend break that experienced walkers and wild campers will favour. There is no accommodation at Amulree and only an infrequent bus service on school days only, nor is there public transport to Ardtalnaig. Wild camping is the solution, and there are many satisfying wild camping spots along the way.

Navigational skills are essential: the route follows a remote moorland track through glens and over passes to reach Amulree. It begins through Ardtalnaig Glen before heading south to enter Glen Almond. The River Almond is a companion for some time, but near Auchnafree the Way abandons the glen and climbs, with a great sense of isolation and mountain views, through Glen Lochan and down by Glenlochan Burn to intercept a minor road west of Amulree.

Although the way onward from Amulree courts the northern shore of Loch Freuchie and threads the pleasant landscapes of Glen Quaich, it intermittently rejoins that minor road before giving up on that once more and striking steeply into the rough, exposed moorland bounds that flank Urlar Burn and eventually lead down through the Birks of Aberfeldy (see opposite) to Aberfeldy and the River Tay.

★ Fonab stone circle

High in the Tay Forest between the River Tay and Pitlochry, the Fonab Stone Circle (Clachan An Diridh: NN 925557) is believed to date from the Bronze Age and stands in the middle of a large clearing, directly crossed by the Way. When the stone circle was built, it would have had magnificent views to the north-east across the River Tummel to Ben Vrackie and the Grampians. The site is still magnificent, and just a little atmospherically mysterious.

The reality is that this is a stunning trail in its own right, rich in history and romance, passing through rugged glens, beside rivers and burns, and by mountains and remote upland lochs

★ Glen Ogle viaduct

Now conveying the Rob Roy Way along the steep eastern slopes of Meall Reamhar, and built between 1866 and 1870, the 460-foot (140-metre) long, 12-arch Glen Ogle viaduct (NN 570264) was part of an ambitious railway link between Callander and Oban on the west coast.

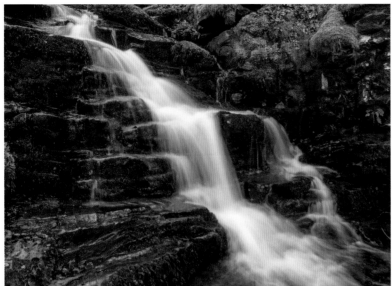

★ Birks of Aberfeldy

Immediately south of the town of Aberfeldy, the Birks of Aberfeldy are in fact the Falls of Moness (NN 851472), visited by Robert Burns during a tour of the Scottish Highlands, who was inspired by the natural beauty to compose a poem to their glory.

Nature on the trail
(above): Golden eagle.
(clockwise): Pine marten; mountain hare; capercaillie; ptarmigan.

STRATHYRE TO KILLIN

(13¼ miles/21.5km)

The use of old railway trackbeds enables a good pace to be set on this stretch, which, from Strathyre rises to a forest trail above the east side of the glen before descending to the Mhor 84 Hotel (the renamed Kingshouse Hotel) on the A84. Beyond the hotel, cyclists will be encountered as a cycle path eventually climbs to meet the old railway route high above Lochearnhead. The age of rail has gone from Glen Ogle, though its memory lingers on as the Way heads through the glen, ignoring the alternative high-level route just after Glen Ogle Cottages and instead heading down to the trackbed of the former Killin Railway (see below) and the River Dochart and its waterfalls just south of Killin.

> The site is still magnificent, and just a little atmospherically mysterious

★ Killin and the Falls of Dochart

This village at the western head of Loch Tay is a delight, renowned for the nearby Falls of Dochart (NN 571323), which are crossed by a narrow, multi-arched stone bridge. Having left the former railway line through Glen Ogle, a branch line – the Killin railway – leads into the village. Opened in 1886, this locally promoted railway line was built to connect Killin to the Callander and Oban Railway main line nearby and carried tourist traffic to the steamers on Loch Tay.

AWAY WITH THE FAIRIES

In Kirkton, a hamlet on the south bank of the River Forth opposite Aberfoyle, you can find at the rear of the ruined kirk the supposed grave of the Reverend Robert Kirk, minister of the parish from 1685 until his mysterious death – or disappearance – in 1692. It was his habit to take an evening stroll upon Doon Hill, close by which, according to local lore, was a gateway to the faerie underworld. Kirk had written a book, *The Secret Commonwealth of Elves, Fauns and Fairies*, in which he described the lives of the faerie people. Legend has it that the faeries spirited him away for revealing their secrets, imprisoning him within a giant tree and leaving a doppelganger behind for a corpse.

It's only 500 yards from the Rob Roy Way to the top of Doon Hill, where you will find the trees festooned with scraps of paper and cloth bearing wishes made to the faeries. If you add one of your own, it is custom to walk round the great pine seven times in a clockwise direction and leave without saying a word, for a spoken wish will remain unfulfilled.

MAPS Day-walk taster

OS Explorer
OL46, The Trossachs; OL48, Ben Lawers & Glen Lyon.

OS Landranger
51, Loch Tay & Glen Dochart; 57, Stirling & The Trossachs.

This page (top): Loch Lubnaig; (middle): Glen Quaich; (bottom): Loch Tay.
Opposite page (top): General Wade's bridge, Aberfeldy (bottom): Falls of Dochart.

● 235

Southern Upland Way

The UK's first officially recognised coast-to-coast long-distance walk, the Southern Upland Way was opened in 1984 and runs from Portpatrick on the west coast to Cockburnspath on the east, between Berwick-upon-Tweed and Dunbar. En route, walkers will experience long, demanding stretches in exposed open upland – and much beauty. In part, this is because this route differs from other classic walking, trails by cutting across it the lines of the hills, rather than following the line of least resistance through glens. The reward is a varied and heart-warming landscape with a fascinating mix of natural and human history that includes a litany of ruined castles and abbeys.

For many walkers, southern Scotland is undiscovered territory, somewhere 'passed through' en route to somewhere else. There may be no commanding summits over 3,000 feet (915m), but more than 80 exceed 2,000 foot (610m). Paradoxically, while great swathes of the region will test even the most experienced walker, there are places where the going is family-friendly and well within, the orbit of those less determined.

From the northern reaches of the hammerhead-shaped Rhins of Galloway, the Way heads into Galloway Forest Park; passing below Merrick, which at 2,765 feet/843m is the highest summit

hereabouts, it heads on to St John's Town of Dalry before curving north and north-east to Sanquhar. Beyond lie the lush, heather-clad Lowther Hills and Daer Reservoir, the trail intercepting the Annandale Way (page 184) at Beattock. Having passed to the south of Moffat, the Way loses itself in a fine line of 'Border Reiving' hills south of Moffat Dale, and heads into Scottish Borders to arrive at St Mary's Loch and Tibbie Shiels Inn. From here, the Way passes into the Tweed Valley Forest Park and on to Galashiels, Melrose – where it meets the Borders Abbeys Way (page 196) – and Lauder, and goes over the foothills of the Lammermuir Hills to reach the east coast.

The section between Moffat and Cockburnspath is also promoted as the Sir Walter Scott Way, and is almost entirely coincident with the Southern Upland Way. Passing close by Scott's home at Abbotsford, the Walter Scott Way was designed to provide a shorter option and add literary interest to the longer route in acknowledgement of the inspiration Scott took from this countryside.

Overall, there can be no doubt that the Southern Upland Way is a masterful creation; but as it is not well known, nor well-travelled, forward planning and self-sufficiency is vital to successful completion of the trail.

AMAZING BUT TRUE ...

Situated at 1,531 feet (466m) above sea level, the old lead mining village of Wanlockhead (NS 873129) is Scotland's highest village. In an atmospheric setting, cradled by the bare and lonely Lowther Hills, the village is a unique and living monument to its mining heritage, which extends back to the 13th century. Following a peak of activity in the 18th and 19th centuries, the last mine closed in the 1950s. The trail from the visitor centre is a must, taking in a mine visit, miners' cottages, and passing smelt mills and spoil heaps, it tells the story of life in this isolated community in the heyday of the mines.

Three Brethren

To tackle the Southern Upland Way in one continuous trek requires fitness, experience and good navigational skills, and even with all three of these would require between 12 and 18 days. Many of the longer sections are arduous and difficult to manage in a single day. Of course, the entire route does not have to be done in one go, and can be conveniently split into two at or near Moffat.

12 days

Start	Portpatrick	
Day 1	Castle Kennedy	13¼ mi / 21.5km
Day 2	Bargrennan	27 mi / 43.25km
Day 3	Dalry	25¼ mi / 40.5km
Day 4	Sanquhar	26½ mi / 42.75km
Day 5	Wanlockhead	7¾ mi / 12.5km
Day 6	Beattock	19¾ mi / 31.75km
Day 7	St Mary's Loch	21 mi / 33.75km
Day 8	Traquair	11¾ mi / 19km
Day 9	Melrose	17½ mi / 28km
Day 10	Lauder	10 mi / 16km
Day 11	Longformacus	15¼ mi / 24.5km
Day 12	Cockburnspath	18¾ mi / 30km

★ The Three Brethren

Three huge cairns (NT 432319), not unlike the Nine Standards encountered on the English Coast to Coast Path (page 32) at the head of Swaledale, stand on a low hill close by Selkirk and boast an outstanding view across the surrounding countryside. They are thought to date from the 16th century, when they were built by the lairds of Yair, Philiphaugh and Selkirk to mark the boundaries of their lands.

FACTS AND FIGURES

START Portpatrick, Dumfries and Galloway (NW 998542)

FINISH Cockburnspath, Scottish Borders (NT 780717)

DISTANCE 214 miles (344km)

HEIGHT GAIN 28,290 feet (8,625m)

DIFFICULTY RATING ◆◆◆◆◆

IS IT FOR ME? Typically, a route of long remote stretches with difficult going, where accommodation is scarce and public transport unavailable, requiring good navigation skills, even for experienced multi-day walkers.

Paradoxically, while great swathes of the region will test even the most experienced walker, there are places where the going is family friendly

PRACTICALITIES

GETTING THERE AND BACK
The whole of Southern Scotland is easily accessible by road, with both Citylink and National Express operating services into the region; there is also a local bus service operator in Dumfries and Galloway that links Portpatrick with Stranraer. There are rail stations at Stranraer, 5 miles (8km) from Portpatrick, and Dunbar, 6 miles (9.5km) from Cockburnspath, which has a local bus service. There are two railway stations on the route itself: one at Sanquhar and the other at Tweedbank, near Melrose (see www.travelinescotland.com).

ACCOMMODATION
The Way visits or passes close to villages and towns with a selection of B&Bs and hotels; plus there are five bothies along the route. Places to stay, however, are sparse in some sections of the Way. There is scope for camping both at commercial and at free campsites (basic or no facilities). Wild camping is legally allowed in Scotland if practised responsibly under the Scottish Outdoor Access Code.

WEBSITES
https://dgtrails.org/southern-upland-way
www.scotlandsgreattrails.com/trail/southern-upland-way

MAPS

OS Explorer
309, 310, 317, 318, 319, 320, 328, 329, 330, 337, 338, 345 346.

OS Landranger
67, 71, 73, 74, 76, 77, 78, 79, 82.

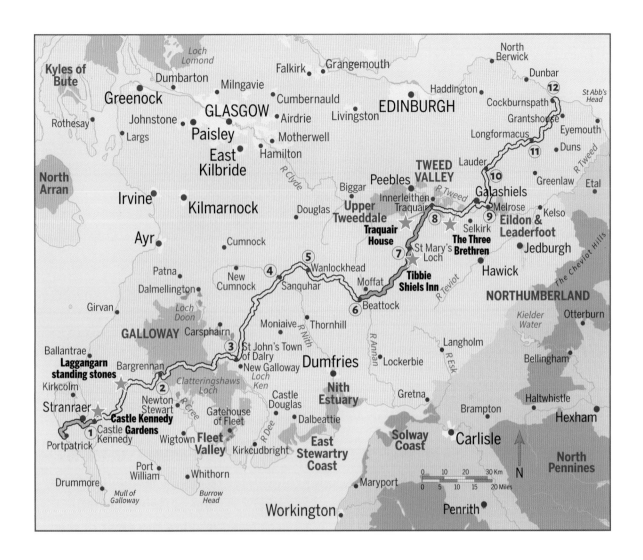

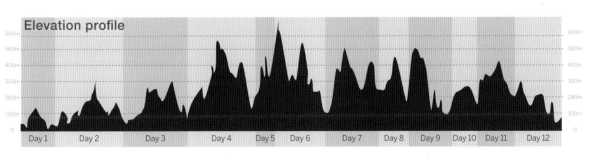

Elevation profile

BEATTOCK TO ST MARY'S LOCH
(21 miles/33.75km)

AND ST MARY'S LOCH TO TRAQUAIR
(11¾ miles/19km)

Moffat is probably a more convenient place to start, and from where the Annandale Way can be followed south until it encounters the Southern Upland Way. As the Way strikes east, it takes on several identities: it is also the Sir Walter Scott Way, the Roman and Reivers Route and, later, it encounters the Borders Abbeys Way (page 196).

From Beattock, the way begins through farmland and forestry, finding a way close by Cornal Burn and around West Knowe to reach Ettrick Head (NT 171063) on the border between Dumfries and Galloway and Scottish Borders. Beyond Potburn, a roadhead is encountered, and this leads alongside Ettrick Water for some distance before finally striking north at Scabcleuch, around more hills and Earl's Hill, to descend to Tibbie Shiels Inn and on along the eastern shoreline of St Mary's Loch.

The onward stretch to Traquair is much shorter, and certainly easier, making the most of the stunning views across St Mary's Loch. Having passed the loch and crossed the A708, a track is pursued across the hillside to the remains of Blackhouse Tower, a forest-stead where James Hogg, the 'Ettrick Shepherd', composed some of his verse. For the most part keeping to the higher ground, the Way heads north-north-east to the village of Traquair and Traquair House, said to be Scotland's oldest continually inhabited house (see opposite).

★ Laggangarn standing stones

Thought to be the last remaining part of a stone circle, the Laggangarn standing stones (NX 219715) may well have marked a route over the moors for more than 4,000 years. The two remaining stones are inscribed with Christian crosses similar to others that date from the years 400–600.

The onward stretch to Traquair is much shorter and certainly easier, making the most of the stunning views across St Mary's Loch

★ Tibbie Shiels Inn

The eponymous Tibbie Shiels was a 19th-century lady who ran the inn (NT 240205) on St Mary's Loch; she hosted many authors and poets, including Walter Scott, William Wordsworth, Robert Louis Stevenson and Christopher North.

Scotland's oldest continually inhabited house, visited by 27 Scottish kings and queens, Traquair House (NT 330354) dates from 1107 and has been lived in by the Stuart family since 1491. Originally a royal hunting lodge, Traquair, for a time, played host to Mary Queen of Scots, and later supported the Jacobite cause without counting the cost (see www.traquair.co.uk).

Nature on the trail (above): Osprey. **(clockwise):** Salmon; short-eared owl; bog rosemary; slow-worm.

PORTPATRICK TO CASTLE KENNEDY

(13¼ miles/21.5km)

Because this western end of the trail introduces walkers to a serene part of the country, the first stage is perfect as a day walk, not least because only a short distance south-east along the coast lies Knockinaam Lodge, today a luxury hotel, but also where Churchill and Eisenhower met to plan the D-Day landings of the Second World War.

Portpatrick is a delightful fishing village, popular with tourists; from it the trail winds north-west along the coast, above bays, cliffs and beaches, to the lighthouse at Portamaggie, where it turns inland to Killantringan. Quiet rural lanes then lead up on to Broad Moor and by Knockquhassen Reservoir. This, in spite of the road walking (which is agreeable enough), is very much a taster of the wild landscapes that are such a dominant feature of the Way. The onward route keeps to the south of the busy ferry port of Stranraer, and again follows tranquil ways and a woodland walk to Castle Kennedy.

★ Castle Kennedy Gardens

One of Scotland's most important historical landscaped gardens, with its collection of rhododendrons, trees and rare species not widely seen in Scotland, Castle Kennedy (NX 110608) is fanned by the warm waters of the Gulf Stream and is rightly regarded as 'one of the showpieces of Galloway'. The original castle was built in the early 17th century as a mansion house for the Earl of Cassilis, Marquess of Ailsa, hereditary chief of Clan Kennedy (see https://castlekennedygardens.com).

MAPS Day-walk taster
OS Explorer
309, Stranraer & The Rhins.
OS Landranger
82, Stranraer & Glenluce, The Rhins.

Opposite page (left): Wanlockhead;
(bottom left): Portpatrick; **(bottom middle):** St Mary's Loch; **(bottom right):** Cockburnspath.

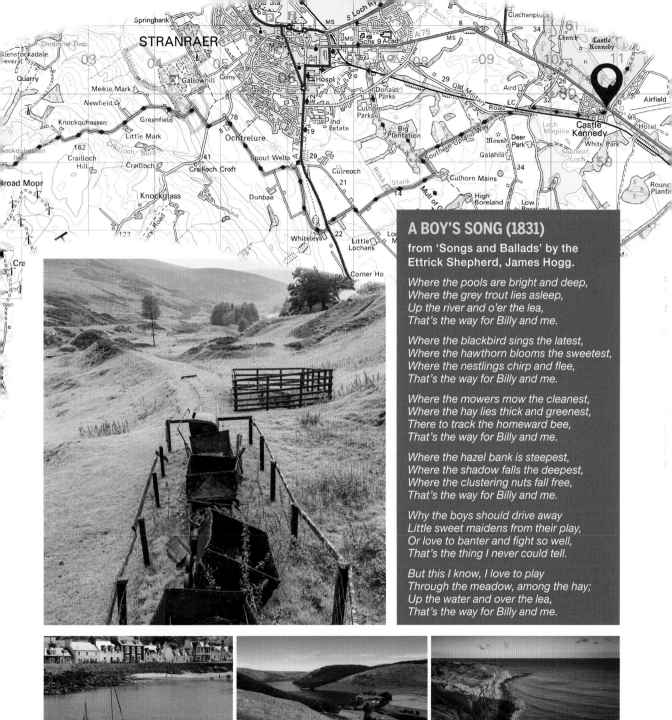

A BOY'S SONG (1831)

from 'Songs and Ballads' by the Ettrick Shepherd, James Hogg.

Where the pools are bright and deep,
Where the grey trout lies asleep,
Up the river and o'er the lea,
That's the way for Billy and me.

Where the blackbird sings the latest,
Where the hawthorn blooms the sweetest,
Where the nestlings chirp and flee,
That's the way for Billy and me.

Where the mowers mow the cleanest,
Where the hay lies thick and greenest,
There to track the homeward bee,
That's the way for Billy and me.

Where the hazel bank is steepest,
Where the shadow falls the deepest,
Where the clustering nuts fall free,
That's the way for Billy and me.

Why the boys should drive away
Little sweet maidens from their play,
Or love to banter and fight so well,
That's the thing I never could tell.

But this I know, I love to play
Through the meadow, among the hay;
Up the water and over the lea,
That's the way for Billy and me.

WALK 31 Speyside Way ⚜

As might be expected, the Speyside Way generally follows the course of the famed salmon river, and links the Moray coast with Aviemore and Newtonmore in Strathspey, on the northern edge of the Cairngorms. When it opened in 1981, the trail extended from Spey Bay to Ballindalloch; a spur to Tomintoul was added in 1990. A northern lengthening from Spey Bay to the fishing village of Buckie followed in 1999, with the route being further extended from Ballindalloch to Aviemore in April 2000. In 2021, the route was extended even further, to, Newtonmore, making use of the former Strathspey Railway trackbed. In general, the walking is not overly difficult, though the stretch between Ballindalloch and Cromdale can be tiresome in wet conditions.

In all, the Way progresses through a theatre of pulse-rousing scenery, including coastline and through the birch woods and pastureland of the Spey, where moors are gradually replaced by uplands of note. From the mouth of the vigorous River Spey, the trail generally follows its glen upstream to Aviemore, Kingussie and Newtonmore. The testing Tomintoul spur climbs into Glen Livet and above Strath Avon to a 360-degree panoramic viewpoint on Carn Daimh (1,870 feet/570m). This spur offers fine scenery and a distillery experience, though transport is needed to return to the spine of the Way.

The route features verdant scenery in the Spey valley in distinct contrast with the neo-tundral conditions on the mountains to the south; in places it follows the river banks closely, elsewhere it crosses open moorland or follows a disused railway trackbed. You progress from the Moray Firth to the Cairngorms and beyond into a glen that saw the birth of legal whisky distilling.

The Scottish Dolphin Centre at Spey Bay, gets the trail off to an intriguing start. Grantown-on-Spey has a hotel – the Grant Arms – that has an exceptional facility for visitors seeking Speyside's wildlife. Surrounding the bustling tourist hotspot of Aviemore, the domed wilderness of the Cairngorms forms the southern skyline and flourishes with wildlife, including red and roe deer, reindeer, red squirrels, grouse, ptarmigan, capercaillie and even the endangered Scottish wildcat. While the Speyside Way is essentially for walkers, it readily appeals to anyone with a yearning for nature at its finest (not to mention fiery malt whiskies), and has an insidious capacity to waylay good intentions. To make matters worse, the Speyside Way connects with the Moray Coast Trail at Buckie and the Dava Way at Grantown-on-Spey, allowing for a more extensive exploration of Speyside.

> **AMAZING BUT TRUE ...**
> Boat of Garten (NH 943189) is a peaceful village in an outstandingly beautiful setting on the west bank of the Spey, between Grantown and Aviemore in the Cairngorms National Park. It grew up around the railway station that opened in the 1860s, and its unusual name comes from the ferry that served the local area prior to the arrival of the railway.

The Spey

The main line of the Speyside Way falls into eight day sections (with an optional and challenging spur to visit Tomintoul).

8 days

Start	Buckie
Day 1	Fochabers *10 mi / 16km*
Day 2	Craigellachie *13 mi / 21km*
Day 3	Ballindalloch *12 mi / 19.25km*
Day 4	Grantown-on-Spey *13 mi / 21km*
Day 5	Boat of Garten *11 mi / 17.75km*
Day 6	Aviemore *6 mi / 9.75km*
Day 7	Kincraig *6½ mi / 10.5km*
Day 8	Newtonmore *13½ mi / 21.75km*

FACTS AND FIGURES

START Buckie, Moray (NJ 419655)

FINISH Newtonmore, Highland (NN 713989)

DISTANCE 86 miles (138km); plus 17-mile (27-km) spur to Tomintoul

HEIGHT GAIN 6,805 feet (2,075m)

DIFFICULTY RATING ◆◆◆

IS IT FOR ME? Using riparian paths, old railway trackbed and moorland tracks, the walking is not unduly difficult in summer; there is limited public transport along the Way so it is best tackled as an end-to-end route.

Nature on the trail (above): Scottish thistle. **(clockwise):** Bottlenose dolphin; red squirrel; wildcat kittens; capercaillie.

★ Scottish Dolphin Centre

Located at the mouth of the River Spey, the Scottish Dolphin Centre (NJ 348653) is a sanctuary for a gamut of wildlife, including bottlenose dolphins, osprey, grey and common seal, visiting otter and many coastal birds. The centre is based in an 18th-century salmon fishing station which itself has a fascinating history.

PRACTICALITIES

GETTING THERE AND BACK
Reaching Buckie is easiest by taxi from Keith station, which is on the railway between Inverness and Aberdeen. The alternative is to take a train to Elgin, then bus to Buckie. Access to Newtonmore is easy by train, being on the main line between Edinburgh and Inverness, or by Express bus.

GETTING AROUND
Local transport between sections of the Way is more complicated; buses are less frequent and some on certain days only or linked to school term-times (see www.travelinescotland.com).

ACCOMMODATION
The Speyside Way passes through attractive villages with hotels, B&Bs and inns. Some close out of season, and most are busy in season, so advance booking is essential. There are hostels at or near Nethy Bridge, Grantown, Tomintoul and Aviemore; and several camping options, both at commercial and at free campsites (basic facilities or none). Wild camping is legal in Scotland if practised responsibly under the Scottish Outdoor Access Code.

WEBSITES
www.speysideway.co.uk
www.scotlandsgreattrails.com/trail/speyside-way

MAPS
OS Explorer
OL57, OL58, OL60, OL61, 424.
OS Landranger
28, 35, 36.

... it so readily appeals to anyone with a yearning for nature at its finest (not to mention fiery malt whiskies)

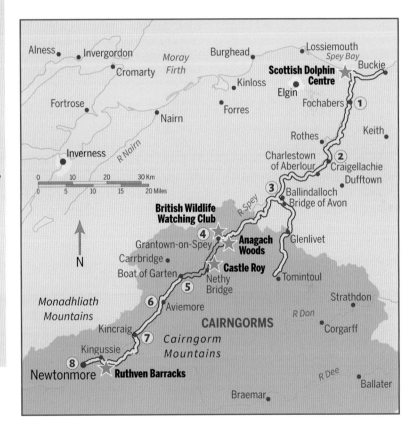

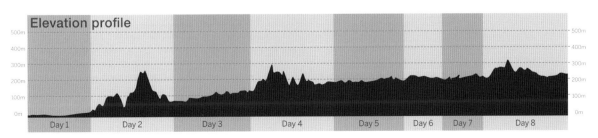

Elevation profile

GRANTOWN-ON-SPEY TO BOAT OF GARTEN

(11 miles/17.75km)

Offering a flavoursome taste of the Speyside Way, this is one of the easiest stretches, following a former railway line as far as Nethy Bridge; thereafter the stretch in to Boat of Garten is dominated by woodlands and the rounded domes of the Cairngorm Mountains to the south. The route leaves Grantown through the atmospheric Anagach Scots pine woodland to Speybridge, where, once across the river, it joins the old railway trackbed as far as Birchfield. From Duackbridge it is possible to deviate to the Loch Garten Osprey Centre before returning and taking an easy route to Garten Bridge. The temptation to continue to Aviemore is hard to resist: either on the tourist steam train from Boat of Garten, or via the highly delightful and easy-going, clear and broad trail for another 6 miles/9.75km. The woodland trees are a haven in season for spotted flycatcher, buzzard and muntjac deer, and this enjoyable stretch persists right to the edge of Aviemore.

★ Anagach Woods

On the edge of Grantown-on-Spey, the Anagach Woods (NJ 034275) feature beautiful natural Scots pine that provide shelter for capercaillie; there are several paths, including an old military road through the woods that make for a perfect evening diversion.

★ Ruthven Barracks

The best preserved of four barracks built in 1719 after the 1715 Jacobite rising, Ruthven Barracks (NN 764997) were destroyed by the Jacobites following defeat at the Battle of Culloden (1746); today they are a Scheduled ancient Monument.

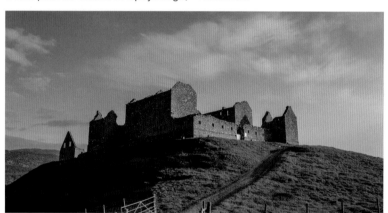

MAPS Day-walk taster

OS Explorer
OL57, Cairn Gorm & Aviemore;
OL61, Grantown-on-Spey & Hills of Cromdale.
OS Landranger
36, Grantown & Aviemore,
Cairngorm Mountains.

★ Castle Roy

Perched on a small glacial mound to the north of Nethy Bridge, Castle Roy (NJ 006219), now in ruins, is a 12th-century fortress built by the Clan Comyn. Two centuries later, the area came under the stewardship of the Clan Grant, and remains so to this day (see https://castleroy.org.uk).

HAVING A WEE DRAM

Speyside has the greatest concentration of malt whisky producers in the world, and there are more than 50 distilleries in this part of Scotland. The oldest is Strathisla at Keith, which dates back to 1786. Why is Speyside such an important whisky-making centre? The drier and warmer weather experienced in the glen and the fertility of its farmland make good barley-growing conditions; and there is the purity and softness of the water of the Spey and its tributaries; while Speyside's oak woodlands originally provided a source of timber for making the barrels where the whisky is aged – the character of the flavour is determined in large part by the quality of the oak.

A good number of the distilleries offer tours and tasting sessions, and whether you are a whisky novice or a connoisseur, walking the Speyside Way will present successive temptations to taste some of the very best single malts, from Cragganmore and Ballindalloch to Aberlour and Craigellachie.

The temptation to continue to Aviemore is hard to resist: either on the tourist steam train from Boat of Garten, or via the highly delightful and easy-going, clear and broad trail

★ British Wildlife Watching Club

Established in 2008 and operated by and from the Grant Arms Hotel (NJ 034279) in Grantown-on-Spey, the British Wildlife Watching Club is a unique enterprise that provides visitors with information on recent wildlife sightings, and where visitors should go to search for wildlife generally. The club enjoys splendid rooms in the hotel (an impressive 50-bedroom Victorian conversion along the main street in Grantown, once visited by Queen Victoria and Prince Albert), including a natural history library and 100-seat lecture room, and exists for anyone interested in wildlife (see www.bwwc.co.uk).

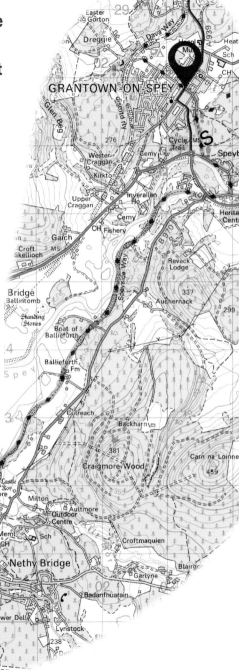

West Highland Way

Several years ago, a reporter asked of the 96-mile West Highland Way which was the best bit. The response was: 'The 95 miles in the middle'. Anyone who has walked the Way will readily identify with the sentiment; after a brief start in a small town centre there is nothing but unadulterated pleasure all the way to the final road walk through Glen Nevis into Fort William.

Since its inauguration in 1980, the West Highland Way has drawn walkers from across Britain, Europe and as far as Australia and New Zealand. They come to take in the lush woodlands of Mugdock, the gentle lands south of the Highland Boundary Fault, the splendour of Loch Lomond to the north of it, and the high mountains that, while not part of the Way, are never far distant. Wilderness comes in the form of open moorland across expansive, water-logged Rannoch Moor, where remnants of the ancient Caledonian pine forest stud the ground as a stark reminder of a distant landscape past. Long stretches follow ancient highways: military roads dating from the 18th century, and drove roads that once resounded to the tread of cattle and sheep herders. History reveals itself in surprising places to those with

the patience to take it in; others intent purely on the joy of walking need only enjoy the invigorating vistas, concealed oases of scenic wealth and the satisfaction that comes from being at one with nature.

The West Highland Way is predominantly a low-level walk but crosses the British watershed no fewer than three times, the last as it crosses from Tyndrum north to the lands of Orchy and Glencoe. With the exception of Conic Hill, a Marilyn that few can resist even though the route passes its summit by, no mountains are encountered. The highest point, 1,798 feet (548m), comes in the shape of a peaty pass at the eastern end of Glencoe, at the top of the so-called Devil's Staircase.

Wayfarers will find food and accommodation dotted along the length of the Way, but there are long stretches where there is nothing and some places where facilities are minimal (and expensive). Time spent forward planning will not go amiss, especially if your experience of multi-day walking is limited. At least in that respect, if the Way proves too much, there are several places where you can opt out, take a bus, train or taxi back to civilisation, and then come back another day.

> **AMAZING BUT TRUE ...**
> While the route is a week-long expedition for most walkers, the fleet-footed have managed to cover the distance in less than a day. Ultra-runner Rob Sinclair set the men's record in 2017 with a time of 13 hours 41 minutes.

Conic Hill and Loch Lomond

PRACTICALITIES

GETTING THERE AND BACK
Both Milngavie and Fort William are served by rail and bus.

ACCOMMODATION
The West Highland Way is not overly endowed with accommodation, so it would be unwise to leave this to chance – or the last minute. The Way is very popular, and accommodation can be fully booked anything up to a year in advance. From Tyndrum to Kinlochleven, accommodation is limited and in some instances expensive: consider spending extra nights in Tyndrum and using taxis or the train (from Bridge of Orchy) to get to and from the trail.

CAMPING
In several stretches of the Way, camping management byelaws are in force between 1 March and 30 September.

WILD CAMPING
is not allowed on or around Conic Hill; on Forestry land; along Loch Lomond (east side) and Glen Falloch from Rob Roy's Cave to Crianlarich.

WEBSITES AND SOCIAL MEDIA
www.westhighlandway.org
www.lochlomond-trossachs.org
Facebook group West Highland Way.

MAPS

OS Explorer
038, OL39, 342, 348, 377,384,385, 392, 399.

OS Landranger
41, 50, 56, 57, 64.

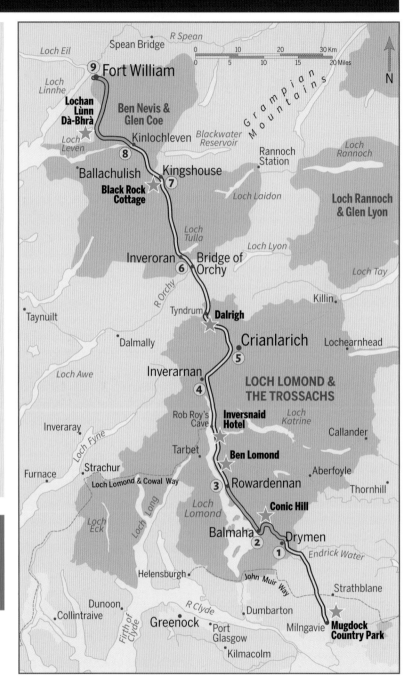

FACTS AND FIGURES

START Milngavie, East Dunbartonshire (NS 553745)

FINISH Fort William, Highland. The traditional end of the Way is at Nevis Bridge (NN 122742), but a new conclusion has appeared at the southern end of the town (NN 099736)

DISTANCE 96 miles (154km)

HEIGHT GAIN 12,375 feet (3,775m)

DIFFICULTY RATING ◆◆◆◆

IS IT FOR ME? Generally a low-level route surrounded by mountains using old highways; long stretches difficult to access by public transport and without accommodation.

The West Highland Way falls into seven distinct stages, and these lend themselves to a comfortable trek albeit it with one long day in the middle. But a six-, eight- or nine-day experience will accommodate those who want to be quicker or more relaxed.

★Conic Hill

Few can resist climbing Conic Hill, which is encountered at the end of Day Two. There are lovely views across Loch Lomond and it's islands. It is not a Munro, but a Marilyn, meaning it is over 150m (492 feet) above the surrounding land.

	6 days	7 days	8 days	9 days
Day 1	Drymen 12¾mi/20.5km	Drymen 12¾mi/20.5km	Drymen 12¾mi/20.5km	Drymen 12¾mi/20.5km
Day 2	Rowardennan 14¾mi/23.75km	Rowardennan 14¾mi/22.75km	Rowardennan 14¾mi/20.75km	Balmaha 7½mi/12km
Day 3	Crianlarich 20½mi/33km	Crianlarich 20½mi/33km	Inverarnan 14mi/22.25km	Rowardennan 7¼mi/11.75km
Day 4	Inveroran 16mi/25.5km	Bridge of Orchy 13½mi/21.25km	Crianlarich 6½mi/10.5km	Inverarnan 14mi/22.5km
Day 5	Kinlochleven 18¼mi/29.5km	Kingshouse 12mi/19.25km	Bridge of Orchy 13½mi/21.25km	Crianlarich 6½mi/10.5km
Day 6	Fort William 14mi/22.5km	Kinlochleven 9mi/14.5km	Kingshouse 12mi/19.25km	Bridge of Orchy 13½mi/21.5km
Day 7		Fort William 14mi/22.5km	Kinlochleven 9mi/14.5km	Kingshouse 12mi/19.25km
Day 8			Fort William 14mi/22.5km	Kinlochleven 9mi/14.5km
Day 9				Fort William 14mi/22.5km

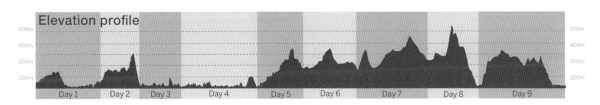

Elevation profile

The West Highland Way can be accomplished piecemeal over several days, some easier than others.

DRYMEN TO BALMAHA
(7½ miles/12km)

A comfortable day across country to the shores of Loch Lomond that allows walkers to 'bag' Conic Hill. Both Drymen and Balmaha are served by bus, and both have accommodation for an overnight stay.

This section begins with gentle walking as far as the Garadhban Forest, through which it wanders easily before crossing the Burn of Mar and getting to grips with the slopes of Conic Hill, although walkers are asked not to use this route in April and May. From the high point, an expansive view opens up of Loch Lomond and its islands, and the sensation is one of walking into the landscape as the route descends steeply to Balmaha.

To prolong the day, walkers might press on to Rowardennan to give a day of 15 miles (24km) – see *Best section for day-walk taster* on page 256.

KINLOCHLEVEN TO FORT WILLIAM
(14 miles/22.5 km)

By a circuitous route, Kinlochleven is accessible by bus, and from it the Way rises steeply through woodland to a military road which passes through the hidden glen of Lairig Mor – a wild and scenic pass bounded by the lofty Mamores. The ruins of Lairigmor croft are a poignant opportunity to reflect on how difficult an existence it would have been for the people who settled here. Fine walking ensues as the route turns a corner to reach a roadhead with a view, south-west, of Lochan Lùnn Dà-Bhrà (Lundavra). The road is a speedy, steep escape directly into Fort William, but the Way presses on into Nevis Forest before finally capitulating and descending to the glen for the walk out. Thankfully, the road walking can be avoided by remaining on the forest trail and, from just above the Braveheart car park, turning up onto a path that circles round the northern end of Cow Hill.

★Lochan Lùnn Dà-Bhrà

Macbeth, King of the Scots from 1040 to 1057, is said to have resided on an island in Lochan Lùnn Dà-Bhrà, probably a crannog. How realistic the story might be is another matter. The lochan comes into view as the roadhead is reached on the final stage to Fort William.

★Ben Lomond

Soaring above Loch Lomond, Ben Lomond is the first really big mountain you'll see when walking the West Highland Way. Rowardennan is the starting point for the difficult walk up to the summit, 3,000 feet (915m) above the Loch.

★Blackrock Cottage

With Beuckle in the background, isolated Blackrock Cottage lies on Rannock Moor and is owned by the Ladies' Scottish Climbing Club.

The splendour of Loch Lomond to the north and the high mountains that, while not part of the Way, are never far distant

BALMAHA TO ROWARDENNAN

(7¼ miles/11.75km) – although public transport does not reach to Rowardennan; a taxi would be needed to return.

This largely follows the shoreline of the loch, but in places at some remove from it. Anyone thinking it might be an easy riparian stroll will be in for a shock, as the route, in all respects delightful, undulates, twists and turns, in and out of woodland before finally revealing Rowardennan at the last moment. High above, Ben Lomond 3,195 feet (974m) rises impressively, and it is not unthinkable to stay over at Rowardennan and add this most southerly Munro to the outing.

The Way wanders easily before crossing the Burn of Mar and getting to grips with the slopes of Conic Hill

Nature on the trail (clockwise): Foxglove; a bluebell field overlooking Loch Lomond; Highland cow; hare.

WORDS TO CONTEMPLATE ALONG THE WAY

On his only recorded visit to Scotland, the poet Gerard Manley Hopkins, 1844–89, came to Loch Lomond from Glasgow in September 1881 and saw the Arklet Falls at Inversnaid. This fine cascade prompted him to pen the following verse on wildness and the natural world. The falls can be viewed from the footbridge over Arklet Water, accessed from steps leading up behind the Inversnaid Hotel.

Inversnaid

This darksome burn, horseback brown,
His rollrock highroad roaring down,
In coop and in comb the fleece of his foam
Flutes and low to the lake falls home.

A windpuff-bonnet of fawn-froth
Turns and twindles over the broth
Of a pool so pitchblack, fell-frowning,
It rounds and rounds Despair to drowning.

Degged with dew, dappled with dew,
Are the groins of the braes that the brook treads through,
Wiry heathpacks, flitches of fern,
And the beadbonny ash that sits over the burn.

What would the world be, once bereft
Of wet and wildness? Let them be left,
O let them be left, wildness and wet;
Long live the weeds and the wilderness yet.

Many parts of the Highlands are traversed by military roads, most of which were built by Major William Caulfield, who built three times as many roads as General Wade. Large stretches of such roads are today followed by the West Highland Way.

MAPS Day-walk taster

OS Explorer
OL38, Loch Lomond South; OL39, Loch Lomond North.

OS Landranger
56 Loch Lomond & Inveraray.

★Dalrigh

Robert the Bruce was defeated by the MacDougalls of Lorne in battle at Dalrigh in Glen Fillan. This followed his coronation as King of Scotland, but further defeat by the English at Methven, near Perth, resulted in him taking to the hills with a small band of supporters. Following the King's loss at Dalrigh, he is said to have cast his sword into a nearby small lochan, now known as the Lochan of the Lost Sword.

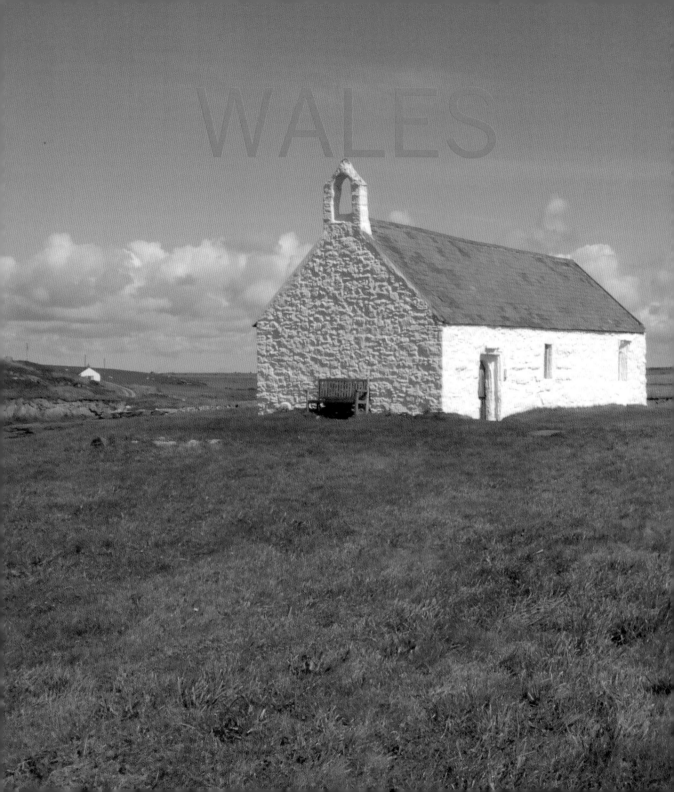

St Cwyfan's Church,
Llangwyfan, Anglesey

Anglesey Coastal Path 🚶

The Anglesey Coastal Path is a developing long-distance route round much of the island's coastline, primarily catering for walkers although some sections are suitable for cyclists and horse riders. The trail falls within a designated Area of Outstanding Natural Beauty (AONB), which covers 95% of the coast, and traverses landscapes that include farmland, coastal heath, dunes, salt marsh, foreshore, headlands, cliffs and a few small pockets of woodland.

The island's name in Welsh, Ynys Môn, was first recorded as 'Mona' in Roman sources, and later known as 'Monez' by the Anglo-Saxons. A sign on the Menai Bridge today proclaims the island to be 'Môn: Mam Cymru' – Anglesey, the Mother of Wales.

The path forms part of the Wales Coast Path, an 870-mile/1,400-km long-distance walking route around the whole coast of Wales from Chepstow to Queensferry, officially opened in May 2012. The Anglesey Coastal Path can be followed in either direction: going clockwise the climb over Holyhead Mountain will come last. The route is well signed throughout. Only rarely does the path venture away from the coast, and then only of necessity: where the path comes inland from Moel y Don by the Plas Newydd estate, and at the Bodorgan Estate on the west of the island between Aberffraw and Malltraeth, where

the Duke and Duchess of Cambridge lived during Prince William's time in service at RAF Valley.

There are few parts of the Coastal Path that are less than striking and inspirational, and once the conglomeration of Holyhead and Holy Island are left behind, the sands of Traeth y Gribin await and then the long and rugged haul to Carmel Head.

Along the north coast, Cemlyn Bay has long been a favoured haunt for birdwatchers, likewise Cemaes Bay further east. The island also has plentiful evidence of occupation from prehistoric times in the form of chambered tombs, hut circles, menhirs and megaliths. Inland from Moelfre, for example, a short diversion leads to Din Lligwy, an ancient village site with hut circles.

Down the east coast, the path encounters huge sandy beaches before it runs on to Trwyn Du lighthouse, looking out to Puffin Island. Along the shores of the Menai Strait, the path is rarely far from the sea, which here is set against the backdrop of the distant northern mountain ranges of Snowdonia and the Lleyn Peninsula. Newborough Warren and its proliferation of pathways and tracks marks a turning point in the path, taking the route through the villages of Malltraeth, Aberffraw and Rhosneigr, and past the Valley airfield to cross finally onto Holy Island, which is remarkable for a jagged coastline for much of its length.

> ## AMAZING BUT TRUE ...
> Heritage Coast (HC) status protects the best stretches of undeveloped coastline. Such is the quality of Anglesey's coast that the island has three separate stretches of heritage coastline: North Anglesey HC, Aberffraw Bay HC and Holyhead Mountain HC.

Menai Bridge

END TO END

The Anglesey Coastal Path has many potential stopping and starting places, but the entire walk might be divided into 12 sections. These can be used to give day walks, although it can be done in fewer.

12 days

Start	Holyhead
Day 1	Porth Trwyn, Llanfaethlu 13 mi / 20.75km
Day 2	Cemaes 12½ mi / 20km
Day 3	Amlwch Port 8½ mi / 13.75km
Day 4	Moelfre 13 mi / 20.75km
Day 5	Pentraeth 5½ mi / 9.25km
Day 6	Beaumaris 13¾ mi / 22km
Day 7	Moel y Don 10½ mi / 17km
Day 8	Llyn Rhos Ddu 8 mi / 12.75km
Day 9	Aberffraw 12¾ mi / 20.5km
Day 10	Four Mile Bridge 13¼ mi / 21.25km
Day 11	Trearddur 8¾ mi / 14.25km
Day 12	Holyhead 11½ mi / 18.75km

FACTS AND FIGURES

START/FINISH St Cybi's Church, Holyhead (SH 247826)

DISTANCE 132 miles (212km)

HEIGHT GAIN 13,990 feet (4,265m)

DIFFICULTY RATING ♦♦♦

IS IT FOR ME? The route features a variety of coastal habitats with some energetic walking; there is a good range of regular facilities and good transport connections.

★ Moelfre

The village area of Moelfre (SH 513865) is remarkable in having more Scheduled Ancient Monuments that anywhere else on Anglesey. The majority are prehistoric, including a Neolithic burial site and a standing stone. There are several Iron Age settlements, too, an indication that the area was inhabited and settled by the time the Romans arrived.

PRACTICALITIES

CLOSURES Part of the path around Carmel Head, between Mynachdy and Ynys y Fydlyn, is closed from 14 September to 1 February each year, when the landowners lock the gates at either end.

GETTING THERE AND BACK Holyhead is on the mainline railway service from London, connecting with other services at Crewe and Chester. There are also reliable local and national bus services across the island (see www.traveline.cymru).

ACCOMMODATION Anglesey is a popular tourist destination, and well provided with accommodation from fine hotels, B&Bs and guest houses to campsites.

WEBSITES
www.visitanglesey.co.uk
www.walescoastpath.gov.uk

★ South Stack (Ynys Lawd)

Reached by means of 365 steps, South Stack lighthouse was built on top of a small island in 1809 to warn ships sailing off the north-west coast of Anglesey. The lighthouse (open to the public) is set against the backdrop of the impressive Gogarth-Mousetrap Zawn sea cliffs, which hold some of the most important breeding seabird colonies in Britain. See www.southstacklighthouse.co.uk.

★ Cemlyn Bay

Separated from Cemlyn Bay by a shingle beach, a lagoon (SH 335931) was designated a Site of Special Scientific Interest and is part of the Anglesey Heritage Coast. This is an important breeding site for Sandwich terns along with common, Arctic and the occasional roseate tern.

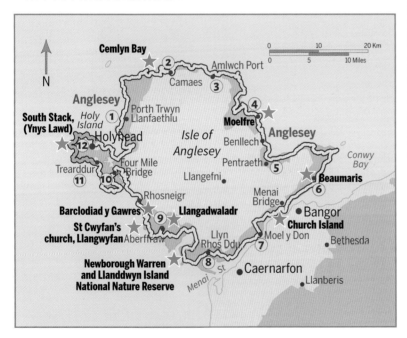

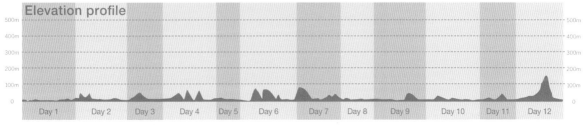

Elevation profile

TREARDDUR TO HOLYHEAD
(11½ miles/18.75km)

From the sands of Trearddur
Bay, the Coastal Path keeps as
close as possible to the coast.
It passes round several small
'porths' or inlets and on to the
South Stack Cliffs Nature Reserve
and then the wide bay known as
Abraham's Bosom. The sea cliffs
of Gogarth overlooking South
Stack lighthouse are said to have
been intimidating rock climbers
for decades. Holyhead Mountain
itself holds no such fears, but the
route to it can be off-putting in
poor weather. The path does not
visit the summit of the mountain,
though only a short deviation is
needed to claim it. After that,
it is a rugged descent to North
Stack and then east down to
Holyhead Broadwater Country
Park and a final loop into town.

★ Beaumaris

Originally a Viking settlement, Beaumaris was developed when Edward I of England
commissioned the building of Beaumaris Castle (SH 607762) in 1295 as part of a
defensive chain of fortifications. The Norman builders responsible for the castle's
construction called it 'Beaux marais' – the 'beautiful marshes' – a description of the
land on which the castle was built. Many regard it as the most technically perfect castle
in Britain.

★ Church Island

Also known as Llandysilio Island, the small
Church Island in the Menai Strait, along a
stretch known as The Swellies, is attached
by a short causeway. The single-chamber
church (SH 551716) is 15th-century,
though Prince Tysilio, the son of a king of
Powys, is believed to have come to the
island in 630 and founded a hermitage.

Along the shores of the Menai Strait, the path is rarely far from the sea, which here is set against the backdrop of the distant northern mountain ranges of Snowdonia

★ Newborough Warren and Llanddwyn Island National Nature Reserve

Originally planted in 1947 to prevent Newborough from being engulfed in sand, Newborough Forest is today an important recreational amenity with numerous paths and trails. Llanddwyn (SH 386625) is a small tidal island in Llanddwyn Bay, named after the church of Santes Dwynwen, the Welsh patron saint of lovers, who reputedly lived there until the 5th century.

★ Barclodiad y Gawres

A fine example of a cruciform passage grave, a notable feature being its decorated stones, Barclodiad y Gawres (SH 328707) is a Neolithic burial chamber, similar to graves found in the Boyne valley in Ireland.

★ Llangadwaladr

The church in this small village is reputed to be the royal burial ground of the kings of Gwynedd. An inscription in the churchyard (SH 383692) on a monumental stone suggests that Cadfan ap Iago (c.569–c.625), King of Gwynedd, is buried there.

★ St Cwyfan's Church, Llangwyfan

Perched evocatively on the small tidal island of Cribinau, St Cwyfan's church is commonly known as the 'Little Church in the Sea' (Eglwysbach y Môr in Welsh), and dates from the 12th century.

Beacons Way 🚶‍♂️▶

The Beacons Way takes a meandering approach to exploring the Brecon Beacons, passing east to west through the principal mountain ranges: the Black Mountains (Mynyddoed Duon), the central Brecon Beacons, and Black Mountain (Mynydd Du). It is a demanding and strenuous route, calling for fitness and good navigational skills as it spans remote and rugged terrain and gathers in 16 major summits, including Pen y Fan.

There is no question that the Beacons Way has been devised with the specific intention of exposing this ruggedly beautiful part of Wales in the best possible light – tackling high mountains, dipping in and out of deep valleys and crossing wild, tussocky moorland. And when that light is right, it reveals the Brecon Beacons and their diverse landscapes and wildlife memorably. The Way has a propensity, happily it might be said, to waywardly deviate off-the-beaten-track into places away from conventional walking routes.

Soon after starting from Abergavenny, the trail crosses Ysgyryd Fawr and descends to Llanvihangel Crucorney, before joining Offa's Dyke Path (page 286) to tackle Hatterrall Hill and parallel the Wales–England border, then dropping into the Vale of Ewyas and Llanthony Priory. Here the route heads for the ridge below Bâl Mawr, follows this south en route to Partrishow and over the slopes of Crug Mawr, before dropping into the valley of the Grwyne Fechan. The trail climbs once more, to the Iron Age hill fort of Crug Hywel before which descends to the town of Crickhowell.

From Crickhowell, the Way skirts Pen Cerrig-calch to reach Cwmdu in the Rhiangoll valley, then heads up onto Mynydd Llangorse and follows it southwards to Bwlch. It crosses the River Usk by an ancient six-arch bridge to enter Llangynidr, and briefly joins the Usk Valley Walk before striking west across the lower slopes of Tor y Foel, making for the head of Glyn Collwn above Talybont Reservoir. The route then crosses the highest peaks in the central Beacons: Pen y Fan and Corn Du, before descending easily to the Storey Arms. There, the trail heads north-west to the top of Graig Cerrig-gleisiad in Fforest Fawr, then continues south-west over Fan Dringarth and Fan Llia to cross the Afon Llia.

A section of the Roman road known as Sarn Helen now follows, before the Way heads west through the Ogof Ffynnon Ddu National Nature Reserve to Penwyllt. The Beacons Way passes by Craig-y-Nos Castle, and up along Fan Hir and Fan Brycheiniog, significant eastern peaks of the Black Mountain rising above Llyn y Fan Fawr, collectively known as the Bannau Brycheiniog. Having traversed the three main summits of the Carmarthen Fan: Fan Foel, Picws Du and Waun Lefrith, and passed above shimmering Llyn y Fan Fach in its secluded hollow, the route descends to Llanddeusant. No sooner does the Way leave the high ground to get to Llanddeusant than it about turns and climbs onto Garreg Las before striking west and then takes a convoluted lowland route to Llangadog.

AMAZING BUT TRUE ...
Crickhowell, with its many Georgian buildings, is named after Crug Hywel, Table Mountain, which overlooks the town. Crickhowell's most famous son is the surveyor Sir George Everest, after whom Mount Everest is named.

Fan y Big

The Beacons Way can be completed in eight days by experienced walkers, or tackled as a series of linear walks. Day lengths vary from 8¾ miles to 15½ miles (14.25km to 24.75km), many involving significant uphill stretches that make them seem longer.

8 days

Start	Abergavenny
Day 1	Llanthony 13½ mi / 21.75km
Day 2	Crickhowell 12½ mi / 20km
Day 3	Llangynidr 11¾ mi / 18.75km
Day 4	Storey Arms 14½ mi / 23.25km
Day 5	Glyntawe 15½ mi / 24.75km
Day 6	Llanddeusant 8¾ mi / 14.25km
Day 7	Trapp (Carreg Cennen) 13 mi / 21km
Day 8	Llangadog 9½ mi / 15.25km

FACTS AND FIGURES

START Abergavenny railway station, Monmouthshire (SO 305136)

FINISH Llangadog railway station, Carmarthenshire (SN 699285)

DISTANCE 99 miles (159km)

HEIGHT GAIN 21,295 feet (6,490m)

DIFFICULTY RATING ◆◆◆◆

IS IT FOR ME? A strenuous route demanding good fitness and navigation skills, best for experienced multi-day walkers; accommodation and transport needs advanced planning.

MAPS

OS Explorer OL12, OL13, 186.

OS Landranger 146, 159, 160, 161.

PRACTICALITIES

GETTING THERE AND BACK Both Abergavenny and Llangadog are served by rail and bus.

ACCOMMODATION There are hotels, B&Bs, campsites and hostels/ bunkhouses near the end points of each day's walk, but relatively scarce in the west, invoking the use of public transport or taxis to reach somewhere to stay.

WEBSITES https://getoutside.ordnancesurvey. co.uk/guides/the-beacons-way www.breconbeaconsparksociety.org/ national-park/the-beacons-way

The Way has a propensity, happily it might be said, to waywardly deviate off-the-beaten-track into places away from conventional walking routes

Wild horses at Llyn Y Fan Fach

★ Beacons Way Art Trail

The National Park Society and the Brecknock Museum Art Trust have developed an art project to celebrate the Beacons Way. Eight Powys artists were chosen to create an artwork to be placed along the route. The images created are a response by the artist to the landscape, ecology or culture of the area through which the trail passes, each work being cast or etched in metal and set into natural stone.

★ Carreg Cennen Castle

Built by one of King Edward I's loyal supporters, John Giffard, in the 13th century, Carreg Cennen (SN 667190) is perched on a limestone precipice high above the River Cennen – a dramatic silhouette that dominates the skyline.

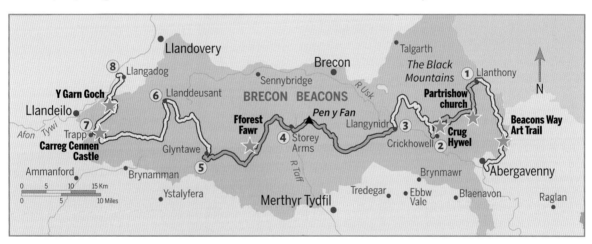

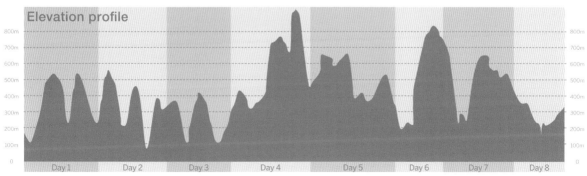

Elevation profile

LLANGYNIDR TO STOREY ARMS
(14½ miles/23.25km)
STOREY ARMS TO GLYNTAWE
(15½ miles/24.75km)

The first stage is a strenuous but rewarding day. Beginning innocuously across the Afon Crawnon and the southern slopes of Tor y Foel, then giving views over Glyn Collwn from the Taff Trail; once Blaen-y-glyn is reached, the hard work begins as the route climbs to a familiar escarpment view of the north-facing slopes of the principal Brecon peaks. Fan y Big comes first, then Cribyn and on to Pen y Fan, the highest peak in southern Britain (2,906 feet/886m) and Corn Du. A straightforward descent leads to Storey Arms.

The second stage into the western Beacons is equally demanding, more remote, untamed and tranquil. This is a good place to look for soaring buzzards, circling red kites and dashing peregrine falcons. A supreme stretch of heather moorland is dealt with over Fforest Fawr (see below), before entering Ogof Ffynnon Ddu National Nature Reserve, a designation that protects its limestone pavements and the associated flora and cave systems.

> This is a good place to look for soaring buzzards, circling red kites and dashing peregrine falcons

★ Y Garn Goch

Directly crossed by the Beacons Way, Y Garn Goch, south of the hamlet of Bethlehem, hosts two impressive Iron Age hill forts of Y Gaer Fawr (SN 690243) and Y Gaer Fach (SN 686242), together the largest in South Wales. The location has been populated since Neolithic times and contains significant Bronze Age burial mounds.

This page (top): Red kite; **(middle):** Blaen y glyn waterfall; **(bottom):** Bannau Sir Gaer reflected in Llyn y Fan Fach. **Opposite page (top):** Crickhowell with Crug Hywel; **(middle):** The twin peaks of Corn Du and Pen y Fan; **(bottom):** peregrine falcon.

★ Fforest Fawr

The first Global Geopark in Wales, the great expanse of Fforest Fawr is a UNESCO Site of Scientific Interest as a habitat for birds, insects, plants and lichen. The area boasts striking waterfalls and the largest cave in the UK, Dan-yr-ogof (see www.fforestfawrgeopark.org.uk).

LLANTHONY TO CRICKHOWELL
(12½ miles/20km)

With a significant amount of ascent required, and crossing three of the major ridges in the Black Mountains, the journey to Crickhowell meets much that is the essence of the Beacons Way, including heart-warming views of the Usk, Honddu, Grwyne Fawr and Grwyne Fechan valleys. Ancient and much-decorated Partrishow church (see below) is well worth a visit.

The day begins briskly, climbing steeply on the Bâl Bach (1,705 feet/520m), only to give up the height gain as it descends to Partrishow. Climbing again on to Crug Mawr (1,805 feet/550m), the trail again loses height, dropping into the Grwyne Fechan valley and then clambering upwards again onto Table Mountain (Crug Hywel – see right). After that, the difficulties relent as the Way takes to Cwm Cumbeth down to Crickhowell.

★ Crug Hywel

North of the town to which it gives its name, Crug Hywel (SO 225207), sometimes known as Table Mountain, is the site of a huge Iron Age Celtic hill fort with an earth and stone ditch.

THE FAN DANCE

Taking in the part of the Beacons Way joining Corn Du, Pen y Fan and Fan y Big, is the gruelling 15-mile (24-km) UK Special Forces selection march while carrying 45lb (20kg) loads, known as the Fan Dance. This test of stamina is the first major indicator of whether a candidate has the physical and mental qualities to make the grade on the selection course.

★ Partrishow church

In a remote corner north of Abergavenny, Partrishow church (SO 278224), was established in the 11th century, and contains a range of intriguing features, including a water stoup, pre-Reformation paintings, oak rood screen and a hermit's cell (see www.abergavenny.org/partrishow.html).

Ceredigion Coast Path 🚶

The Ceredigion Coast Path follows the Welsh Heritage Coast from Cardigan northwards along Cardigan Bay to Ynyslas, near Borth, to the north of Aberystwyth. Like the rest of the coastline in Wales, the trail forms part of the Wales Coast Path, an 870-mile (1,400-km) long-distance walking route round the whole coast of Wales from Chepstow to Queensferry. But the Ceredigion Coast Path is a fine jaunt in its own right, crossing a diverse landscape that includes the dune system at Ynyslas, high cliffs, sea caves, sandy bays and storm beaches.

Several of the sections along the coast are undulating and challenging, but only towards the end – into the Dyfi Estuary National Nature Reserve – are there any comparatively lengthy days. Cardigan, on the Teifi estuary, is where the Ceredigion and Pembrokeshire Coast Paths meet. A statue of an alert otter standing by the riverside marks the official starting point of the Ceredigion path. Cardigan is a pleasing destination in itself, but what follows along the coastal path is intensely inspiring and sure to please wildlife enthusiasts: harbour porpoise, bottle-nosed dolphin and Atlantic grey seals are often seen offshore, and there is always the prospect of seeing an osprey, chough or soaring buzzard.

The northern end of the path feeds into Ynys-hir, the first RSPB reserve in Wales, which, along with the Dyfi reserve of sand dunes and salt marsh, has been of underlying importance in achieving for the area the only designated UNESCO Biosphere in Wales. Offshore, you may win a glimpse of Borth's 'submerged forest', an ethereal collection of ancient tree remains stretching for nearly 3 miles (5km) along the shore. Legend has it, that they are part of the lost kingdom of Cantre'r Gwaelod.

Ceredigion is very much a coastal county, with 50 miles (80km) of shoreline, but rises inland to the Cambrian Mountains and the county of Powys. Roughly central along the coast, Aberystwyth is a thriving, diverse and vibrant settlement, located, as its name suggests, at the mouth of the River Ystwyth; the town has been a major player in Wales since the establishment in 1872 of the University College of Wales, and the National Library of Wales is here, too.

The Ceredigion Coast Path may now be subsumed into the Wales Coast Path, but it has lost none of its individual identity or intrinsic appeal.

AMAZING BUT TRUE ...

The mainland part of the Ynys Lochtyn promontory has some delightful inlets and sea arches. The English composer Edward Elgar took a holiday near here in 1902 and enjoyed wandering atop the cliffs. It was while doing so on one occasion that he overheard people singing on the beach below, and this inspired one of his most popular and moving compositions, the *Introduction and Allegro for Strings*.

St Caronnog, Llangrannog beach

END TO END

The Ceredigion Coast Path can be accessed by road at a number of spots, so it can readily be split into five distinct sections.

5 days

Start	Cardigan
Day 1	Aberporth 13¼ mi / 21.5km
Day 2	New Quay 12½ mi / 20km
Day 3	Llanrhystud 13½ mi / 21.75km
Day 4	Aberystwyth 9½ mi / 15.25km
Day 5	Ynyslas 10 mi / 16.25km

FACTS AND FIGURES

START Cardigan, Ceredigion (SN 177458)

FINISH Ynyslas, Borth, Ceredigion (SN 609940)

DISTANCE 59 miles (95km)

HEIGHT GAIN 12,515 feet (3,815m)

DIFFICULTY RATING ◆◆◆

IS IT FOR ME? There's a variety of coastal terrain with several demanding ascents/descents; good range of regular facilities and good transport connections.

★ Pen Dinas

To the south of Aberystwyth, Pen Dinas is an Iron Age hill fort, an indication that the promontory on which it stands has been used by man from an early age. The hill is topped by a towering monument (SN 584802) erected in the 1850s as a memorial to the first Duke of Wellington.

GETTING THERE AND BACK
Bus services operate to Cardigan and all the intermediate points along the coast, while Aberystwyth and Borth are also on the Cambrian railway line. See www.thecambrianline.co.uk and www.trawscymru.info.

ACCOMMODATION
There is plentiful accommodation of all standards along the Welsh coast, but it is a popular tourist and weekend destination so advance booking is essential for visits during the summer months.

WEBSITE
www.discoverceredigion.wales

MAPS
OS Explorer
OL23, 198, 199, 213.
OS Landranger
135, 145, 146.

This page: Ynyslas.
Opposite page (top): Grey seal; (middle): otter, (bottom): Wellington Monument, Pen Dinas.

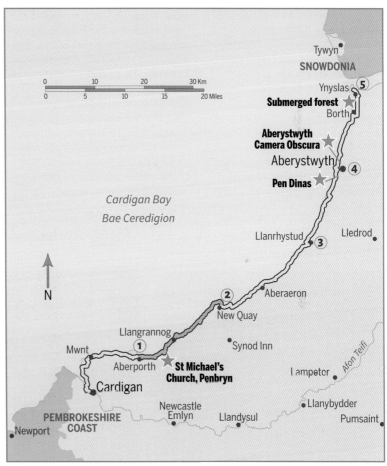

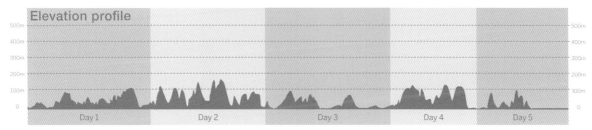

Elevation profile

ABERPORTH TO NEW QUAY
(12½ miles/20km)

Between Aberporth and Llangrannog, the scenery is characterised by sea cliffs, promontory forts and sheltered beaches, all part of the Heritage Coast. Aberporth has two small bays framed by headlands. From here, the Path takes a relaxed meander above coves, caves and the sea; it's worth dallying to take in not only the scenery but the wildlife, too. There are comforting views of the long sandy beach of Penbryn and the Iron Age promontory fort at Ynys Lochtyn beyond. Between Penbryn and Llangrannog lie two steep climbs and associated descents; the Path then heads up to the ramparts of the Iron Age fort of Castell-bach, before descending into the village of Llangrannog, making this one of the most challenging stretches.

The onward stretch to New Quay, a place that the renowned Welsh poet, Dylan Thomas, moved to in 1944 to escape the Blitz, is arguably the most stunning part of the Coast Path, and includes the iconic Ynys Lochtyn, the coves of Cwmtydu and Cwm Soden; it is longer than the first section but less demanding. Part of what makes this section so special is that it lies athwart two types of Palaeozoic rock, Silurian and Ordovician, named after two Celtic tribes that used to occupy Wales. This feature is particularly impressive around the promontory of Ynys Lochtyn, which is topped by the Iron Age hill fort of Pendinas Lochtyn.

CEREDIGION

Ceredigion is named after Ceredig, the son of the 5th-century Celtic leader Cunndda, who was chief of the northern British tribe that recaptured this area from Irish invaders.

The county has undergone something of an identity crisis: having been a recognised region since the time of Ceredig, in 1536 it transformed into Cardiganshire. Later, the county became part of Dyfed; but between 1974 and 1996, the historical name Ceredigion was revived by the district council and Ceredigion County Council was embraced by the new unitary authority in 1996.

A statue of an alert otter, standing by the riverside, marks the official starting point of the Ceredigion Coast Path

★ **St Michael's Church, Penbryn**

On a hillside on the western side of the Hoffnant valley, Penbryn church (SN 293521) is reputed to be the oldest in the diocese of St David, dating from the 12th century.

★ Submerged forest

Between Ynyslas and Borth, an ancient petrified forest is visible at low tide; the stumps of hazel, pine, birch and willow protruding from the sands have been radiocarbon dated to 3,500 years ago. The forest is mythically linked with Cantre'r Gwaelod, the 'Welsh Atlantis', an ancient sunken kingdom thought to have extended many miles into what is now Cardigan Bay.

★ Aberystwyth Camera Obscura

At the top of Constitution Hill in Aberystwyth is the world's largest Camera Obscura (SN 584827), giving a spectacular bird's-eye view of more than 1,000 square miles, in a 360-degree sweep round Aberystwyth. The Camera Obscura is accessible via the Aberystwyth Cliff Railway, the longest cliff railway in Britain.

Glyndŵr's Way

Named in commemoration of Owain Glyndŵr, a descendant of the princes, of Wales and the medieval Welsh nationalist leader who organised rebellion against the English king, Henry IV, Glyndŵr's Way (Llwybr Glyndŵr) wanders across the open moorland, undulating farmland, woodlands and forests of mid-Wales. This is a demanding walk, with plenty of hills to contend with in a relatively infrequently trodden part of Wales; often remote and rough, but a route that can be tackled at any time of year. As it is not so well known as other National Trails, there are times when you may have the trail to yourself.

Unlike other National Trails, Glyndŵr's Way has little thematic connection with geographical features, historic sites or routes; instead it links towns, villages and other locations that enjoy an association with Glyndŵr. As a result, on paper the Way is something of an on-its-side-V-shaped wander, not committed to a particular range of hills or drove roads but to the history of one man and his endeavours; a varied walk and all the better for its meanderings. There are green hills aplenty and satisfying panoramas to offset the effort involved. One perverse characteristic of the Way is its penchant for ascending hills only to descend from them almost immediately, and then to repeat the process, sometimes three times a day. That makes for tiring but hugely rewarding days.

Glyndŵr's Way will appeal to anyone who enjoys the solitude and open spaces of the countryside with a bit of a challenge thrown in. Making the most of some of the finest landscapes in central Wales, its tour includes the serene Radnorshire Hills, the banks of the Clywedog Reservoir and heather-clad Pumlumon, source of the River Severn and the Severn Way (page 126). There are heart-warming views over craggy Cadair Idris to summits of longing in Snowdonia, Lake Vyrnwy and the Cambrian Mountains. It is well worth making the short detour to reach the high point of the trail at Foel Fadian (SN 828953: 1,530 feet/510m), from which views extend along the majestic Dulas valley to Machynlleth and the sea.

In spite of its hills, reservoirs and woodlands, there is no escaping the fact that Glyndŵr's Way takes delight in threading a congenial way through active, living farmland, a landscape that is very much lived in and worked. Anyone wanting to make a complete circle of this exploration of Wales should note that Buttington near the end of the trail in Welshpool is linked to the start in Knighton by the Offa's Dyke Path (page 286), which passes through the delightful Shropshire Hills Area of Outstanding Natural Beauty.

AMAZING BUT TRUE ...

Owain Glyndŵr instigated a Welsh revolt against English rule in September 1400, leading a campaign for Welsh independence. In the summer of the following year he regularly harassed the English, rapidly gaining control of Mid Wales. Over time, his rebellion was suppressed, and he lost the last of his strongholds in 1409. Glyndŵr escaped capture and is believed to have died in 1415.

Clywedog Reservoir

Glyndŵr's Way finds a route through some sparsely populated parts of the country; the southern sections, between Knighton and Machynlleth are especially noteworthy in that regard. So, some long days are unavoidable, and the Way is arguably best done between April and September. Nine hearty days should suffice.

9 days

Start	Knighton	
Day 1	Felindre	15½ mi / 25km
Day 2	Abbeycwmhir	15½ mi / 25km
Day 3	Llanidloes	15¼ mi / 24.5km
Day 4	Penfford-Lâs (Staylittle)	11¾ mi / 18.75km
Day 5	Machynlleth	16½ mi / 26.75km
Day 6	Llanbrynmair	15¾ mi / 25.5km
Day 7	Llanwddyn	17¾ mi / 28.75km
Day 8	Meifod	15 mi / 24km
Day 9	Welshpool	11¾ mi / 19km

FACTS AND FIGURES

START Knighton (Tref-y-clawdd), Powys, at the town clock (SO 285723)

FINISH Welshpool, Powys (SJ 226073)

DISTANCE 135 miles (217km)

HEIGHT GAIN 23,355 feet (7,120m)

DIFFICULTY RATING ◆◆◆◆

IS IT FOR ME? Physically demanding walking often in remote countryside, sometimes on infrequently trodden paths; limited accommodation and transport requiring advance planning.

MAPS

OS Explorer
OL23, 200, 201, 214, 215, 216, 239.

OS Landranger
124, 125, 126, 135, 136, 137, 147, 148.

Tormentil

PRACTICALITIES

GETTING THERE AND BACK
Mid Wales is not well served by rail other than at Knighton, Llangynllo, Machynlleth and Welshpool; nor do many bus services connect directly with the trail, although some helpful services run to and from Llanidloes, Machynlleth and Welshpool. National Express connects Welshpool with Shrewsbury and London.

ACCOMMODATION Although the Way passes through several villages, accommodation is limited and pre-booking is essential. There is a limited supply of hostel/bunkhouse-type accommodation, not all of it en route. Several farms offer overnight B&B accommodation.

CAMPING The Way passes many active hill farms, which can pose a problem for anyone wanting to wild camp along the route; it is essential to obtain permission from the landowner first if this is your planned means of accommodation.

WEBSITES
www.nationaltrail.co.uk

★ Dyfnant Meadows Nature Reserve

Partially designated as a Site of Special Scientific Interest, Dyfnant Meadows (SH 999155) is an area of species-rich grassland that supports important plant species, such as tormentil, heath bedstraw, devil's-bit scabious and butterwort.

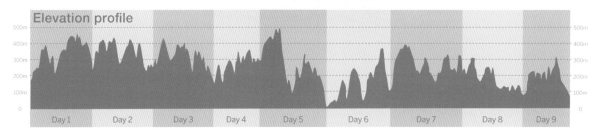
Elevation profile

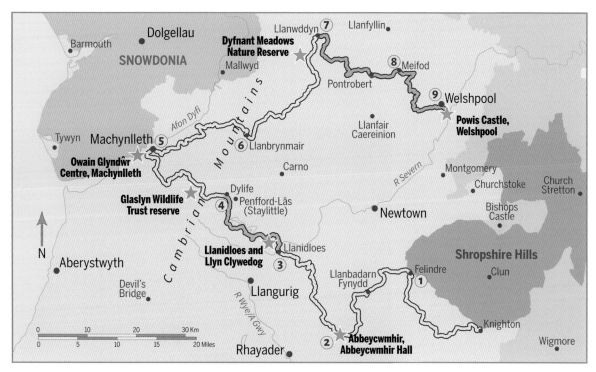

★ Abbeycwmhir

The village name derives from Cwmhir Abbey, the Cistercian monastery built here in 1143 and the largest abbey in Wales, although never fully completed. Located in Nant Clywedog and surrounded by hills, the village is said to be the burial place of the last native Prince of Wales, Llewellyn ap Gruffydd. Tradition says Llewellyn's body was buried at Cwmhir, and there is a memorial stone in the ruins of the old abbey. His decapitated head, however, severed following an ambush in woodland at Aberedw, was sent to London after being shown to the English troops based on Anglesey.

★ Abbeycwmhir Hall

The hall at Abbeycwmhir is an outstanding example of Victorian Gothic Revival architecture, described as neo-Elizabethan; it was built in 1834 for a London lawyer, and was doubled in size 35 years later.

Best sections for
Weekends/Short breaks

LLANWDDYN TO MEIFOD
(15 miles/24km)

MEIFOD TO WELSHPOOL
(11¾ miles/19km)

Capable of being split into two days at Meifod, this final run in to Welshpool is comparatively easy, with the hardest part of the trail now over. As far as Dolanog, the trail favours farmland and valleys, as well as a riverside stroll above the Vyrnwy once Pont Llogel is reached. Beyond Dolanog more woodland awaits, and then pleasant walking to Meifod village, where the River Vyrnwy (Afon Efyrnwy) is crossed by Broniarth Bridge, and up onto Broniarth Hill, the first real uphill stretch. Quiet rural lanes ensue before a final ascent up onto Y Golfa (SJ 182070), and a splendid romp down into Welshpool.

★ Powis Castle, Welshpool

Set on a rock above Welshpool and built around 1200, Powis Castle is a medieval fortress and country mansion, the seat of the Earl of Powis and renowned for its formal gardens and landscaped estate. Of especial note, the castle houses more than 1,000 items from India and East Asia, assembled by two generations of the Clive family: Robert, who became known as 'Clive of India', and his son, Edward. This is the story of the East India Company that dominated trade with the East from the end of the reign of Elizabeth I to Victorian times.

... will appeal to anyone who enjoy the solitude and open spaces of the countryside with a bit of a challenge thrown in

★ Glaslyn Wildlife Trust reserve

The rippling expanses of heather moorland are stunning in August when the heather is in full bloom; this is the ancient county of Montgomeryshire's largest nature reserve, set at the heart of the Cambrian Mountains.

This page (top): Llyn Clwedog;
(bottom): Town Hall, Llanidloes.
Opposite page (top): Powis Castle;
(bottom): Glaslyn Wildlife Trust reserve.

★ Llanidloes and Llyn Clywedog

A delightful small market town at the very heart of Wales, and the starting point for the Severn Way (page 126), Llanidloes is the first town on the river and lies close to the Llyn Clywedog reservoir. Glyndŵr's Way passes beneath the dam before taking a course along the southern shore of the lake. This is a splendid interlude in which to observe wildlife, notably red kite and buzzard. Here, too, is the Bryntail Lead Mine, associated with the 19th-century mining and processing of lead ore.

LLANIDLOES TO DYLIFE
(13½ miles/21.75km)

Notwithstanding the transport logistics that will need to be resolved, this stretch begins at the lovely market hall in the centre of Llanidloes and briefly follows the Severn Way out of town. It heads over the river and up into woodland, before striking out for the impressive Llyn Clywedog dam and the site of the Bryntail lead mine. Beyond the dam, the Way soon touches on the shores of the reservoir, and then climbs over the shoulder of Mynydd y Groes to a picnic site near Cwmbiga. This might be a suitable conclusion to the day, but a fine continuation leads past the hamlet of Penfford-Lâs and on to Dylife and its 17th-century drover's inn and guesthouse.

★ **Owain Glyndŵr Centre, Machynlleth**

Standing on the site of the famous parliament held in 1404 at which Owain was crowned Prince of Wales, the building housing this National Heritage Centre was given to the town of Machynlleth by Lord Davies of Llandinam in 1912. The Centre, open to the public, hosts an interactive and informative exhibition on the life, times and vision of Owain Glyndŵr (see www.canolfanglyndwr.org).

THE DEATH OF LLEWELLYN AP GRUFFYDD

Following the death of Llewellyn ap Gruffydd, also known as Llewellyn the Last, in a skirmish with the English at Builth on 11 December 1282, his severed head was taken with a report of the battle to Edward I. In response, the Welsh poet Gruffydd ap yr Ynad Coch wrote in anguish:

See you not the rush of the wind and rain?
See you not the oaks thrashing each other?
See you not that the truth is portending?
See you not that the sun is hurtling the sky?
See you not that the stars have fallen?
Do you not believe in God, foolish men?
See you not that the world is ending?
Ah, God, that the sea would cover the land!
What is left us that we should linger?
Head cut off, no hate so dreadful,
Head cut off, thing better not done,
Head of a soldier, head of praise,
Head of a warlord, dragon's head,
Head of fair Llywelyn, harsh fear strikes the world,
An iron spike through it. Lem ad in dicivid essedic

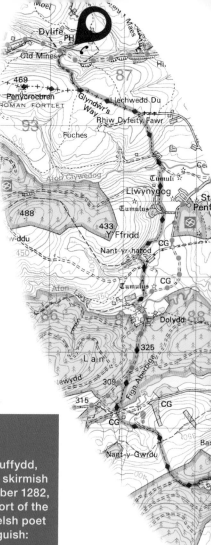

Nature on the trail (clockwise):
Goshawk; raven and buzzard; cattle on the moor; ragged robin; yellow bedstraw.

MAPS Day-walk taster

OS Explorer
214, Llanidloes & Newtown; 215, Newtown & Machynlleth.

OS Landranger
136, Newtown & Llanidloes.

WALK 37 Offa's Dyke Path 📍

Named after, and loosely following, a dyke constructed on the orders of King Offa, the King of the Anglo-Saxon kingdom of Mercia from 757 to 796, to divide his realm from those of his rival neighbours in what is now Wales. That the 'dyke', an earth embankment, existed is not in dispute, but much else is open to conjecture. There is no direct evidence, for example, to associate the dyke with the king, though throughout history no one else has laid claim to it. Nor is it clear why it was built: was it meant to be defensive or was it simply a boundary defining feature? Or, maybe, both? Certainly, this was a time of trouble for Offa, who was frequently in conflict with the Welsh kingdoms; and a monkish biography of King Alfred the Great refers to '…a certain vigorous king called Offa … [who] had a great dyke built between Wales and Mercia from sea to sea'.

Setting all that aside, the dyke, which runs from Sedbury Cliffs, near Chepstow on the banks of the River Severn, to Prestatyn in Denbighshire, North Wales, throws down a challenge few walkers with a taste for long-distance walking can resist. Taking in eight different modern-day counties, and crossing today's border between England and Wales no fewer than 20 times, the Path offers an intimate and at times demanding exploration of the border region known as the Welsh Marches – in medieval times, the 'Marcher Lords' would have ruled here.

On its journey, the Path courts the River Wye before crossing , the river at Monmouth and heading into the Brecon Beacons National Park, reaching it at Pandy and then charging up onto the delightful ridge of Hatterrall Hill in the Black Mountains. Further on, it traverses the Shropshire Hills and the Clwydian/Dee Valley range of hills, which, together with the Wye Valley, make up three Areas of Outstanding Natural Beauty encountered en route. The southern and northern stretches can be demanding, especially in poor weather, with many ups and downs, though most are gentle. In between, there are several flirtations with the Severn Way (page 126) and the Montgomeryshire Canal, which make for easier walking.

Like many other National Trails, Offa's Dyke Path can be walked all year, though spring and early summer offer the richest spread of wild flowers and an abundance of birdsong in the hedgerows.

> **AMAZING BUT TRUE …**
> Wintour's Leap (ST 541961) is a viewpoint high on the wooded cliffside above a looping meander of the River Wye where it encounters Offa's Dyke Path north of Woodcroft. It's named after Sir John Wintour, a well-known local mining and timber entrepreneur in the 17th century. During the Civil War he sided with the Royalists: on one occasion, to flee Parliamentarian forces, legend has it he leapt on horseback from the top of the cliff to be subsequently picked up by boat from the river. History records his survival, for he was later captured and spent time in the Tower of London.

Beginning and End, Prestatyn

The Offa's Dyke Path is a mix of high- and low-level stretches, and visits several large towns and villages: Monmouth, Hay-on-Wye, Kington, Knighton and Welshpool. These, and many places in between, are ideal stopping-off points, but there are not many sections where facilities and services are few and far between. An itinerary of 11 days, gives individual days of between 13½ and 20 miles (21.5 and 32km), and may call for some logistical forward planning.

11 days

Start	Sedbury Cliffs
Day 1	Monmouth 18¼ mi / 29.5km
Day 2	Pandy 16 mi / 25.75km
Day 3	Hay-on-Wye 16 mi / 25.75km
Day 4	Kington 15 mi / 24km
Day 5	Knighton 13½ mi / 21.5km
Day 6	Montgomery 16¾ mi / 27km
Day 7	Four Crosses 17½ mi / 28km
Day 8	Pentre 20 mi / 32km
Day 9	Llandegla 12¾ mi / 20.25km
Day 10	Bodfari 17¼ mi / 27.75km
Day 11	Prestatyn 14½ mi / 23.5km

FACTS AND FIGURES

START Sedbury Cliffs, Chepstow (ST 552928)

FINISH *Beginning and End* sculpture, Prestatyn, Denbighshire (SJ 061838)

DISTANCE 177 miles (285km)

HEIGHT GAIN 28,845 feet (8,795m)

DIFFICULTY RATING ◆◆◆◆

IS IT FOR ME? A mix of high-level energetic walking and low-level easier going, encountering towns fairly regularly and with reasonable transport connections.

This page (left): Moel Famau; **(right):** Hay Bluff.
Opposite page: St Michael's Church, Llanfihangel Tal-y-llyn.

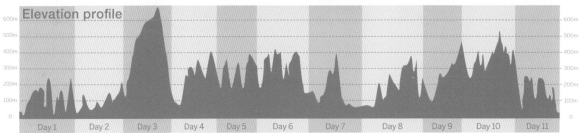
Elevation profile

Taking in eight different modern-day counties and crossing today's border between England and Wales no fewer than 20 times

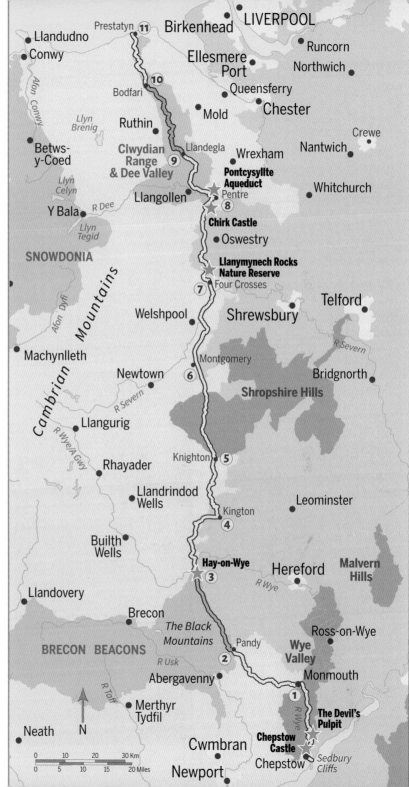

LLANDEGLA TO BODFARI
(17¼ miles/27.75km)

On this penultimate stage of the trail, much time is spent high in the Clwydian Hill Area of Outstanding Natural Beauty. After a farmland start, the route heads for high ground but bypasses several, admittedly lowly, hills that might readily be included: Moel y Plâs and Moel Gyw, for example. And while Foel Fenlli and its ramparts of an Iron Age hill fort appear to be passed by maps, it is easily included. After which, the way tumbles down to Bwlch Penbarras, then Moel Famau and the ruins of its early 19th-century tower – in the shape of an Egyptian obelisk and built in 1810 to commemorate the golden jubilee of George III's accession to the throne – are easily reached on a broad track. An obvious green track continues over Moel Dywyll and Moel Llys-y-coed and around Moel Arthur, site of another hill fort, here associated with King Arthur. After crossing a minor road above Llangwyfan, the Path heads for Penycloddiau's heathery crest, before finally relinquishing the high ground and heading down to the River Wheeler and the village of Bodfari.

On this penultimate stage of the trail, much time is spent high in the Clwydian Hills

★ Chepstow Castle

Holding a commanding defensive position on a limestone cliff overlooking the River Wye, Chepstow Castle is cited as the oldest surviving post-Roman stone castle in Britain, construction having begun in 1067. The first Norman stronghold in Wales, this is the southernmost of a chain of castles built in the Welsh Marches. Today, it is beautifully preserved and a prime illustration of how castles evolved.

★ The Devil's Pulpit

With a splendid view over Tintern Abbey in the valley below, the Devil's Pulpit (ST 542995) is a limestone pillar from where the Devil is said to have preached to the Cistercian monks below in an endeavour to persuade them to desert their order.

★ **Pontcysyllte Aqueduct**

This remarkable structure (SJ 270420) is a navigable aqueduct that carries the Llangollen Canal across the River Dee in the Vale of Llangollen, and a UNESCO World Heritage Site. It is a feat of pioneering civil engineering of the Industrial Revolution – a human-engineered waterway, completed in the early 19th century. Its inscription cites it '... as a masterpiece of creative genius, and as a remarkable synthesis of expertise'.

★ **Hay-on-Wye**

This delightful market town is certain to waylay the intentions of anyone with a love of books. With more than 30 bookshops, Hay is regarded as 'The Town of Books', and is home to the Hay Literature Festival. For good measure, the town is also the location of two Norman castles.

PANDY TO HAY-ON-WYE
(16 miles/25.75km)

Although there is no extant
evidence that the dyke was
ever built along this stretch, the
elevation along the eastern face of
the Brecon Beacons nonetheless
makes it a soul-warming
introduction to the entire walk.
Soon after leaving the hamlet of
Pandy, the Path ascends into the
Brecon Beacons National Park,
and continues through grass and
heather along the ridge of Hatterrall
Hill, with views to the west over the
Vale of Ewyas and the 900-year-old
ruins of the Augustinian Llanthony
Priory. The Path continues along
a broad ridge to Hay Bluff, on the
way passing the highest point of
the entire trail, an undistinguished
summit (SO 255350: 2,306
feet/703m). From Hay Bluff, a
popular place to keep your eye
open for semi-feral ponies, the
route eases down to the River Wye
and Hay, the book capital, arguably,
of Britain.

Hatterrall Hill

CASTLES

The Welsh borderlands had the
highest concentration of
motte-and-bailey fortifications
in Britain. After the Norman
conquest of England, King
William I set out to subdue the
Welsh and in the later Norman
and medieval periods his
descendents built stronger
castles to secure the frontier.
Welsh-borders castles along or
close to Offa's Dyke Path
include:

- Chepstow
- St Briavels
- Monmouth
- White Castle, Llanvetherine
- Longtown
- Montgomery
- Powis
- Chirk
- Dinas Bran

★ Chirk Castle

Just a short distance off-route, Chirk
Castle (SJ 268380) is well worth the
deviation. The castle was completed
during the time of Edward I as part of his
plan to conquer the Welsh princes, and is
built on an outcrop above the rivers Dee
and Ceiriog – an imposing and sombre
statement of the king's intent.

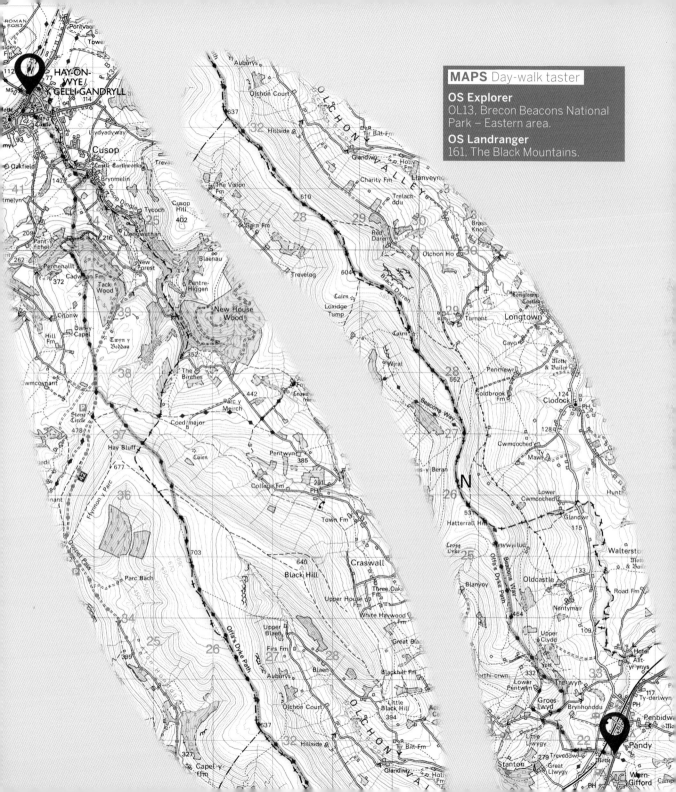

MAPS Day-walk taster

OS Explorer
OL13, Brecon Beacons National
Park – Eastern area.

OS Landranger
161, The Black Mountains.

Pembrokeshire Coast Path

Lying almost entirely within the Pembrokeshire Coast National Park, this National Trail pursues a complex, convoluted, challenging and breathtaking route that embraces windswept clifftops, secluded coves, sandy beaches and estuaries. There is a demanding repertoire of short and steep ascents and descents, often on narrow paths, with towns and villages on the way that, speak of a time when fishing and smuggling were at the opposite ends of a bustling maritime trade. On its tortuous route, the trail takes in no fewer than 14 harbours, almost 60 beaches, 40 Iron Age hill forts, as well as Norman and medieval castles, Napoleonic forts and countless secret coves. With the exception of Milford Haven and Ministry of Defence locations, the trail simply follows the coastline of Pembrokeshire, providing an ever-changing geology and diverse flora, fauna and birdlife, for which the area is especially renowned.

Opened in 1970, the Pembrokeshire Coast Path was the first National Trail in Wales. It passes through a landscape of social, cultural and maritime history, which embraces Neolithic cromlechs and Iron Age forts, and the routes taken by Norman and Viking invaders. But there are quiet, remote and wild interludes, too, which give rise to the description of Pembrokeshire in 'The Mabinogion', a 1,000-year-old collection of folk tales, as the 'Land of Mystery and Enchantment'. Echoes of that sentiment still ring round this last mighty outpost of Wales, which pierces the Celtic Sea, and is haunted by myths and legends.

The trail, which unavoidably is also part of the Wales Coast Path, represents an arduous physical challenge, with overall height gain and loss in excess of 35,000 feet (10,670m). With deviations to avoid high tides, stormy conditions and to reach off-route accommodation, daily distances may vary, and could possibly take the overall length to more than 200 miles (320km).

Exposed to Atlantic prevailing winds, the Pembrokeshire Coast Path is nevertheless unquestionably a dazzling trail; it is one that takes in miles of breathtaking coastal scenery – some of the finest in Britain – and covers every form of maritime landscape, including volcanic headlands, sedimentary cliffs and glacial valleys.

AMAZING BUT TRUE ...

There is a feeling of isolation about St David's, situated on a remote peninsula at the south-western tip of Wales; but in the Dark Ages, the holy city of Wales was an important centre of the Celtic world, lying at the crossing of routes linking Ireland, Brittany, Cornwall and England. St David's is the smallest city in Britain. Its cathedral occupies the site of a monastery allegedly founded by St David early in the 6th century, nestled into the valley of the little River Alun and built so as not to be seen from the sea by Viking raiders.

Near Tenby

The trail can be completed in 12 days, giving daily distances no higher than 20¾ miles (33.25km), and while this is within the abilities of regular multi-day walkers, given the terrain of the Pembrokeshire Coast Path it is a demanding pace. The direction of travel is a matter of choice; it is given here as north to south.

	12 days	15 days
Start	Poppit Sands	Poppit Sands
Day 1	Newport 13½ mi / 21.75km	Newport 13½ mi / 21.75km
Day 2	Goodwick 13½ mi / 21.75km	Pwllgwaelod 9½ mi / 15.25km
Day 3	Trefin 17¾ mi / 28.75km	Strumble 10½ mi / 16.75km
Day 4	St Justinian 14¼ mi / 22.75km	Trefin 11½ mi / 18.5km
Day 5	Newgale Sands 15 mi / 24.25km	Whitesands Bay (St David's) 12¼ mi / 19.75km
Day 6	Marloes 17 mi / 27.5km	Caerfai 8½ mi / 13.75km
Day 7	Sandy Haven 20¾ mi / 33.25km	Nolton Haven 11¾ mi / 19km
Day 8	Pembroke 20¼ mi / 32.5km	Marloes 12¼ mi / 19.75km
Day 9	West Angle Bay 14½ mi / 23.25km	Dale 12½ mi / 20km
Day 10	Broad Haven 15 mi / 24.25km	Milford Haven 16½ mi / 26.75km
Day 11	Tenby 16½ mi / 26.75km	Pembroke 12 mi / 19.5km
Day 12	Amroth 7½ mi / 12km	Angle 11¾ mi / 18.75km
Day 13		St Govans 17 mi / 27.25km
Day 14		Lydstep 13½ mi / 21.75km
Day 15		Amroth 12¼ mi / 19.75km

FACTS AND FIGURES

START Poppit Sands, St Dogmaels, Pembrokeshire (SN 152485)

FINISH Amroth, Pembrokeshire (SN 172072)

DISTANCE 186 miles (299km)

HEIGHT GAIN 35,140 feet (10,715m)

DIFFICULTY RATING ◆◆◆◆

IS IT FOR ME? Physically challenging with successive steep ascents/descents often on narrow paths; good transport connections via a shuttle bus for piecemeal completion.

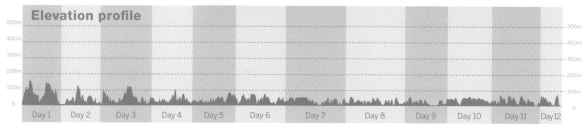

Elevation profile

Day 1 Day 2 Day 3 Day 4 Day 5 Day 6 Day 7 Day 8 Day 9 Day 10 Day 11 Day 12

PRACTICALITIES

BE AWARE

For all its attractions, the southern part of the Coast Path lies within a Ministry of Defence firing range; advance checking about firing times is paramount if road walking is to be avoided. At Quoits Mill, Monkton, west of Pembroke, the trail follows a minor lane that floods at high tide, making it impassable for walkers, who will need to decide between diverting onto a busy road or waiting for the water to subside.

GETTING THERE AND BACK

St Dogmaels is accessible by rail via Haverfordwest then bus to Cardigan, followed by the 405 walker bus (Poppit Rocket), which also goes to Poppit Sands. At the southern end of the trail, Amroth is accessible by rail to Kilgetty, then bus to Amroth. There are also bus services between Tenby and Amroth.

GETTING AROUND

The Pembrokeshire coastal bus services cover the entire route, and have delightful names, such as the Coastal Cruiser, the Celtic Coaster, the Strumble Shuttle, the Poppit Rocket and the Puffin Shuttle. Between them, they make it easy to tackle the trail in day segments spread over weeks or months.

ACCOMMODATION

Although sparse in places, there is generally a good choice of accommodation along the Coast Path and plenty of campsites, although it is illegal to wild camp in Wales.

WEBSITES

www.nationaltrail.co.uk
www.pembrokeshirecoast.wales
www.visitpembrokeshire.com

This page: Ceibwr Bay.
Opposite page: Newport.

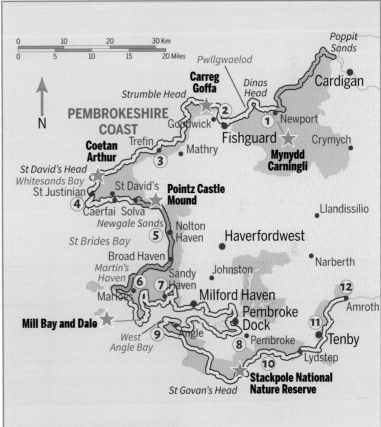

MAPS

OS Explorer
OL35, OL36, 177, 198.
OS Landranger
145, 157, 158.

Unquestionably a dazzling trail, one that takes in miles of breathtaking coastal scenery

SOLVA TO MARTIN'S HAVEN
(21½ miles/35.5km)

There is almost a sense of torment about this section, with the Path anxious not to miss any of the many coastal indentations. This stretch also has several ups and downs, some very steep, though they are less demanding once beyond Newgale, where the Path parallels Newgale Sands. A short deviation round Nolton Haven is the only break in clifftop walking until Broad Haven is encountered.

Beyond Broad Haven, Old Red Sandstone cliffs are a striking feature, though they are not so high, as sea cliffs go. In spring, there is an abundance of wild flowers to colour the route as it rounds Borough Head and a host of rocky inlets, before romping along to the headland at Martin's Haven. A short distance off-route towards the end, Marloes Beacon (SM 784084) is a diminutive summit, but one blessed with an outstanding view. Someone has gone to the trouble to calculate that it is the 19,340th highest peak in the British Islands!

An ideal illustration of the nature of the trail, one on which the walker spends long stretches in their own company

★ Mynydd Carningli

South of Newport, Mynydd Carningli (SN 062371) dominates the scene and hosts prehistoric and historic remains, as well as being a Biological Site of Special Scientific Interest. The summit features one of the largest hill forts in Wales, thought to be more than 2,000 years old. The mountain forms part of the Preselli Hills. Geologist and archaeologist Herbert Henry Thomas (1876–1935) proposed the theory that the 'bluestones' that form the inner circle of Stonehenge on Salisbury Plain were quarried and transported from Mynydd Carningli more than 4,000 years ago; that would represent an amazing feat of endeavour: a gruelling journey of at least 200 miles (320km) with a crossing of the Severn estuary thrown in for good measure. Others suggest that the bluestones reached Stonehenge by glacial transportation.

★ Carreg Goffa

High above Aber Felin, to the east of Strumble Head, a memorial stone (SM 926404) erected in 1897 commemorates the defeat of the last attempted invasion of Britain by a French force on 22 February 1797, when 1,400 Napoleonic troops landed at Carregwastad Point.

★ Pointz Castle Mound

A short distance inland from the trail, Pointz Castle (SM 830237), a scheduled ancient monument, consists of the well-preserved remains of a motte and ditch that dates to the medieval period, and as such is an important relic of the medieval landscape.

★ Coetan Arthur

Close by St David's Head, Coetan Arthur (SM 725280) is one of many prehistoric sites attributed to King Arthur. This collection of huge stones formed part of a passage grave linked to a round barrow. Erected around 5,000 years ago, however, this is a burial chamber inland from a collection of hut circles on the headland nearby. The headland itself possesses much – ancient field patterns, enclosures and defensive banks and ditches – that will interest even the most incurious passer-by.

Nature on the trail (clockwise):
Sea anemones; razorbills; puffin on Skomer; shore crab; Arctic tern.

POPPIT SANDS TO NEWPORT
(13½ miles/21.75km)

Walkers need to be self-sufficient on this first stage of the Coast Path because, apart from a diversion inland to Moylgrove, there are no facilities or services until Newport Sands come into view. But that is an ideal illustration of the nature of the trail – one on which the walker spends long stretches in their own company.

No sooner has the walk begun than it encounters Cemaes Head, a headland that is the highest part of the Path (574 feet/175m) and from where steep cliffs plunge airily to the sea. There are plenty of ups and downs to contend with before the Path drops to the rocky inlet at Ceibwr Bay. Before long, the Coast Path encounters the Witches' Pool (Pwll y Wrach), from which it climbs once more to the top of sea cliffs and round the lump of Foel Goch, gradually descending to the sands at Newport; to the south rises the imposing and mystical dome of Mynydd Carningli (see page 298).

There is almost a sense of torment about this section, with the Path anxious not to miss any of the many coastal indentations

★ Mill Bay and Dale

Close to St Anne's Head at the entrance to Milford Haven, Mill Bay has a special place in British history, for it was here that the Earl of Richmond, Henry Tudor, landed in 1485, while his ships and over 4,000 men landed further up the coast at Dale. Henry travelled through western Wales, gathering support as he ventured east eventually to engage Richard III in battle at Bosworth, and so became King Henry VII, founder of the Tudor dynasty which lasted until the death of Elizabeth I in 1603.

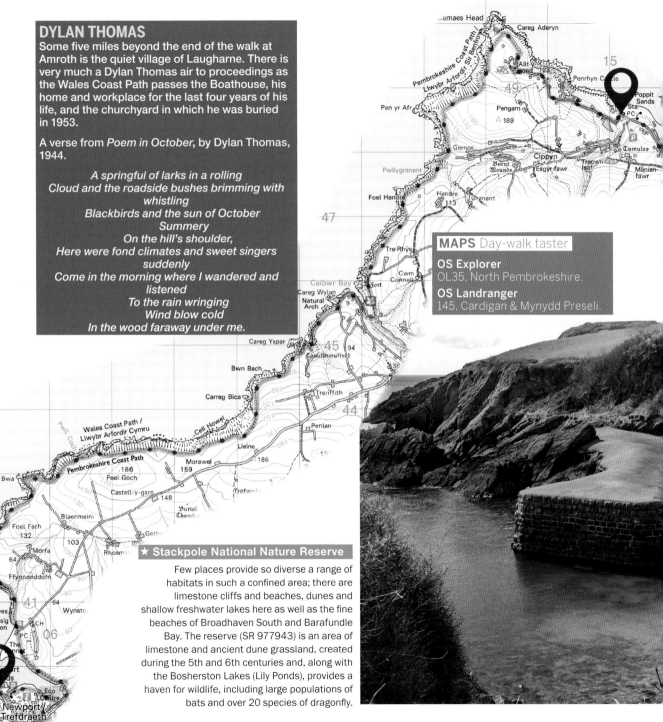

DYLAN THOMAS

Some five miles beyond the end of the walk at Amroth is the quiet village of Laugharne. There is very much a Dylan Thomas air to proceedings as the Wales Coast Path passes the Boathouse, his home and workplace for the last four years of his life, and the churchyard in which he was buried in 1953.

A verse from *Poem in October*, by Dylan Thomas, 1944.

*A springful of larks in a rolling
Cloud and the roadside bushes brimming with whistling
Blackbirds and the sun of October
Summery
On the hill's shoulder,
Here were fond climates and sweet singers suddenly
Come in the morning where I wandered and listened
To the rain wringing
Wind blow cold
In the wood faraway under me.*

MAPS Day-walk taster

OS Explorer
OL35, North Pembrokeshire.

OS Landranger
145, Cardigan & Mynydd Preseli.

★ Stackpole National Nature Reserve

Few places provide so diverse a range of habitats in such a confined area; there are limestone cliffs and beaches, dunes and shallow freshwater lakes here as well as the fine beaches of Broadhaven South and Barafundle Bay. The reserve (SR 977943) is an area of limestone and ancient dune grassland, created during the 5th and 6th centuries and, along with the Bosherston Lakes (Lily Ponds), provides a haven for wildlife, including large populations of bats and over 20 species of dragonfly.

MAPS

OS LANDRANGER

ENGLAND

1. **Chiltern Way** *map nos:* 164, 165, 166, 175, 176
2. **Cleveland Way** *map nos:* 93, 94, 99, 100, 101
3. **Coast to Coast Path** *map nos:* 89, 90, 91, 92, 93, 94, 98, 99, 100
4. **Cotswold Way** *map nos:* 150, 151, 162, 163, 172
5. **Cumbria Way** *map nos:* 85, 89, 90, 96
6. **Dales Way** *map nos:* 97, 98, 104
7. **Derwent Valley Heritage Way** *map nos:* 110, 119, 128, 129
8. **Hadrian's Wall Path** *map nos:* 85, 86, 87, 88
9. **London's Capital Ring** *map nos:* 176, 177
10. **North Downs Way** *map nos:* 177, 178, 179, 186, 187, 188, 189
11. **Peddars Way and Norfolk Coast Path** *map nos:* 132, 133, 144
12. **Pennine Way** *map nos:* 74, 75, 80, 86, 87, 91, 92, 98, 103, 109, 110
13. **Ribble Way** *map nos:* 98, 102, 103
14. **Ridgeway** *map nos:* 165, 173, 174, 175
15. **Severn Way** *map nos:* 126, 127, 135, 136, 138, 150, 162, 172
16. **Shropshire Way** *map nos:* 117, 126, 127, 137, 138, 148
17. **South Downs Way** *map nos:* 185, 197, 198, 199
18. **South West Coast Path** *map nos:* 180, 181, 190, 192, 193, 194, 195, 200, 201, 202, 203, 204
19. **Thames Path** *map nos:* 163, 164, 173, 175, 176, 177
20. **Two Moors Way** *map nos:* 180, 181, 191, 202
21. **Yorkshire Wolds Way** *map nos:* 100, 101, 106, 107

SCOTLAND

22. **Annandale Way** *map nos:* 78, 85
23. **Arran Coastal Way** *map no:* 69
24. **Borders Abbeys Way** *map nos:* 73, 74, 79, 80
25. **Fife Coastal Path** *map nos:* 59, 65, 66
26. **Great Glen Way** *map nos:* 26, 34, 35, 41
27. **John Muir Way** *map nos:* 56, 63, 64, 65, 66, 67
28. **Loch Lomond and Cowal Way** *map nos:* 55, 56, 62
29. **Rob Roy Way** *map nos:* 51, 52, 57
30. **Southern Upland Way** *map nos:* 67, 71, 73, 74, 76, 77, 78, 79, 82
31. **Speyside Way** *map nos:* 28, 35, 36
32. **West Highland Way** *map nos:* 41, 50, 56, 57, 64

WALES

33. **Anglesey Coastal Path** *map nos:* 114, 115
34. **Beacons Way** *map nos:* 146, 159, 160, 161
35. **Ceredigion Coast Path** *map nos:* 135, 145, 146
36. **Glyndŵr's Way** *map nos:* 124, 125, 126, 135, 136, 137, 147, 148
37. **Offa's Dyke Path** *map nos:* 116, 117, 126, 137, 148, 161, 162, 172
38. **Pembrokeshire Coast Path** *map nos:* 145, 157, 158

Publishing information

© Crown copyright/Ordnance Survey Limited, 2022

Published by Milestone Publishing Limited under licence from Ordnance Survey Limited.
Pathfinder, Ordnance Survey, OS and the OS logos are registered trademarks of Ordnance Survey Limited and are used under licence from Ordnance Survey Limited.
Text © Milestone Publishing Limited, 2022

This product includes mapping data licensed from Ordnance Survey
© Crown copyright and database rights (2022)
OS 150002047

ISBN 978-0-31909-206-4

First published in Great Britain 2021 by Trotman Publishing. This edition first published 2022 by Milestone Publishing.

While every care has been taken to ensure the accuracy of the route information, the publishers cannot accept responsibility for errors or omissions, or for changes in details given. The countryside is not static: hedges and fences can be removed, stiles can be replaced by gates, field boundaries can be altered, footpaths can be rerouted and changes in ownership can result in the closure or diversion of some concessionary paths. Also, paths that are easy and pleasant for walking in fine conditions may become slippery, muddy and difficult in wet weather, while stepping stones across rivers and streams may become impassable.

If you find an inaccuracy, please contact Milestone Publishing, 21d Charles Street, Bath, BA1 1HX

Printed in India by Replika Press Pvt. Ltd. 2/22

A catalogue record for this book is available from the British Library.

Milestone Publishing credits

Series Editor Kevin Freeborn
Author Terry Marsh
Layouts Patrick Dawson
Cartography Cosmographics
Picture research and proofreading Kate Michell

Photography credits

Front cover: stocker1970/Shutterstock.com

Back cover: left keith 316/Shutterstock.com; centre Ondrej Fendrych/Shutterstock.com. Outer flap Patrick Dawson; Inner flap John Hodgson.

Interior: Terry Marsh, the author, supplied the following pictures pages 3, 24, 26, 32, 37, 37, 38, 48, 51, 52, 53, 54, 58, 59, 102, 107, 107, 108, 109, 112, 126, 130, 190, 193, 194, 195, 255, 257, 258, 260, 286. Page 286 Jonathan Young.

Other images were sourced as follows: page 22, John Cassell, Public Domain, Wikimedia Commons; 34, Rydal Mount; 36, Rydal Mount; 90, Tony Hisgett from Birmingham, Wikimedia Commons; 91, Ethan Doyle White, Wikimedia Commons; 91, Poliphilo, Wikimedia Commons; 110, Marcin Floryan, Wikimedia Commons; 123, Stephen Simpson, Public Domain, Wikimedia Commons; 130, Llywelyn2000, Wikimedia Commons; 147, Tim Heaton, Wikimedia Commons; 164, Brian Robert Marshall, Wikimedia Commons; 165, Chris Wood, Wikimedia Commons; 167, Pitou250, Public Domain, Wikimedia Commons; 172, Herbythyme, Wikimedia Commons; 172, 173, Nilfanion, Wikimedia Commons; 189, Beshoffs, Wikimedia Commons; 216, Mark Nightingale, Wikimedia Commons; 224, Gary Campbell-Hall from Edinburgh, Wikimedia Commons; 230, Trevor Littlewood, Wikimedia Commons; 231, W.H. Worthington, Wikimedia Commons; 240, Andrew Bowden from London, Wikimedia Commons; 240, Andy Stephenson, Wikimedia Commons; 246, Scottish Dolphin Centre; 281, Kieranpkelly, Wikimedia Commons; 281, Restharrow, Wikimedia Commons; 284, Arthur Cadwgan Michael (1881–1965), Public Domain, via Wikimedia Commons; 298, Helge Klaus Rieder, Public Domain, Wikimedia Commons; 299, Llywelyn2000, Wikimedia Commons.

The following images were supplied by Shutterstock.com page 1 pavla; 4, 39, 72 Michael Conrad; 6, 30 John Ray Gordon; 7 John spreadbury; 11, 89, 131 Martin Fowler; 13 Robert Coppinger; 14 Stefan-Kadar; 16 SarahHowardPhotography; 19 Chrislofotos; 20 Konmac; 20 Stephen Tucker; 21 AdamEdwards; 21, 23 Peter_Fleming; 22, 94, 144 SuxxesPhoto; 23 Barry and Carole Bowden; 23 Bildagentur Zoonar GmbH; 23, 85 Giedriius; 23 Rural Revolution; 26 Andrei Petrus; 27, 30, 222 Dave Head; 28 Tim-Hill; 29, 174, 179 Iortek; 29, 96 Richard Bowden; 30 MCWorldEnt; 31 David Havel; 31 Paulpixs; 31 Scott M Ward; 31 Steven Ward; 37 sagulpol2807; 38 Mike Russell; 39 Henri Koskinen; 39 juerginho; 39 Matt Gibson; 39 Simon Whitfield; 40 Dean Clarke; 42 Frank Fischbach; 44, 122 1000 Words; 44 chrisontour84; 44 John Corry; 45, 46, 122 4 season backpacking; 45 sophiablu; 46 Dave Porter; 47 Nigel Jarvis; 47, 70 PJ photography; 47 Simon Charles A Johnson; 47 Stephen Ellis35; 51 Janet Griffin; 51 Jarmo Honkanen; 51, 62, 68 Kevin Eaves; 51 Rick Ollerton; 52 BabichAndrew; 53, 89 Philip Bird LRPS CPAGB; 58 J. Jackson UK; 59 Neal Rylatt; 60 albinoni; 60 DMC Photogallery; 61 Henrik Larsson; 61 John Ruberry; 61, 107 julian hodgson; 61, 241 Mark Medcalf; 61, 154 Peter Turner Photography; 61 ShaunWilkinson; 61, 101 tony mills; 64 Jean Waring; 66 Kristin Greenwood; 66 Alex Manders; 66 Jayvic; 66 Rob Atherton; 66 Simon Annable; 66 Tim M; 67 Morphart Creation; 67 Paul K Martin; 68 Liang Mi; 68, 243 mountaintreks; 68 peter g lawson; 69 Irina Borsuchenko; 69 jack perks; 69 Mariusz S. Jurgielewicz; 69 Mike Busby; 69 noicherrybeans; 69 Rudmer Zwerver; 69 Tony_Traveler85; 73 Ger Bosma Photos; 73, 118 Phil messenger; 73, 101, 111, 125 Sandra Standbridge; 73 Violaman; 74 Barry Paterson; 74 Jaime Pharr; 74 The Old Major; 75, 184 Nigel Eve; 75 Shiarn Briggs; 77 Colin Ward; 78, 83 Hanging Bear Media; 80 AnyaWhy; 80 Chris Mole; 82 Fotosin; 82 iolya; 83 cktravels.com; 83 elRoce; 83 mikecphoto; 83 Numage; 84, 86, 167 BBA Photography; 84 Charles Bowman; 84 HipKat; 84 ileana_bt; 84 L F File; 84 pcruciatti; 85 arjma; 85 Guy William; 85 James Alex Duncan; 85 Nancy Kennedy; 85 WilcoUK; 88 Chris Dukes; 89 Jordon Sharp; 89 Peter Titmuss; 90,146 Gillian Pullinger; 90 Tim Smalley; 92 Bora Zrinyi; 93 John Miller; 96 Adrian Swinburne; 98, 173 Andy333; 98 Nicoleta Lungu; 98 Scott Darby; 99 M Rose; 99, 115 Phil Silverman; 100, 140, 162, 186, 292 Jo Jones; 100 Richard Bowden; 100, 170 Sebastien Coell; 101, 125, 300 Erni; 101, 131, 146 Nicola Pulham; 106 Michael Dewsbury; 106, 233, 265 Pete Stuart; 106 TomSpecial; 107 Quaker268; 108 peter jeffreys; 109 PORNPIPAT CHAROENTHAI; 111 Brookgardener; 111, 159 colin robert varndell; 111 Karel Bartik; 111 Peter J Barker; 111 Pieter Bruin; 111 WonderPhotoSpain; 111 Yorkshire Scenes; 114 JS Rowley; 116 Keith Heaton; 116 Michael J P; 117 derek oldfield; 117 Matt_Turner; 120 Droneski Imaging; 121 Juneisy Q. Hawkins; 122 Steve Simmons UK; 122 urbanbuzz; 123 A G Baxter; 124, 155 Charlesy; 125 Alan Tunnicliffe; 125 Pawel Piotr; 125 Svitlyk; 130 Everett Collection; 131 Russell Drye; 133 Ian Merton; 133, 167 Ian Schofield; 133 Maciej Olszewski; 133 Pichit Kaewbutta; 133 slowmotiongli; 133 Tomasz Klejdysz; 134 UAV 4; 136 EddieCloud; 138 Andrew Roland; 138 Shaun Barr; 138 Simon Edge; 139 Graham King; 139 JudyPreyesh; 139 SnapHound Photography; 141 Costea Andrea M; 141 Emi; 141 Kevin Wells Photography; 141 nat_us; 141 Szymon Bartosz; 142 Lilly Trott; 146 GybasDigiPhoto; 147 Ricky Howitt; 147 Veronique Stone; 149 ColleenSlater Photography; 149 KatyKing27; 149 Mark Heighes; 149 matushaban; 149 Neil Bowman; 149 Scott Dunwoodie; 149 Yuri Kravchenko; 150, 156, 225 ian woolcock; 154 SAKhanPhotography; 154, 290 Valery Egorov; 155 Davis Dorss; 155 Gerry White; 155 Helen Hotson; 156 travellight; 158 AlanMorris; 158 Dennis Jacobsen; 158 Martin Pelanek; 158 Ondrej Prosicky; 158 Pav-Pro Photography Ltd; 159 David JC; 159 Malt House Photography; 159 Tom_Sanderson; 159 Twymanphoto; 160 Piotr Wawrzyniuk; 162, 165 Chris Lawrence Travel; 164 Lance Bellers; 165 Jacek Wojnarowski; 166, 167 Mistervlad; 168 Adrian Baker; 176 Sebastian Hulse; 177, 181 EMJAY SMITH; 177 evergoodstudios; 178 Duncan Cuthbertson; 179, 181 AlmacUK; 179, 262 northallertonman; 180 Des-Green; 180 Peter Yeo; 181 jps; 181 Mark Jenner; 181 UniquePhotoArts; 182 Naj Ativk; 186 robert f cooke; 188 GarethTandy; 188 Heartland Arts; 189 leon mcgarrity; 192, 193 Allan Napier; 193 Apilak Premsakakul; 193 LouieLea; 193 Martin Prochazkacz; 194 Mark Godden; 195 13threephotography; 195 Swen Stroop; 196 Jule_Berlin; 198 alanf; 198 hipproductions; 198 Scott Pryde; 198 Tom Curtis; 200 inson Calfort; 201 dvlcom; 201 WApted; 202 pql89; 204 Heather Raulerson; 205, 206, 221 David McElroy; 206 Winnie Ho; 207 Jiri Vondrous; 207 wonderlustpicstravel; 208 andy morehouse; 210 Fulcanelli; 210 JeniFoto; 212 Kev Gregory; 212 TTphoto; 214 Sue Burton Photography; 217 Riska Parakeet; 218 Bill McKelvie; 218 Pecold; 219 evenfh; 219 Gilbert S. Grant; 219, 299 Julian Popov; 219 RWM Photography; 221 Cliff Hands; 226 Dmitry Naumov; 226, 227 Maritxu; 226 Skully; 227 Samib123; 228 AndyMitchell; 230 Alistair McDonald; 230 NOT FOUND; 231 douglasmack; 232 Cedarkae B; 233 Mark Medcalf; 233 AndrewSproule; 233, 241, 246 Mark Caunt; 233 Steve Simkins; 233 Zhecho Planinski; 234 Jan Durkaj; 234 Steve Meese; 235 cornfield; 235 Edinburghcitymom; 235 Franke de Jong; 235 Terry Kettlewell; 236 Anthony Ackers; 241 Grigorii Pisotsckii; 241 Milosz Maslanka; 241 zdenek_macat; 242 Carole MacDonald; 243 John Messingham; 243 Lytd11; 243 Peter R Foster IDMA; 244 fasphotographic; 246 grafxart; 246 Greg Kushmerek; 246 Marek Rybar; 246 Patrik Stanek; 248 Jan Holm; 248 PK289; 248 Roddy MacLean; 249 JanTrautscholdPhotography; 250, 256 Gary_Ellis_Photography; 253 Dougie Milne Photography; 254 John A Cameron; 255 Julietphotography; 256 Akan Zhussup; 256 Jamie Ballantine; 256 Juraj Kamenicky; 257 Joe Dunckley; 262, 264 Gail Johnson; 263 Andrew Astbury; 264 stiffan67; 265 Andrew Chisholm; 265 Jalegr; 266 Mark R Croucher; 268 andreac77; 269 Tappix; 270, 291 Harjit Samra; 270 JazzLove; 270 Tim Scanlan Photography; 271, 272 Billy Stock; 271 Helen J Davies; 271,274, 288 Richard Whitcombe; 274 Dominic Rowley; 274 Jonathan Hughes; 275 James LePage; 276 Electric Egg; 276 yui; 277 Colin Burdett; 277 Iolo ap Gwynn; 278 totajla; 280 Wieland Teixeira; 282 tornadoflight; 282, 284, 285 Wozzie; 283 MaxineA; 283 yackers1; 285 Dani Vincek; 285 F-Focus by Mati Kose; 285 Karin Jaehne; 285 weha; 288 steve bridge; 289 Scp photography; 290 Robert Deller; 291 cornfield; 292 Jo Jones; 292 Renee Denise; 294 Tony Baggett; 296, 297 Alan Foster; 299 Greens and Blues; 299 JeremyRichards; 299 Mica Stock; 299 Simon T May; 300 Dparish; 301 FOOTSTEP LOG.

FSC MIX Paper from responsible sources FSC® C016779 www.fsc.org